# EVERY MAN
# A KING
The Autobiography of
# HUEY P. LONG

Evangeline Oak, St. Martinville.

"And it is here under this oak where Evangeline waited for her lover, Gabriel. This oak is immortal, but Evangeline is not the only one who waited here in disappointment. Where are the schools, the roads and highways, the institutions for the disabled you sent your money to build? Evangeline's tears lasted through one lifetime—yours through generations. Give me the chance to dry the eyes of those who still weep here."—From Huey P. Long's speech. Campaign, 1927-28.

# EveryMan a King

## The AUTOBIOGRAPHY HUEY P. LONG

Introduction by T. HARRY WILLIAMS

DA CAPO PRESS

Library of Congress Cataloging in Publication Data

Long, Huey Pierce, 1893–1935.
  Every man a king: the autobiography of Huey P. Long.
      p.    cm.
  Includes bibliographical references and index.
  Originally published: New Orleans: National Book Co., 1933.
  ISBN 0-306-80695-9 (alk. paper)
    1. Long, Huey Pierce, 1893—1935. 2. Legislators—United
States—Biography. 3. United States. Congress. Senate—Biog-
raphy. 4. Governors—Louisiana—Biography. 5. Louisiana—Poli-
tics and government—1865–1950. I. Title.
E748.L86A3   1996                                    95-42402
                                                         CIP

First Da Capo Press edition 1996

This Da Capo Press paperback edition of *Every Man A King*
is an unabridged republication of the edition published in
New Orleans in 1933, with the addition of an introduction by
T. Harry Williams and an index reprinted from the 1964
edition. It is reprinted by arrangement with Russell B. Long,
Palmer Long, and Christopher R. Brauchli.

Published by Da Capo Press
A Member of the Perseus Books Group
http://www.dacapopress.com

*"Ill fares the land, to hastening ills a prey,*
*Where wealth accumulates and men decay."*

**GOLDSMITH**

# INTRODUCTION

In August, 1933, George R. Allen, a newspaper man who did public relations work for Senator Huey P. Long, wrote an interesting letter to the Louisiana leader. Allen had been able, he said, to persuade the North American Newspaper Alliance to run an article in its syndicated service extolling Long's program in Louisiana. But the editor of North American, to maintain a pretense of neutrality, had insisted that Allen prepare also an anti-Long article to appear first. Allen had readily agreed. "In the first article I will give the opposition their day," he told the Senator, "and in the second I will knock it into a cocked hat."

Long was duly appreciative of Allen's artistry. Few American politicians have had as shrewd and as sensitive a regard for the uses of the printed word as this apparently unlettered man who burst so explosively on the national scene in the 1930's. His knowledge of the techniques of public influence was uncanny and apparently instinctive. It came into play when he ran for his first political office at the age of twenty-four and was constantly enlarged and refined thereafter. In that initial race he hit on the device of putting his cause before the voters through the medium of printed circulars which he tacked on trees and poles all over his district. He continued to use the circular mechanism throughout the rest of his career, in his races for governor and United States Senator, and to popularize his policies after winning power. It has been estimated that between 1928 and 1935 some 26,000,000 of these documents were distributed all over Louisiana. Long's circulars were no mere abstracts that shrilled forth a few biased sentiments. They were, naturally, partisan and slanted, but they were lengthy compositions—an average product would run from 1,000 to 1,800 words—and they were packed with political and economic information.

They were also extremely well written. Long wrote the copy for every circular or, if he was busy with other matters, sketched out to a subordinate the points he wanted made. It was not just that he was intent on presenting the most effective case to the public. This man who seemed to be purely political had a real interest in literary exposition and an itching desire to represent himself in print. Many of his intimates have opined that if he had not been a great politician he might have been a great actor or preacher. It is very possible that he might have been, if not a great writer, at least a talented one. He constantly sought to create media for the expression of his writings. After he became governor he founded his own newspaper, the *Louisiana Progress*, which became, when he went to the Senate, the *American Progress*. It was a weekly, although sometimes irregular in appearance, and for years Long contributed a column to it. Often the column was only an excerpt from one of his Senate speeches, which were his own compositions, but just as often it was something special he had taken time to put together. He also wrote some articles about himself for the popular magazines.

But, like every aspiring writer, he wanted above all to enshrine his name in the most enduring form of publication—books. And the name Huey P. Long appears as the author on the title pages of three volumes. His part in the preparation of the first one published was, however, only nominal. *Constitutions of the State of Louisiana* appeared in 1930. It was a comparative compilation of the various constitutions from 1812 to 1921, relating articles in the earlier documents to the 1921 version. Most of the actual work seems to have been done by a lawyer friend, aided by assistants assigned by Long, although Long, a master of legal lore, could well have done the job himself if he had not been in the turmoil of his governorship. The purpose behind the project was to enable Loyola University to grant him an honorary degree. A solid piece of scholarship, the book became a widely used reference tool in Louisiana.

In the fall of 1932, after he had taken his Senate seat and already had become a national figure, Long decided to write his autobiography. He began work on it almost immediately and continued intermittently until the task was completed in 1933. Necessarily, because of the press of Senate duties, Long had to get away to New Orleans or Baton Rouge to do his composing. He dictated the whole manuscript, utilizing several secretaries and often striding up and down the room and acting out some episode he was describing. He did a lot of revising and rewriting, and finally, after having his newspaper friend Allen read the finished draft, he made a last revision. The book appeared in October, 1933, approximately a year after its conception. The title, *Every Man a King*, was drawn from a slogan that Long had employed in his campaigning and that he would later use as the name for a campaign song. (His literary activities included the writing of words for songs to which a more musically inclined friend put the notes.)

Long's third book was published in 1935. Entitled *My First Days in the White House*, it was a description of how he would handle the problems of the depression when President. Some Long associates think that this work was ghostwritten for him by a Washington journalist. But reliable evidence indicates that he dictated at least large portions of it himself, although possibly some other writer edited the raw material. *My First Days* reveals much about Long's philosophy of sharing the wealth, and it is hilariously funny—for example, he makes Franklin D. Roosevelt a member of his cabinet—but it does not have the personal or historical importance of *Every Man a King*. The latter book has more body. It is truly autobiographical and details with adequate, if not complete, frankness the rise to power of one of America's most remarkable politicians.

Huey P. Long was born in 1893 in Winn parish (county), the seventh in a family of nine children. There is a myth about his background that colors everything that has been written about him. It is that the Longs were abjectly poor, were without education or culture, were, in Southern terminology, "hillbillies" or "trash." Long himself helped to father the myth—he operated in an age when politicians found it profitable to boast of a log cabin origin—but it has little foundation. Winn parish, with its thin soil and cutover timber patches, was undeniably poor in comparison with the more favored cotton and sugar parishes. It could not show an array of planter magnates, but it did have a substantial number of small farmers who worked hard and enjoyed a fairly comfortable living. The Longs were as well off as most people in Winn and, indeed, something above the average. Rather than scorning culture, they were highly respectful of it and eager to acquire it. Every member of the large family secured at least a touch of a college education. Huey Long, as he relates in the autobiography, had relatively little formal schooling at the higher levels—he exaggerates somewhat the work he took at Tulane University—but from boyhood he educated himself with a program of voracious reading. It is unlikely that many college graduates of the period had, for example, as wide a knowledge of history, or as much of a sense of history, as this product of the north Louisiana hills.

The members of the Long family, it needs to be noted for an understanding of the autobiography, were all intelligent and extremely individualistic in their relations with one another. Huey Long hints at this characteristic in referring to two of his brothers, whom, curiously, he does not name. The older brother mentioned in the early pages is Julius, who helped finance Huey's education and with whom he formed a law partnership. Yet Julius and Huey eventually broke and became bitter personal and political enemies. The younger brother described later who wanted to run for office is Earl Long, who was destined to be a political figure in his own right and three times governor. He and Huey broke too, although before Huey's death they were reconciled. All the brothers and sisters were in some degree interested in politics and active in it throughout their lives.

Perhaps there was something in the stark environment of Winn parish that was conducive to political interest. Winn had a tradition of dissent and protest that was rare in the rural South. In 1861 the parish had opposed secession and had shown but a scant enthusiasm for the Confederate cause. In the 1890's it had been the center of Populist strength in the state. In the early 1900's it had nurtured a Socialist party—more agrarian than Marxian, perhaps, but still daring to wear the collectivist label—that garnered a respectable vote in presidential elections and even won a number of local offices. Huey Long and his brothers and sisters grew up in an atmosphere of hot political debate, and many of the debaters challenged the basic assumptions held by many Americans. None of the Longs was a Populist or a Socialist. But the doctrines of these two factions, which Huey Long heard constantly in his youth, could not help but enter into his thinking. His own political philosophy was a kind of neo- or modified Populism. Drawn from his observation of local issues and conditions and his wide reading in past and current history, it was a down-with-the-big-man and up-with-the-little-man creed. He expressed it in definite terms when in 1918, at the age of twenty-four, he ran for his first office, and he never deviated significantly from it thereafter.

In the autobiography Long states that he decided to run for a place on the Railroad Commission because he was not old enough to try for any other office. The explanation is disingenuous. Although the age element may have had some influence, Long was moving with calculated shrewdness. For a politician who wanted to go to the top, the commission was the best possible starting point. Shortly to be renamed the Public Service Commission and given enlarged supervision over all utilities, it was potentially one of the most powerful agencies in the state. It had been a moribund body. But after Long, who won an easy victory, took his seat, things changed fast. The commissioner launched a series of spectacular actions that he had undoubtedly planned from the moment he set eyes on the office. He instituted and prosecuted complaints and lawsuits against the biggest corporations in the state, with the gigantic Standard Oil Company heading the list of victims. Not all the decisions had the effect that Long claimed. But for the first time the commission had become an active, meaningful agency—and in the process Huey P. Long had become a figure with a state reputation, a man to be reckoned with as candidate for governor.

There can be no doubt that Long had planned from the first to run for governor. In fact, some of those closest to him think that he had mapped out a whole sequence of offices to be secured on a regular schedule—governor, United States Senator, and, finally, President. But he failed in his first try for the governorship in 1924, although he ran a strong third. A variety of factors combined to undo him. He got in the middle of a fight over the Ku Klux Klan. Of the two other candidates, one was pro-Klan, the other, anti-Klan; Long, seeking to avoid the issue, lost votes in both camps. He lacked adequate finances and did not have an effective state-wide organization. The story in the autobiography, that rain on election day held back his full country vote, which has received wide credence, is without basis. What defeated him was an inability to roll up much of a vote in populous south Louisiana and the city of New Orleans. He tried to remedy this situation before running for the governorship again in 1928. To strengthen himself in the southern parishes he indorsed Senator Edwin S. Broussard's bid for re-election in 1926, in return for a pledge of Broussard's support. He also sought to create a more efficient organization in New Orleans. The Broussard deal worked. But Long was unable then and later to set up a combination in New Orleans that could cope with the ruling Old Regular machine. He finally, toward the end of his career, broke the Old Regulars, but he never won an election against them in the city proper.

Still, with more abundant finances and better organizational support, Long was able to win in 1928. He did not have the required majority of the popular vote in the first primary. But he was razor close, and when the third ranking candidate pulled out, with most of his leaders declaring for Long, the second runner also withdrew. Huey Long was governor, and a momentous change in the power structure of Louisiana was about to take place. The new governor was determined to do many things, but first and foremost he meant to strike a deathblow at the hierarchy that had long controlled the state.

After Reconstruction, in all the Southern states the places of power were taken over by the upper income groups, the old planter class and the new and rising business interests. For generations these hierarchies ruled Southern politics, exercising their power through the medium of the one-party system, manipulating and combining factions in the Democratic organization. Occasionally rebels rose to challenge the existing order. They were men who claimed to speak for the masses and who demanded for the masses some voice in the councils of government and some share in the material rewards that government could bestow. In Southern historical writing they are called the demagogues. The demagogues made much noise and won some elections, but they did not alter in any fundamental way the nature of power relationships. Despite their violent denunciations of the ruling classes, they did little to raise up the masses. Some of them had no real interest in reform and were easily deflected into race baiting or into collaboration with the hierarchy. Those that had a program were unable to put it through, and for a fundamental reason—they lacked the ability, or more probably the will, to destroy the organization of the oligarchy and were eventually overthrown by it.

No demagogue had dared to defy the Louisiana hierarchy. Composed of the usual upper income groups and others peculiar to the local scene—the

Standard Oil Company and gas and shipping interests—and allied with the New Orleans Old Regulars, the machine seemed especially strong and
secure, and it was unusually conservative and com-
placent. It was capable of meeting demands for social
change and absorbing and blunting them. It had, for
example, to deal with the threat posed by the Progressive movement, which affected Louisiana and the
South somewhat later than other sections. John M.
Parker, who won the governorship in 1920 and who
had Long's support, advocated some Progressive
ideals, and as governor he steered some Progressive
measures to enactment. But Parker, a man of ability,
was himself a representative of the planter class, in-
hibited by his own standards and those of his group,
and though he pushed harder than some associates
thought he should, he did not push too hard. The
Louisiana of the 1920's could hardly be said to be
a modern state. It had less than 300 miles of cement
roads, only 35 miles of roads with other surfacing,
only three major bridges in the state highway system,
an inadequate educational arrangement from the state
university down to the elementary level, and archaic
hospital and other public services. Both the place
and the time were ripe, overly so, for a leader who
would demand change. But few could have guessed
what kind of change would come after 1928.

Long had promised change in both his campaigns.
That he would succeed in getting much seemed
doubtful to supporters and opponents and disinterested observers. He took with him into office only a
minority of pledged followers in the legislature, and

everybody knew the vast power of the opposition to contain its enemies. Besides, Long was one of those demagogues. He would make a token effort for reform and then go to denouncing Negroes or Yankees and recalling Confederate glories in the Civil War and Southern suffering during Reconstruction. That was the way it always had been.

It was not going to be anything like that way. Long was the one Southern popular leader who promised something and then delivered. He was governor from 1928 to 1932. In 1930 he ran for the United States Senate, defeating the incumbent with ease. He could not take his seat, however, because of a conflict with his lieutenant governor, Paul Cyr. Long and Cyr had broken, and Huey would not go to Washington until he had made certain that one of his own men would succeed to the governorship. Not until January, 1932, could he safely leave the state. He was in the Senate after that date, but he was, in effect, still governor. His friend, O. K. Allen, was governor in name only. Long ran the administration and the state, ran both, his enemies charged, like a dictator.

The Long program of legislation was put into force over the period between 1928 and 1935. Although it took some time to enact, it was an impressive accomplishment. By 1935 Louisiana had 2,446 miles of cement roads, 1,308 miles of asphalt roads, twice as many miles of gravel roads as when Long took office, and over forty bridges in the state highway system. Appropriations for education, especially at the higher level, were increased, and the providing of free textbooks caused a 20 per cent jump in public school enrollment. In a notable attack on ignorance, free night schools were set up that aided over 100,000 adult illiterates of both races. State hospitals and other public institutions were expanded and enlarged and their services were humanized. Repeal of the poll tax opened the political doors to a host of new voters, and the new, significant issues that Long introduced aroused popular interest in politics to a degree unmatched in any other Southern state. The huge costs of the Long program were met in a manner that anticipated the New Deal—by heavier taxes, especially on corporations, and by the issuance of bonds that increased the state debt to what was by the standards of that time an astronomical figure.

It took Long years to pass his program because he had to proceed against the implacable opposition of the ruling classes. The governor's announcement of his principal demands in 1928 led to an attempt in the following year to impeach him. He narrowly defeated the move by resorting to the device that became famous in Louisiana political history as the "round robin"—a sufficient number of state senators to block impeachment were persuaded to sign a document that they would not vote to convict. Long thus saved himself and continued to press toward his objectives. That this episode had a profound influence on him cannot be doubted. There is some question, however, as to its exact impact, and even his closest associates differ on this point. According to one version, Long was a fairly typical Progressive or liberal governor. Like similar executives in all sections, he entered office full of ideals and fired with a desire to pass legislation to

help the masses. He met unreasoning and even un-
scrupulous resistance from the conservatives, and this
development changed him, making him more rancor-
ous and ruthless, ready to use extreme methods to
reach his goals. There is some merit in the analysis.
The impeachment unmistakably hardened Long, and
the stratagems of the opposition and his own stratagems to overcome theirs induced in him a measure of
cynicism about the democratic process. But another
explanation probably is closer to the mark. It is that
from the very first Long knew pretty much what he
was going to do and moved to do it, at his own
schedule and on his own terms. He was an artist in
power, like Abraham Lincoln or Franklin D. Roosevelt, and as he manipulated power he became in-
creasingly fascinated with its uses.

Long's first objective after going into office was
to perfect the organization that had elected him. He
shortly welded together an extraordinarily effective
machine. It covered the whole state and was one of
the instruments that eventually enabled him to control
the legislature almost completely. Before Long appeared on the scene, parish politicians, the "leaders"
in local parlance, had exercised an inordinate influence in their own areas and on the state generally.
The leader was usually, although not always, the
sheriff, and if enough sheriffs could agree on a candidate and make a deal with the New Orleans Old
Regulars, they could dictate the election of a governor.
Long abruptly abolished this pattern. In his arrangement the sheriff might have a place, but he was only
one of several leaders. Deliberately Long would set up

in a parish a plural or committee type of organization. There were several leaders who divided power among themselves and watched one another and reported on the others to Long, and no one of them was strong enough to defy the big boss at Baton Rouge. Moreover, Long was accustomed to dealing directly with the voters. He was capable, as his local leaders uneasily knew, of invading their parishes and turning their own people against them.

But no machine, no matter how artfully constructed, can endure on symmetry alone. It has to be able, as Long was fully aware, to pass out material or prestige awards to its followers. The Long organization was deliberately geared to be abundantly appreciative. Its ability rested on a firm and frank basis of patronage and price. Immediately the regime reached out to grasp control of existing boards and bureaus, and then by constantly creating new agencies to perform new functions it kept enlarging the jobs at its disposal. Thus the number of state employees was steadily increased, some of them being added unnecessarily but with a candid admittance that depression conditions obligated the state to hire people. More jobs were made available through the huge road building program, which in part was a state public works project. Finally, the Long organization was self-sustaining in a financial sense. The road contractors, the contractors on other works, the distributors of highway machinery and supplies, and the companies that wrote the state's insurance were required to render regular contributions to the machine's campaign treasury, and for obvious reasons these interests met the assessments. The state employees had to pay a percentage of their salaries before an election, the so-called "deducts." Surviving Long leaders will argue that these dealings were moral because they were open and known to the public. The organization was not beholden to any secret donors, they contend, and was hence independent and free to act in the public interest.

If Long had simply created an efficient machine, his achievement, while noteworthy, would not have been unusual, nor would it have won him the attention he secured in his own time or entitle him to the unique place he has in the annals of American politics. He went far beyond the pattern of previous leaders in the South or any section. He was the first mass or popular leader to set himself, not just to establish a machine of his own or to bring his enemies to terms, but to overwhelm utterly the existing organization and force it to enter his own apparatus. He systematically deprived the opposition of political sustenance, until finally he brought even the Old Regulars to their knees. At the time of his death by assassination in 1935, he had compelled most political elements in the state to affiliate with his organization. Each had a place and received certain rewards—but he defined the terms. A Long henchman was governor, and Long appointees filled all the executive offices. Long followers dominated the legislature, and a Long majority sat on the state supreme court. More, a series of far-reaching laws passed by an obedient legislature gave the governor, that is, Long, a controlling influence over local governments. There was still opposition, bitter and organized, but it seemed that the old power, structure had been destroyed, that, in fact, one man had become the power structure of an American commonwealth. Nothing quite like it had ever been witnessed in the nation's history.

It was, without exaggeration, an imaginative and imposing edifice of authority, and the man who had envisioned and put it together was very possibly the most daring of all American politicians. Most observers of the political scene would add that Long was also the most dangerous of our leaders. In his own time he was called a dictator and likened to Adolph Hitler or Benito Mussolini. The comparison was natural in the 1930's and has won wide credence. But later students will wonder about this easy application of the dictator label. Long, a remarkably introspective politician, wondered about it himself. Not surprisingly, he denied the charge. What is surprising was that some of his reasons were perceptively sound. He was well aware, for example, that his machine was largely a personal creation and dependent on the magnetism of his name. (The Long machine of later years was similarly dependent on Earl Long's name.) He realized too that he had concentrated too many powers in his own hands, powers that he but no successor could wield. On numerous occasions he warned his associates not to attempt to emulate him. He knew, finally, that his so-called dictatorship would not survive him. (The Long machine was, in fact, *voted* out of office five years after his death.) Long was not an American Hitler. Rather, he was an American boss, typical in many ways of the type, atypical in that he came to grasp for too much power, to look on power as something to be gained for the sheer pleasure of its use. It is fashionable to denounce Long as a power grabber. But no politician should be judged by just one aspect of his character or career. This is especially applicable to the great politician, the "shaker," the leader who picks things up and changes them, who leaves behind him a different, if not always a better, world. Such a man has to be evaluated in the round, to be rated by what he did to and for society and to and for himself.

Thus it is proper for detached commentators on the art of politics to point out that Huey Long had more power than any democratic leader should have. But they should also emphasize that unless he had been willing and able to take power he could not have done the things that he did—that he could not have lifted Louisiana from a condition of near feudalism into the modern world almost overnight or inspired thousands of poor white people all over the South to a vision of a better life or introduced into all of Southern politics, which had been pervasively romantic, a saving element of economic realism. The commentators might want to add, as a footnote, that in the Long story there is a great tragic query about politics and life itself. Robert Penn Warren poses the question in *All the King's Men*. How much evil may a good man have to do to do good—and how will he himself be changed by what he does?

In the autobiography Long hints at the problem the politician may have with power, but he does not tell us everything we would like to know about his own use of it. One of his purposes in writing the book was to further his ambitions, and naturally he was not going to expose methods he had already employed or tip his hand as to what he might do in the future. Having a large element of impudence in him, he could not resist boasting about the ease with which he outwitted opponents about what one reviewer called "his devilish resourcefulness," but this was as close as he got to the issue. One could wish that he had let his mind play freely and frankly on this central question in statecraft and given us the results of his experience.

Perhaps he intended to be more philosophical in a later volume, which would treat his national career and his accession to the office he was surely aiming at, the presidency. For *Every Man a King* is a partial autobiography carrying the author up to what he obviously considered a mid-point in his life. It is a story of preparation for greater tasks. When Long wrote the book, he had been in the Senate only a few months. He was just on the verge of his break with Roosevelt. His titanic struggle with the President that helped to turn the New Deal to the left was yet to come. So also was the campaign to sell to the country the economic nostrum known as Share Our Wealth. Long discusses SOW in his book and reveals the interesting information that he thought out the essence of the idea as early as 1918. There is room to doubt that he meant ever to translate the formula into working legislation. But he certainly believed that as a symbol it would be potent enough to carry him into the highest office. In the meantime, as a first install-ment he would give his countrymen an account of his life.

Apparently Long had the manuscript in final form by the summer of 1933. He asked George R. Allen to act as his agent in New York in dealing with print-ers, binders, jacket designers, and the like. Allen was to award the jobs on the basis of cost and speed of delivery and to deal with no shop that did not employ union labor. The journalist spent most of August talking to various companies. He ran into all kinds of vexatious problems, shifting cost estimates and delayed schedules, but he was finally able to an-nounce that he had signed agreements. The Senator was shocked at the dark ways of the Eastern pub-lishers. "Be careful with these people up there," he warned Allen. "Don't get tied up to where they can back out on you to our disadvantage again. They seem to be a cagy set. I have never seen anything like it." Actually, Allen had negotiated fairly good terms. The cost of printing an edition of 50,000 was approximately $8,000, a not unreasonable figure. And the first copies came off the press in the remarkably quick time of three weeks. They appeared in resplend-ent gold jackets which bore five pictures of the author. Although the work had been put together in New York, the title page carried the imprimatur of the National Book Company of New Orleans, which was the property of Long and some of his associates.

This company handled the sales of the book, sending out three hundred review copies and circularizing bookstores and rental libraries all over the country.

The author displayed more than the normal eagerness of a writer to see his product sell. Long had the additional motive of hoping that a wide distribution would enhance his political fortunes. The book was deliberately priced at the low figure of a dollar, and countless copies were distributed free to members of the Share Our Wealth Clubs. Once when Will Rogers was complaining that one of his books was not doing well, Long laughed and said: "Why don't you do what I did, give them away." Whatever the method, sale or gift, most of the edition was eventually disposed of. Seekers of a copy in recent years have found the book almost impossible to come by.

This new edition is presented in the belief that the book is what practically all reviewers, even hostile ones, hailed it as when it first appeared—an important political testament that deserves the attention of all serious students of politics. The present version is reproduced from the original edition with no revisions and, except for the omission of several photographs, no deletions. It contains, in fact, an addition. To conserve space Long cut out a proposed index. The editor has supplied one.

T. HARRY WILLIAMS

*Baton Rouge, Louisiana*

# CONTENTS

# LIST OF ILLUSTRATIONS

# EVERY MAN
# A KING
The Autobiography of
# HUEY P. LONG

# CHAPTER I

BENVENUTO CELLINI, famed Florentine autobiographer, musician and sculptor, said that when one whose career has been above the ordinary, reached the age of sixty years, he should compile an autobiography for the world.

I am now thirty-nine, some twenty-one years short of that time when, according to Cellini, I should begin to compose such a work. But there is a fable to the effect that Cardinal Mazarin, on his death bed, grieved over the fact that he was near death at the age of fifty-two. A physician is said to have declared that his years of service in the Fronde were four years in one; that, therefore, he was dying at an age past eighty.[1]

If newspapers, magazines and some biographers of this country and other nations find the public so interested in me that they should continue to write

---

[1] The conversation between Mazarin and his physician is given by Dumas, as follows:

"Monseigneur," said Guenaud, seating himself by the bed, "your eminence has worked very hard during your life; your eminence has suffered much."

"But I am not old, I fancy. The late Monsieur de Richelieu was but seventeen months younger than I am when he died, and died of a mortal disease. I am young, Guenaud; remember, I am scarcely fifty-two."

"Oh! monseigneur, you are much more than that. How long did the Fronde last?"

"For what purpose do you put such a question to me?"

and to publish garbled accounts of my career, then perhaps I should write of myself.[2]

In the year 1892 my father, Huey P. Long, and my mother, Caledonia, with their six children moved from Tunica to the community of Winnfield, Louisiana, the Parish Seat of Winn Parish (County) and it was there that I was born August 30, 1893. Land was very cheap at the time my parents settled there and they were able to buy a 320-acre tract, a small part of which was under cultivation. When I was born my parents were living in a comfortable, well-built, four-room log house. A year later we moved into a better house which was built on the same premises.

My earliest and more or less inchoate recollections are that, in the time of my childhood, any person of brawn had some place or opportunity to hew out what was required of him in life. My sympathies were attracted to the persons who had no such physical asset, whose fight for subsistence was one of living

---

"For a medical calculation, monseigneur."

"Well, some ten years—off and on."

"Very well; be kind enough to reckon every year of the Fronde as three years—that makes thirty; now twenty and fifty-two make seventy-two years. You are seventy-two, monseigneur; and that is a great age." While saying this, he felt the pulse of his patient. This pulse was filled with such fatal prognostics that the physician continued, notwithstanding the interruptions of the patient: "Put down the years of the Fronde at four each, and you have lived eighty-two years."

[2] Three purported biographies have been written on Huey P. Long, not including magazine articles, and newspaper feature stories. The latest is entitled "The Kingfish," published by Putnam.

from hand to mouth, of which there seem to have been more than a few among the people I knew.

Our community was a kindly one with the philosophy of "live and let live"; no one went hungry or in need of clothes if any one in the neighborhood had things beyond his own immediate requirements. I was frequently sent by my parents with food and clothing of the best kind to some less fortunate family living in the neighborhood. Such people did not need to make their wants known—not even was it necessary that they disclose their identity. If there was a fair sign from which it might be reasonably suspected that someone was in need, we shared with him the best we had.

Among the first of the strange families to have moved into our locality was a Methodist preacher with a number of small children. There were not enough people of his faith to furnish sufficient contribution for his church work. I made frequent trips to their home, sometimes more than once a day, carrying provisions to feed the children.

Years later, when one from this family was among the foremost of the sinister-controlled members of the Legislature undertaking my ruin as Governor I sent someone to him and I said to my messenger:

"Tell him one thing: I am still glad my folks didn't let them starve." But there is and always has been a Providence who understands and who does not forget.

I must have been about eight years old when I saw the first sheriff's sale which I remember. By that

time a railroad had been built into the community.[3]
A farmer's place was to be auctioned by the sheriff
for a debt owed to a store. Before the sale, standing
on the steps of the courthouse, this farmer begged the
crowd not to bid for his home. He plead that it would
be taking it away from his children; that if given time
to raise another crop he could pay his debts.

No one in the crowd offered a bid. The creditor
remained silent until the sheriff was about ready to
declare "no sale," when he took courage and made his
bid.

The poor farmer was out; I was horrified. I could
not understand. It seemed criminal.

This marked the first sign, in my recollection, of
a neighborhood, where the blessings of the Creator
were shared one with the other, being transformed
into a community yielding to commercial entice-
ments.

A small railroad built a line into Winnfield and
located a depot on my father's farm. Soon other railroads entered the same vicinity and Winnfield became
a village. Within ten years the town grew to about
3000 inhabitants. One side of my father's farm became part of the business section, and another part of
it was occupied by residences.

The surrounding territory soon abounded with sawmills and lumber camps. The sparse farm population

---

[3] The Arkansas Southern Railroad was extended from El
Dorado, Arkansas, to Winnfield, Louisiana, in the year 1900.
This line was later purchased by the Rock Island System and
extended to Little Rock, Arkansas, on the north, and Alexandria,
Louisiana, on the south.

increased. But the more remote rural section was never thickly settled and is not now.

I recollect a trip to one of these sawmill camps near my home a few years later when a schoolmate and myself auctioned off a wagon load of books. We had only a banjo and a pair of scissors left in the wagon. We sold them, too.

Returning home that night, after we had calculated our profits, the mule pulling the wagon made a run away going down hill, tearing up the wagon and the harness. Bang went the profits!

The free and easy life and practises of the incoming railroad and sawmill workers rather excited my father, lest his sons might become contaminated by them. With some of the first money which he acquired from the sale of town lots carved from his farm, he bought another farm ten miles back in the country from Winnfield, to which he early announced his intention of moving.

The family home was never moved to this farm; however, we did some of the work there. A few crops of cotton and corn were raised.

I managed to keep as a closed secret the fact that I smoked and chewed tobacco. But when the time came for me to leave town and go to the country farm, I usually managed to smuggle a little along. On one occasion a plug slipped out of my back pocket while I was riding on a spring seat of the wagon. My father picked it up.

"If you stay alive until you are twenty-one, it will be the wonder of this world," he muttered, taking the tobacco away from me.

Practically everybody in the neighborhood, male and female, had done some of the work of planting corn, cotton and potatoes; all had picked cotton; most of them from time to time had worked on the railroad or at the lumber camps and sawmills.

From my earliest recollection I hated the farm work. In the field the rows were long; the sun was hot; there was little companionship. Rising before the sun, we toiled until dark, after which we did nothing except eat supper, listen to the whippoorwills, and go to bed.

Sometimes we split a few rails, or hewed a cross tie or two; occasionally we cut wood or drove a team of mules. The cotton boll-weevil had made its appearance and added to the already uninteresting and unprofitable work. My every sympathy has gone out to those who toil.

At the age of ten, I made my first attempt to run away from home. I got less than fifty miles. I made another effort a few years later, but was caught some twenty miles away from Winnfield.

I had read in the Scriptures of the tears and greetings given for the prodigal son on his return. But when I reached home one of my sisters, in a shrill voice, shouted:

"Come in, tramp!"

While at home I was, under compulsion, a regular attendant of all religious ceremonies. On Sunday morning about nine o'clock we went to Sunday School. Church services immediately followed. On the same Sunday in mid-afternoon I went to the church for the young people's religious society meeting. On Sunday night we returned for more church services. On Wednesday night we attended prayer meeting. We went to every funeral within ten miles. Most of us read the Scripture from cover to cover.

At about the age of thirteen I took up the work of a printer. I mastered the trade fairly well, working in a printing office most of the time while not actually attending school. The compensation was rather good in comparison with what was paid for other work. A book auctioneer, with a large collection of books of all kinds and descriptions, came to Winnfield. He hired me to help in handling the books. I took my pay in books.

A school mate of mine made an arrangement by which he secured some books to auction in nearby and smaller towns. I helped him in some of the towns, with none too great success except to acquire a considerable stock of books. At times we found jobs selling stocks of merchandise at auction.

At the age of fifteen I was sent as a representative in debating from the Winnfield High School to the State High School Rally which was held at the Louisiana State University in Baton Rouge, the Capital of the State. I fared badly, but was given honorable mention.

The following year, April, 1910, I was again sent to the State Rally as debater, declaimer, mile runner and member of the relay team. I made no showing worthy of mention in any of the contests except in debating, in which I won third place and a scholarship to the Louisiana State University.

# CHAPTER II

CONDITIONS were not very good in the Winn-field community along in 1910.

There were nine children in our family. I was six-teen years old. My parents had been able, with the help the six older children had given, to send them to college until they were practically finished or graduated.

I saw no opportunity to attend the Louisiana State University. The scholarship which I had won did not take into account books and living expenses. It would have been difficult to secure enough money.

I secured a position travelling for a large supply house which had a branch office in New Orleans. My job was to sell its products to the merchants and to advertise and solicit orders for it from house to house. Along with the work of soliciting orders from house to house and from merchants, I tacked up signs, dis-tributed pie plates and cook books and occasionally held baking contests in various cities and towns.

I dropped out of the employment of the concern for about four months to attend school at Shreveport, after which I took up the same work.

In the summer of 1911, I secured employment with a packing company as a regular travelling salesman with a salary and expense account. For the first time in my life I felt that I had hit a bed of ease. I was permitted to stop at the best hotels of the day. My territory covered several states in the south. According to the lights and standards of my associates, I had arrived.

On one of my trips back home, I brought a newly invented product, a safety razor. My father undertook to use it. After moistening his face, he stood in front of the looking glass just over the mantel and began to shave. One of my older brothers, a college graduate, was seated on a trunk in the rear of the room. Observing the lather drying and becoming thin, he undertook to advise my father, with a grain of satire.

"Pa," he said, "they say that thing works a little better with lather."

My father paused and looked at my brother.

"I'll just swear," he said, "I have certainly raised smart sons. I'll bet, young man, that the wonder of your life is how pa ever got this far."

The life of a drummer was entirely too easy for me. I turned in a goodly volume of business. I was easily convinced by other drummers that so long as I reported large sales I need not worry as to my expense account or as to the regularity of my work. I found this was not true in my case and that I was working for a strict disciplinarian; after being given a few warnings, which I did not heed, I was summarily discharged.

I undertook to secure my reinstatement without avail whereupon I went back to Houston, Texas, where I stayed for some months. I secured employment at various occupations, but I was not able to get another position as a travelling salesman.

Finally I left Houston for Memphis, Tennessee,

but I found no opening for a travelling salesman there, and for several weeks I was without any employment at all. I went from park to depot and depot to railroad yards, sleeping wherever I might be permitted to lay my head and eating what I could get when I could get it. I gave up my effort in Memphis and left for Oklahoma.

Uptown in Oklahoma City was and still stands the office of the Dawson Produce Company. I went there and called for the manager. I met Mr. K. W. Dawson himself, the owner of the business. He was a very serious but kindly faced gentleman.

I immediately felt at ease and asked to secure some kind of work as a salesman in the vicinity of Norman, Oklahoma, so that I might earn enough money to attend the University there and study law. I was almost penniless at the time but undertook not to disclose it.

Mr. Dawson told me to return the next day. On the following day he told me that there were four towns, including Norman, which were being worked by a salesman whom he could use in the office; that if I wished to make those towns as my territory he thought I could work their trade and attend school all the time necessary to carry on a year's law classes.

I gladly took the job and was given an order book with a price list and the accounts which I was to collect. This occurred January 2, 1912. But how was I to get to Norman?

Snow and sleet covered the ground. The wind was cold and cutting.

I surveyed my belongings. I had exactly three nickels.

There was an interurban line which ran half way the route to Norman, from Oklahoma City to Moore. The fare for that first nine miles was fifteen cents. I pondered—whether I should ride the first nine miles for the fifteen cents and walk the remaining nine miles or try to walk the entire eighteen miles, as cold as it was, and have the money when I reached Norman. I took the course of walking the full distance.

I reached there about midnight and walked the streets of the town the balance of the night, spending some time to warm myself at an oil mill where work was being done.

On the morning of January 3, 1912, bright and early, I ventured forth on my new employment. Immediately, I sold one merchant some fifty sacks of potatoes. I finally secured pledges for sufficient orders to account for an entire carload. What luck!

I went to telephone the orders to Mr. Dawson, intending to ask his permission to draw some amount of money on the business. Of course, I placed the call "collect." I had eaten breakfast and had not a cent left.

Word came back that the collect telephone call was declined.

I faced the task of securing twenty-five cents in order to place my telephone call from Norman to Oklahoma City. In my back pocket was a new leather purse which had been sent to me as a Christmas gift. It had been put to no use whatever. It couldn't have been. I found a way to pawn it to a second-hand furniture store, outside the business section of the town, for the necessary amount.

I again placed the telephone call for Mr. Dawson. When he answered I informed him that I had sold a carload of potatoes in Norman at list price.

"I am sorry," he answered, "we are out of potatoes and will be for some time."

I had walked; I had starved; I had disposed of everything of value I had on the face of the earth. So, I planned to leave Norman the best way I could. I would not give up without one more effort. Boldly I went to a bank to see the president and undertook to borrow twenty-five dollars. At least the banker wasn't crazy.

So my plan was made to leave Norman.

I strolled over to the Santa Fe depot.

While there I noticed a well groomed, rather stout looking gentleman, who appeared to be as aimless and purposeless as I was. He seemed unsettled and nervous. He either spoke to me or I to him. One word brought on another. He asked where I was going. I told him I hadn't exactly decided, but that maybe I would go south, or maybe north. Then he said:

"One train is due here any minute."

"I am not thinking about the train," I replied.

"Then, how are you going?" he asked.

"How do most people go that don't ride?" I asked.

"You don't mean you are going to walk?"

"Out of here just like I walked in," I answered.

He introduced himself to me as R. O. Jackson. In the conversation which followed I told him how I had secured employment in Oklahoma City, of walking into the town, of my disappointment in making certain sales which could not be filled, of my inability to stay there long, and of my decision to leave.

He reached into his pocket and pulled out several bills. He offered to hand me one of twenty dollars.

"I do not want you to give me twenty dollars or anything else," I said. "The chances are, however, that whatever you hand me will be a gift. If I can make it here at all, I can do it on five dollars. If you will lend me five dollars, and I can't pay it back, then you can feel that I at least saved you fifteen."

He handed me the five dollars.

My new friend and creditor did not leave me after lending me the money. On the following morning, when I approached the mercantile establishments of Norman, I was frequently informed that Jackson had been to one or the other asking that they give as much of their business as possible to the Dawson Produce Company. I met Mr. Jackson on the street the following morning.

"What are you going to do for law books?" he asked me.

"Go without any until I can get some money to buy them," I replied.

"My brother-in-law owns the drug store here that handles the law books. He will credit you." [4]

I was at the University from January until May, 1912, where I spent the happiest days of my life. I attended my law classes regularly and I earned,

---

[4] The Drug Store handling law books in Norman in 1912 was owned by Barborough Brothers, one of whom is the brother-in-law of R. O. Jackson.

on the average, nearly $100.00 per month for my work as a salesman.

My previous experience did not make much of a mark on me. I spent my money as I made it. What I did not spend, I either loaned or gave away to other boys at the University more in need than myself.

I left that school at the end of its session in the spring of 1912, expecting to return that autumn. I secured a job with a manufacturing house of Kansas City, Missouri. I was one of the regular salesmen for the concern.

Eventually, other salesmen were placed under me —men doing work similar to that which I had done in the early days with the supply company.

I was soon located in Memphis, Tennessee, with headquarters at the Gayoso Hotel. My territory embraced parts of Texas, Oklahoma, Louisiana, Arkansas, Tennessee, Illinois, Kentucky, Mississippi, and Alabama.

I had begun to help certain others. I could not see a way to return to the University of Oklahoma, a fact which gave me much grief and heartache.

During Christmas week, 1912, I came back to my home in Louisiana on a month's vacation. I spent much of my time in Shreveport. I invited Miss Rose McConnell, whom I had met while attending school in Shreveport, to go with me to the Grand Opera House to see the opera "Lohengrin."

A few days later I was arrested and charged with having shot at some one, but at a time during the hours when I had been at the Grand Opera House. Miss McConnell had kept the stubs torn off the theatre tickets. We located all the people who had been near us at the show and I was released.

We were married the following year in Memphis, Tennessee. I was nineteen years old.

Late in the summer of 1914, when war clouds had gathered in Europe, I spent a final few weeks on the road with the Chattanooga Medicine Company at a better rate of pay, and in October entered Tulane University at New Orleans as a law student. I undertook to carry the work of a three-year law course in one year in order that I might be admitted to the bar in the following spring. I had a few hundred dollars and a brother had promised to lend me $400.00 more.

My wife and I settled in a dingy two room apartment in the city of New Orleans. I attended such classes as the hours would permit, studying many other subjects without the help of class instruction.

I entered a contest to become one of the school's debaters, and was chosen by the University to debate against a girls' college. That was the year, I think the only year, when that girls' college won the debating contest from Tulane.

I studied law as much as from sixteen to twenty hours each day. My weight fell to 112 pounds. While I passed such of the examinations as I was permitted to take at Tulane, it was not possible under the scholastic rules of the University for me to take the other examinations so that I might secure a diploma.

My money gave out completely during the last months of the spring. I faced the alternative of becoming a lawyer very quickly or of abandoning the effort.

I went to Chief Justice Frank A. Monroe, of the Supreme Court of Louisiana, in New Orleans.

"My name is Long. I am a special student at Tulane University," I said to the Judge.

"All right, Mr. Long, what can I do for you?"

"Judge, I don't know that you can do anything for me, but I want to give you the facts about my situation and get your advice on what I should do and if possible, your help."

The old Chief Justice appeared responsive. I felt perfectly at ease.

"Under your rules here I cannot take an examination for the bar until the last part of June. I would like to wait until June if I could. I am married. I have no money. I have borrowed to get to where I am now. I want to know if it's at all possible for the court to give one an examination other than on the day set by the rules."

"This court can do anything that a majority of its members want to do," he replied. Then he continued: "The only difficulty I can see for you is in getting the bar committee to examine you. Looks to me like they ought to be reasonable."

"Well, Judge, if it's not asking too much, just how would you advise me to go about getting the bar committee."

"Why, just go to them like you came to me. If you are well enough up on your subjects they can examine you orally. We'll try them out. Let me know how you make it."

I sought a meeting of the bar committee for the next day, and was able to arrange it. I was passed by the bar committee, whereupon Chief Justice Monroe assembled a majority of the court, gave the necessary examination, and on the 15th day of May, 1915, at the age of 21, I was sworn in and declared a full-fledged lawyer in the State of Louisiana.

# CHAPTER III

I ARRIVED at my old home town of Winnfield some few days after I had been admitted to the bar, ready for the practice of law. My first few months' effort netted me no returns. I gave up the office I had occupied.

With no money and apparently with no chance of earning any through the practice of law, I undertook to secure employment as a travelling salesman. I couldn't secure a position. I had no law books except a copy of the Civil Code, a volume of the Code of Practice and a "formulary."

I found a small ante-room, located over the Bank of Winnfield. It was about eight feet wide by ten feet long. It had no electric lights and only one window in it. The bank trusted me for the rent of that ante-room at $4.00 a month. I secured a white pine top table, placed my three law books on it, had painted a fifty-cent tin sign, and again undertook to herald to the world:

"Huey P. Long, Lawyer."

A shoe store opened on the street immediately next to the bank. The proprietor promised that, whenever I was wanted at the telephone, he would call me.

### THE CHANCE FOR A LAWSUIT

There had been a character living in the Winnfield community for a lifetime by the name of Cole John-

18

son. He seldom worked except for roasting a few peanuts and selling them on the streets. He was known to lead a shiftless life, occasionally playing seven-up and poker around the swamps. He had a voice like a screech owl; in fact, his physical appearance reminded one of that remarkable bird.

Cole Johnson, as he was known to the community, became ill and was sent to the Charity Hospital in Shreveport. In the meantime, Mr. Oscar K. Allen, now the Governor of Louisiana, who had been reared on a farm three miles from that of my father, between our farm at Winnfield and the farm out in the country, had become the neighborhood pride concerning what was known as the "yan-side element," meaning the people living beyond the bayou east of Winnfield.

Cole Johnson had secured credit at Mr. Allen's store, and Mr. Allen learned something no one else seemed to know—that the man had initials. He entered Cole Johnson's account on his books under the name of "C. G." Johnson.

When it was reported that Cole Johnson had died at the Charity Hospital at Shreveport, the "yan-side" relatives and neighbors, living some sixteen miles from Winnfield, called at the Allen store and asked him to telephone to the hospital and ask for the body. Mr. Allen complied and gave instructions that the body of "C. G." Johnson be sent to Winnfield.

On the following morning a casket arrived. It was turned over to the relatives and neighbors who immediately loaded it on a wagon and carried it sixteen miles into the rural section. There the casket was placed in a room to be opened for public view at sunrise.

But the mourners at the wake concluded they would have a view of the remains before the arrival of other friends and neighbors. When the lid of the casket was lifted there was exposed to view the body of a dark-skinned African gentleman. The casket was immediately closed, put back in the box, loaded on a wagon and sent to Winnfield without the loss of a moment's time. A messenger, riding horse-back ahead of the caravan, brought Mr. Allen news of the incident.

When the body of the deceased colored gentleman was hauled up in front of the Allen store it was learned that Mr. Allen was absent. Some said he had gone fishing. Anyway, he had left word that I should be called in to advise with the neighbors and relatives.

In due course the mourners called at my office. The spokesman was a tall and angular gentleman, about forty years of age, red-faced, with a prominent chin. He began:

"Lawyer, Uncle Cole Johnson died up in the Charity Horspittle in Shreesport, and we had Oscar Allen phone for his body. They sent us a colored man. We set up with him until nearly morning before we found it out. We want to know what to do for our rights."

"Where is the body?" I asked.

"It's right down here in the street, beside this building now."

I looked out of the window to the street; my office was in the second and last story of the building. The

coffin was within my easy view. Several of the neighbors were standing about.

"Well, just what do you want done?" I asked,
when I had resumed my seat, facing the gentleman.

"We want damages, and we want Uncle Cole's
body."

"Well, I think we can get Mr. Johnson's body, all
right," I answered, "but damages—against whom do
you expect to recover?"

"Anybody. That horspittle, first."

"Why, gentlemen," I began to give my first legal
advice, "the law is that money devoted to charity cannot be recovered in a damage suit. In other words, the
State gives the hospital money to care for the sick
people, and the law will not allow that money to be
taken away from that purpose in a damage suit."

"What's that?" a new voice chimed in. "Do you
mean to say there ain't nothing coming to me for
hauling that colored man sixteen miles and back, and
setting up with him until four o'clock in the morning,
thinking all the time he was Uncle Cole?"

"Not against the hospital, gentlemen," I replied.

The chief spokesman took the reins.

"Then what about Oscar Allen? He's in on this
thing. Somebody's going to pay me for setting up all
night beside that colored man."

I managed to dismiss the callers with the assurance
that I could not be retained to secure damages on their
behalf from anyone for the mistake.

My first legal advice was to my friend and lifelong
associate, now Governor Allen. I suggested to him
that his fishing trip, whether for fish or not, be pro-

longed until proper exchange was made and the body of Cole Johnson was buried. This was done and Mr. Allen returned.

I received no fee, but at least I had rendered legal advice in a prominent matter and for a noted citizen. It should be recorded that the hospital actually sent the body of "C. G." Johnson, as directed by Mr. Allen. Cole Johnson had been there entered under his usual name.

I managed for several months to pick up a little "chip and whet-stone" practice. The bank from which I was renting my office pressed me pretty hard for the $4.00 per month rent. It was hard to get.

I had established a little checking account at the bank, and on one occasion gave a check which overdrew it by a dollar or two. I had thought that, if I ever should overdraw for a dollar or so, the bank would take care of that much.

I went to the bank and met one of the officers.

"I have a little overdraft here," I said.

"Overdraft?" he questioned back.

"Yes," I said, "it's just for a few dollars."

"Now, maybe I can correct you. You have no overdraft here, but a check came in this morning and there is no money to your account to pay it."

"Well, of course, you know I'll pay it and it's good," I replied.

"Huey, the banks we do business with don't wait on checks to be paid as long as we have been waiting on your office rent. Now, you ought to have known better than to have written this check. We really had no right to hold it till you got here; it should have been returned marked 'Insufficient Funds' before now."

"Now I understand you," I replied.

"Well, if you understand that, then understand that we expect that office rent paid, and tbat may keep you here a while longer than you will be if things go like they are now. I looked that office over and there ain't anything to move," he said.

I had bought a typewriter and was in arrears trving to pay for it at the rate of $10.00 a month. I had bought the revised statutes of the State, a filing cabinet, an oak table and typewriter desk, on all of which my payments amounted to an additional $20.00 per month. I still occupied the ante-room, had no telephone and worked at night by the light of a kerosene lamp.

After securing funds to satisfy the check and the office rent, I had to wait but a few davs when onportunity came my way to make a call on the bank.

There came to my office a widow, Martha E. DeLoach, who some nine and a half years before had made a deposit of some insurance monev in what was known as the Winn Parish Bank. which had consolidated with the Bank of Winnfield. An officer of that institution had taken her funds to his own use. This officer paid the widow part of the money and gave his note for the balance, which note she accepted. He had left the State and his whereabouts were unknown.

Mrs. DeLoach said she had been to other lawyers of the town, but had been advised that upon accepting the settlement from the bank officer she had released any claim she might have had against the bank.

I filed suit and brought the bank into court. Upon my starting to try the DeLoach suit, the court ordered that I furnish bond for the costs to the amount of $100.00.

It began to look as though the widow's suit would be dismissed.

I took a last chance. I went to see Senator S. J. Harper.

"Senator," I said, "are you a director of the Bank of Winnfield?"

"Yes, I am one of the first directors it ever had, and I am still a member of the board."

"Well, the lawyers of the bank have asked me to get up a bond of $100.00 for Mrs. DeLoach. I can't make the bond."

"Is that so?" he answered, rather friendly.

"Yes, and here's the bad part of it. Mrs. DeLoach hasn't anything and I haven't anything either that's worth $100.00 on a bond. If I could furnish the bond I am sure to win it."

"It doesn't look exactly fair," the senator said, "for them to dismiss that woman's suit because she can't make a bond. That won't look right."

"But it's going to be done tomorrow morning if I can't make the bond," I rejoined. "Would you help me to get somebody to sign that bond?"

"No," he replied, "I wouldn't like to be put in the position of trying to get someone to sign a bond against the bank that I'm a director of."

"Now, wait a minute," he pondered. Then continued: "Could you put that bond up in cash?"

"Why, yes. In fact, I think if I could deposit half

the cash for the time being, that the clerk would waive giving any bond at all until the costs ran above $50.00."

"I'll lend you the $50.00. You give me your due bill."

"Senator," I added, "if it is that easy to get $50.00, how about letting me give you my note for $60.00? I need $10.00."

"Make it for $75.00," said the senator.

I executed the proper instrument. The senator opened his safe and counted out the $75.00.

The DeLoach case was won very easily. All I had to do was to present the petition and prove that the Bank of Winnfield had bought the assets of the Winn Parish Bank, in which the money had been deposited, to get judgment.

My wife being very economical, we lived modestly for a few dollars per month. No children had been born to us up to that time, but we were very happy.

I had begun a state-wide agitation against a new law of the State which had severely restricted the right of recovery for injury or death incurred in the course of work. I created quite a sentiment against the law.

The State Legislature met in May, 1916. My friend, S. J. Harper, of Winnfield, was a member of the State Senate. I prepared for him certain amendments which he was to offer in the Committee on Capital and Labor, of which he was a member.

It was my first time to have seen a legislature in session. The formalities, mannerisms, kow-towing and easily discernible insincerities surrounding all of the affairs of the session were, to my mind (untrained to such a scene), disgusting.

I was twenty-two.

I ran across a rather elderly gentleman whose name was Faust. He had traveled considerably.

Early one afternoon Mr. Faust sat with me in a restaurant near the Capitol Building. I said to him:

"Everybody talks guarded, like he was afraid he would slip on something if he ventured very far."

"Son," said the elderly Mr. Faust, "it's something like this in all State capitals. You're fighting on a bad side to get much encouragement."

"Do you know what I'm trying to do?" I asked.

"Yes, I think I know what you are trying to do, but I don't think you do."

"How do you mean that?"

"Well, just as fast as you can you're trying to fence yourself out of getting a pretty good start as a lawyer."

"Well," I replied, "suppose the people change this whole thing? They can if they want to," I asked.

"If they knew what they wanted to do they could. I doubt that much you say will ever be heard of by many people, and not one out of a hundred of them will pay you much attention."

"But the people of Louisiana are pretty liberal, I think."

"The State is the worst yet," he said. "Why do you think Standard Oil located here?"

"What about New Jersey?" I asked.

"It doesn't compare with Louisiana."

In the course of a few days a meeting of the Committee on Capital and Labor of the State Senate was assembled in the evening to consider, among other things, the Harper amendment which I had prepared. Upon my asking to be recognized I was generally ordered to sit down.

One time when I rose the committee chairman asked,

"Whom do you represent?"

"Several thousand common laborers," I said.

"Are they paying you anything?"

"No," I replied.

"They seem to have good sense."

The attendants guffawed.

Several speeches were made condemning my activities against the law. I was referred to as an impostor by one or two lawyers and members of the Senate, but still I could not secure recognition to speak.

One lawyer there told a story of a fly alighting on the hub of a wagon passing through a sand bed which said to itself:

"See what a dust I am raising!"

He referred to my having been admitted to the bar of the State for only one year, and urged ignoring such contemptuous furor as I had undertaken to create.

At about the hour of midnight a motion was made that consideration of the amendments be terminated and that the committee adjourn.

I had stood for about all the legislative practices that my system could tolerate. Neither the rulings and orders of the chair nor anything else could have hushed me at the time. Without being recognized I rose at the foot of the table and began to speak. I was not interrupted. I said:

> For twenty years has the Louisiana Legislature been dominated by the henchmen and attorneys of the interests. Those seeking reforms have, from necessity, bowed their heads in regret and shame when witnessing the victories of these corrupting influences at this capitol. But, gentlemen, with all this, not until 1914 did they possess the brazen audacity to command the General Assembly of Louisiana to pass unanimously a law by which a laborer's family should not receive over an average sum of $300.00 for a life upon whom they depend for education and support, though it be lost while in the honest discharge of duty. . . .
>
> Yet, there are those here representing the combined corporations, who declare that they merely seek justice. What a subterfuge! Exposure seems to be an irresistible converter. There are hours when the infidel invokes God and the anarchist calls on the government. There are times when the people cling to that which they have repudiated. Can it be that these gentlemen, after exposure seems imminent, will now attempt to invoke the term "justice" after their continued practices of fraud and deceit? We are afraid of such conversions.

Most of the amendments proposed by Senator Harper were lost on the vote of the committee, but enough sentiment was aroused that many of them were adopted following debate on the floor of the Senate.

There was a suit filed by a farm family against a lumber company involving a tract of timber. The case had been tried and lost in the lower court and was then pending on appeal. The lawyer handling the case for the family was one of the ablest of his time. With one of his clients he met me on the street one day.

"We can win this case on appeal if a good brief is written on a plea of estoppel," he told me. "If you will get up a brief in the case on that plea I will see that you are paid $100.00, if we win."

I took the record of the case, looked up the point of law and wrote a brief which, when printed, consisted of only a few pages. Before it was printed I carried it to the attorney in the case.

He read it.

"That will win it," he said.

"Is that all we are going to write?" I asked.

"That is the law and that's enough," he answered.

We won the suit on the appeal, the decision of the lower court being reversed.[5]

My practice soon grew to such proportions that it approximated, in the number of cases handled, as much as that of the balance of the bar of Winnfield combined. This was due to energy to handle every case, however small or difficult it might be.

One of the hardest fought cases I ever had was for $22.50. It was tried in three courts, finally reaching

[5] C. M. Sanders et al vs. Tremont Lumber Co., 143 La. Reports, page 181.

the Supreme Court, involving costs and expenses of several hundred dollars. I finally won it.[6]

Once I had reached the stage that I had a law library and law office, equipped sufficiently to care for the work, my energy was equal to the handling of one side of nearly every case brought to the bar of Winnfield.

It became my problem to develop some means by which I could compel the interests from whom I won timber in lawsuits to transport my timber, or else to pay me a fair price for what I had won. They operated tram railway lines for their timber only.

I awaited the day when the concern with which I was most often engaged in litigation was extending its tram railway line into a large body of timber which it thought it owned. When this railway track had reached a point where a certain land title began, I brought suits for that particular tract.

This railway line was placed in the position that if I won the suits, either it could not cross the land at all, or in order to acquire the right to cross, it would have to declare its railroad to be a common carrier.

When I had won that suit the president of the concern called to see me.

---

[6] Shreveport Mill and Elevator Co. vs. John Stoehr, 139 La. Reports, page 719. The amount involved was $22.50. The Supreme Court in the case held: "Where a merchant, having contracted to furnish to a baker hard wheat flour of a certain brand, ships flour of another brand, representing it to be of the same grade as the brand ordered, and the baker uses only enough of it to find out that it is of an inferior grade, he is not required to pay for the portion which he used in testing the flour, and which proved to be of no value to him."

"Now, I don't want you to sue us any more," he said. "The next time any one comes to you with a claim, make out a deed for me and write me just about what you think is a fair settlement, and I will send you a check."

Some few days after that, two farmers, claiming timber rights located near the land over which the other litigation had occurred, brought through me claims against the same company. I made out two deeds, one for $750.00, and the other for $500.00. I forwarded them to the president of this company, with a letter asking that he send me the money in accordance with his statement to me. Checks came back by an early mail, without a word of comment.[7]

I never sued that company again.

An opportunity seemed to appear to make it possible for me to move to the City of Shreveport, when a vacancy occurred in the United States Attorney's office there. I undertook to secure the position of Assistant United States Attorney. I received such assurances as to convince me that the position was practically mine for the asking. Later, a severe opposition developed from all the corporations of my territory, which I could not overcome.

Probably that was my evil day. Once disappointed over a political undertaking, I could never cast it from my mind. I awaited the opportunity of a political contest.

---

[7] Conveyance records of the Parish of Winn, Louisiana, deeds of E. A. Ford and S. R. Newsom to the Urania Lumber Company.

In participating in local politics I learned some very early lessons.

We had a great friend, Joe Anders, who, while possessing some very loyal followers, had a certain vicious opposition, including his brother, Ben L. Anders.

When election matters had reached fever heat in the fall of 1916, Joe Anders came to Winnfield late one Sunday afternoon. I met him in the rear end of a general store.

"Huey," he said, "my wife is distantly related to the man that's running against your brother. I found out yesterday that Ben had cut his eye around to see whether or not I was leaning so strong to you fellows as I had been."

"All right, Joe," I said. "What have you got on your mind?"

"Well, now, I've got an idea. If we can work this thing I can handle the men that are with me. Maybe we can turn Ben and the whole opposition crowd to you fellows. Suppose I turn against you today and help my wife's kinfolks?"

I thought a minute. I suggested that we consult with a few of our strategists.

Our crowd grew to about four. Joe had planned the matter out in pretty good form.

"Now, fellows," he said, "let me go back home and phone the old doctor that's handling that man's campaign against you. If he will tell me to come down, I'll get a couple of witnesses to come along to watch me, to go back and report what happens. Then I'll run back and slowly change over and about

Saturday before election I'll take to the saddle. I can drive every one of the enemies to you."

At that point one of our number spoke up:

"Joe, I didn't know you knew just how valuable you could be. Start out a little bit before Saturday."

Joe's brothers and all his other enemies swung to our camp. On election day we voted the strength of Joe Anders and the strength of his opposition. It took several days for the opposition to verify the correctness of the returns.

When Joe Anders was moving out of the Hood's Mill neighborhood to take a job as a policeman in Monroe, his brother, Ben L. Anders, wasted two boxes of shells shooting his shot gun to celebrate the advent.

"Ben," I said, "I hear that you boys have been celebrating around Hood's Mill."

"Yes, the community has made great strides," he said.

America was about ready to go into the World War. State Senator Harper, who had befriended me in many ways, was one of the foremost workers against America entering it.

Senator Harper published a book, which he called "Issues of the Day—Free Speech—Financial Slavery." A grand jury of the United States Court indicted him at Alexandria, Louisiana, charging violations of the law under the Espionage Act.

I accompanied Senator Harper to Shreveport to arrange to secure his bond.

I am quoted in the issue of the Times-Picayune of February 22, 1918. The statement was as follows:

Some time ago Senator Harper announced that
he would be a candidate for Congress from the
Eighth District in the coming September election.
He announced that his platform was solely one
that this war in which we are now engaged should
be supported by a conscription of war profits and
certain amounts of swollen fortunes, as well as a
conscription of men. In the book which he published, he quoted many government statistics and
newspaper reports to show that two per cent of
the people living in the United States own seventy
per cent of its wealth, and he went so far as to say
that if the war profiteers were not forced to bear
their just share of this nation's war costs, that the
country must face financial slavery for the future. Senator Harper was indicted for publishing
this book.[8]

I have told United States Attorney Moore that
we regard this indictment as nothing less than an
attempt to coerce a reputable official of this State,
whose views are not in accord with the war profiteers and I have demanded that this case be called
immediately and disposed of. If it is within our
power, we are going to force this case to trial at
the next term of court.

We recognized that in the selection of the jury was
practically the decision of the case. We feared that
the judge was hostile and would charge the jury, al-

---

[8] Senator Harper's stand for taxing of wealth for war instead
of issuing bonds is now recognized as a sound principle of government, although his comments came near resulting in his wreck-
age. The road to reform is usually strewn with bones of mar-
tyrs.

most to the point that they should bring in a conviction.

Unsolicited, the Government offered to give us a delay. We declined. Every day of adverse publicity was to our disadvantage.

We found out that the prospective jurors and ourselves were being closely shielded, either by agents of the Government or by some one else.

I ventured upon the expedient to take advantage of such surveillance. I would take off Juror A, whom we did not desire to serve on the jury. Always where I could be seen, I would buy him a drink. I would buy him something to eat. I would talk with him in close, confidential tones, even to the point of whispering in his ear about everything under the sun except the Harper case. I did that with several of them, all prospective jurors whom we wanted excused.

When the time came to select the jury, each talesman with whom I had associated or talked in such a confidential way, was asked if I had not talked to him about the case. The truthful, but unbelieved answer would come back that I had not mentioned the case to him. The prosecution, fully convinced the juror was lying, would excuse such juror and exhaust one of the Government's six challenges.

They were about to exhaust near to their last on such a talesman, when a Winnfield political enemy called the prosecuting attorney aside.

I was convinced that the government had discovered the prank to which they had fallen a victim.

The court being again called to order after a recess, the Judge began to read statements which I had made

in the newspapers. It seemed apparent that I was
to be sent to jail. But to our great astonishment,
after reading the entire list of statements I had made,
the Judge concluded:

"The Court-cannot let this and other matters pass
without a reprimand."

To the devil with the reprimand as far as we were
concerned! All we wanted was a chance to clear our
client.

The Harper case went on to tiresome lengths.
Upon evidence being closed, two of the Government
prosecutors presented arguments for conviction, and
my brother alone presented argument for the defense.
He was acquitted.

I managed to forge into some political recognition
of my own in local politics.

A Parish School Superintendent's election by a
School Board of nine members had resulted in a 5 to
4 defeat for our candidate on a secret ballot. I reas-
sembled 5 of the board members before daylight the
next day, took their affidavits and at noon marched
them into an open meeting, where they presented a
resolution declaring our candidate elected, which was
adopted 5 to 4 by a viva voce vote. The Supreme
Court held our viva voce election legal and the secret
vote illegal. Our candidate took office.[9]

---

[9] State ex rel, etc. vs. Mixon, 142 La. Reports, page 714.

# CHAPTER IV

## BEGINNING THE LIFE OF PUBLIC OFFICE AND "CITY" LAWYER

M Y legal and political opposition to the vested interests took on larger proportions from month to month. I was being called to different parts of the State to handle cases in the Courts.

But "save the mark" when we ran into a battle against one of these corporations before a State board. We didn't have the chance of a snowball in a fire.

I had concluded to wage a fight on a wide scale to reform both the personnel and the conduct of certain State departments. Somehow, in my youthful enthusiasm, I felt perfectly equal to the task. Had I known then the hill I had picked to climb, it is certain that my plans to free these departments from corporate influences would have been less ambitious.

What a fight lay ahead! Always my cases in Court were on the side of the small man—the under-dog. I had never taken a suit against a poor man and have not done so to this day.

I find in the newspaper files the following letter which appeared in the columns of the New Orleans Item and other papers of the State, on March 1, 1918, viz:

THINKS WEALTH SHOULD BE MORE EVENLY DISTRIBUTED

The Editor of the Item:

A conservative estimate is that about sixty-five or seventy per cent of the entire wealth of the

United States is owned by two per cent of the
people. Sixty-eight per cent of the whole people
living in the United States own but two per cent
of its wealth. From the year 1890 to 1910, the
wealth of this nation trebled, yet the masses
owned less in 1910 than they did in 1890 and a
greater per cent of the people lived in mortgaged
and rented homes in 1900 than in 1890, and more
lived in rented and mortgaged homes in 1910 than
did in 1900. Reports from the Committee on Industrial Relations, appointed by the President,
showed that wealth is fast concentrating in the
hands of the few.[10]

But the greatest cause for industrial unrest is
that of education. Authorities on education tell us

---

[10] President Wilson's Industrial Relations Commission of
1916 declared the cause of the distress among the people to be:
"1. Unjust distribution of wealth and income. . . ." The report
further says: "The rich, 2% of the people, own 60% of the
wealth; the middle class, 33% of the people, own 35% of the
wealth. The poor, 65% of the people, own 5% of the wealth.
This means in brief that a little less than 2,000,000 people,
who would make up a city smaller than Chicago, own 20%
more of the nation's wealth than all the other 90,000,000." The
Federal Trade Commission in 1930 showed the trend of 1%
of the people owning 59% of the country's property, much
worse than in President Wilson's time, even.

The Saturday Evening Post said, in its editorial columns on
September 23, 1916, under the heading of "ARE WE RICH
OR POOR?"—the following: "The man who studies wealth in
the United States from statistics only will get nowhere with the
subject because all the statistics afford only an inconclusive suggestion.

"Along one statistical line you can figure out a nation bustling
with wealth; along another, a bloated plutocracy comprising 1%
of the population lording it over a starveling horde with only
a thin margin of merely well-to-do in between."

that eighty out of every one hundred people in the
United States never enter high school; only fourteen out of every thousand get a college education; 690 out of every thousand never finish the
fourth grade in school. Does such a condition
give the ordinary man his proper return of the
nation's prosperity? What do you think of such a
game of life, so brutally and cruelly unfair, with
the dice so loaded that the child of today must
enter it with only fourteen chances out of a thousand in his favor of getting a college education
and with 986 chances against his securing the
lucky draw? How can this Nation prosper with
the ordinary child having only twenty chances in
a thousand of securing the first part of the game?

This is the condition, north, east, south and
west; with wealth concentrating, classes becoming
defined, there is not the opportunity for Christian
uplift and education and cannot be until there is
more economic reform. This is the problem that
the good people of this country must consider.

HUEY P. LONG.

I was twenty-four years of age.

Through a careful perusal of the State Constitution I found that there was no minimum age limit prescribed for a Railroad Commissioner. I was, therefore, eligible for election. Five candidates, including
myself, entered the race for Railroad Commissioner
from the North Louisiana District in the summer of
1918.

My headquarters were established in the small residence of my father-in-law in Shreveport, from which
my wife, with the help of the family and friends in

the neighborhood, mailed out literature and answered letters. Although our first child was only one year old my wife conducted my campaign "headquarters" with courage and efficiency.

The motor car was a new thing in our country. Its appearance was generally considered to be resented among the country population but I paid no attention to this supposed prejudice. I borrowed sufficient money to buy an automobile in which to travel over the district.

Soon, however, my funds ran out. Politics involving personally running for office was something new to me. I went to the office of O. K. Allen. He was the Tax Assessor of the Parish.

"Oscar," I began, "I haven't a penny in the world that I can get my hands on to continue this race. I don't see that I can go any further."

"How much money have you got?"

"Not a penny. I was afraid my gasoline would give out before I could reach Winnfield. If it had I would have had to beg for some."

"Well," he said, "I can get some money."

"Get me five hundred dollars if you can."

He negotiated his own note at the bank and brought me back the money in cash. I left the town and renewed my work.

I canvassed the farmers in person and spent most of my time at night tacking up my campaign posters in the neighborhood being canvassed. Occasionally, so intense was my campaign, I called people from their beds at all hours of the night to talk politics.

Nothing in my campaigning seemed to please

farmers more or cause them to recollect me nearly so favorably as to call them from their beds at night. All over the neighborhoods flew the news of my working through the nights.

I ran second—some two thousand votes behind the incumbent in the first primary. A second primary was ordered and was soon on in full force.

The final reports of that contest gave me a majority of 636 votes. My opponent congratulated me upon my victory.

I thus became Railroad Commissioner just as I entered the age of twenty-five.

Immediately following the second primary I announced a change of residence from Winnfield to Shreveport.

I had done certain legal work for some of my Winnfield friends connected with the oil business in Caddo Parish, of which Shreveport is the parish seat. They paid me in oil stock. I bought additional stock from some of them.

Several companies in which I was interested were very successful. We finally had a very large concern which gave promise of becoming an even larger affair.

It was just at this time the big companies threatened to begin pipeline embargoes, designed to freeze out small companies and independent operators.

We feared the worst for our company.

More than one hundred other independent oil concerns with thousands of stockholders, were in the area affected by this pipeline embargo. They had all been encouraged to develop the field to the fullest extent. The pipelines of the oil trust were paying $1.55 per barrel for the oil and begging for more of it.

Like a flash, however, all the independents were told they would take no more of their oil. I had gone to sleep one night with transactions all ready to be closed for options and equities I had acquired which meant I might some day be mentioned among the millionaires, to awake in the morning to read that nothing I had was of value because the three pipeline companies said so.

A meeting was held at the Shreveport Chamber of Commerce, attended by officials of the Standard Oil Company and the other pipeline companies allied in the embargo.

The faces of the Standard Oil group bore expressions of self-content. About these men there was that undefinable something that betokens freedom from money cares and anxiety as to the future. But the faces of the men in the independent group told a different story. Care, and in some cases, desperation, was written in every line.

Some of the other big companies had not at that time issued any announcement that they were going to proceed to an embargo. An officer of one of them arose.

"I think maybe we can work this thing out," said the pipe line officer, "provided we all stop drilling any more wells. My company has not said it will refuse to take this oil."

"But you are going to," the Standard Oil vice-president authoritatively announced.

The official of the other pipeline company subsided.

"And this a free country," I spoke for the first time. I continued: "You've done this before and got by with it, but this time, go do it and see when you hear the last of it." [11]

I left the meeting.

The following days I had occasion to learn considerably more of the courses pursued and the results from such oil controversies. Elderly oil operators informed me that nothing was ever gained fighting the big companies.

As I walked through the lobby of the Youree Hotel in Shreveport early one morning a rather dynamic oil operator approached me.

"Son," he began, "I was at that Chamber of Commerce meeting the other night. You've got fire. If you are willing to pitch what you have got in the oil field in the bucket, you've got the position that you can make these guys sick, if you fight them long enough."

"I am going to fight them," I replied, "but I doubt that I will ever know enough about the question to go very far."

"Guys like you can go where a wise guy will never tread."

With the State faced by an oil embargo and "freeze out," I undertook to bring the large oil companies operating pipelines before the Railroad Commission

---

[11] This was the beginning of the oil controversy in reshaping Louisiana's tax policy. The agitation resulted in heavier taxes on the business of producing oil and gas.

for regulation. Louisiana had a law that gave us a measure of control over them.

I was not successful in securing much action from my two associates, except that in a meeting held at Shreveport, several independent oil operators were allowed to come before our body to make certain representations of facts about conditions existing in the operation of pipelines.

The oil trust officials did not even appear. They seemed to know their ground. Nothing said at the meeting was disputed. It could not have been.

I prepared a condensed statement of findings together with a set of recommendations based upon the presentations made to the Commission by the independent oil operators.

My ultimate hope was to force an extra session of the Legislature, or if not that, to force the oil question as an issue in the state-wide political campaign soon to start.

To a meeting of the Railroad Commission held in the old Capitol, at Baton Rouge, on March 25, 1919, I took several prepared copies of these proposed findings, making no mention of this fact until the Commission had gone into executive session.

Then I presented my report and argued for its adoption.

One commissioner seemed to be willing to sign. The Chairman hesitated. He read and re-read from portions of the proposed findings.

The old Capitol building is situated on a high bluff immediately overlooking the Mississippi River. When the argument had reached its height I looked out of the window and saw an oil tanker steaming up the river. I pointed to it.

"Look at that, Shelby," I said. "There now is a ship coming up the river loaded with Mexican crude to go in the tanks where they will not let us put our oil."

Chairman Shelby Taylor took one look at the ship. He reached for a pen and signed the document. Michel put his name on it.

I handed the paper to the Secretary, who engrossed it as a Commission document. I had the copies of the findings which I had in my possession certified by the Secretary, some of which I handed to the newspapers that night. Next day it was given sensational publicity.[12]

News that the Commission had issued such a finding swept through the City of Baton Rouge the next morning like a hurricane.

Adjacent to the Capital City was located its large refinery and oil tank farms, the largest in the world.

Lawyers and agents representing the Standard Oil Company flocked to the City at an early hour of the morning following the Commission's findings to see what could be done to remedy the situation. In the meantime the Commission had gone into session to hear other cases.

The Chairman lived and practiced law in Baton Rouge; he appeared to be ill at ease. He stormed at the Secretary as we sat behind the table listening to the evidence and arguments in other cases.

---

[12] All Louisiana newspapers of March 26, 1919.

"Where is that document? I've been made a fool of; hand it to me and I will tear it up," I heard him say in muffled tones.

I intervened, exhibiting a number of certified copies.

"This document is issued," I said, "and I have plenty of copies; I have given plenty of others to the press."

Governor Pleasant declined to call any extra session to deal with the oil question though sentiment favored it.

I issued several statements but the Governor was adamant.

With a new Governor to be elected in January, 1920, an opening campaign meeting for the preceding July 4th, was scheduled at Hot Wells, a health resort in the center of the State. All candidates for Governor were invited to speak.

I was permitted to speak on the oil trust fight at this meeting.

A newspaper, unfriendly to me, carried, in its report of the meeting:

### "LONG WAS THE SENSATION"

"When he concluded, John R. Hunter, of Alexandria, who presided over the meeting, referred to the Long speech as being 'as hot as this boiling water that bubbles up from Hot Wells at 116 degrees. . . .'

"He recited the history of the Standard Oil at Pine Island and at Chrichton, charged that they had driven oil prices down and frozen out the little fellows until they got control.

" 'It was weak-backed Democrats like Pleasant that drove the Third District Democrats from the Democratic Party' he charged. 'Thank God, he opposed me when I was running for Railroad Commissioner.'

"Mr. Long said that if there ever was an institution that stood convicted before the people, that it is Standard Oil. 'This octopus is among the world's greatest criminals. It was thrown out of Texas following its raid in Spindle Top; it was ousted from Kansas; it was forced to terms in Oklahoma by the famous Oklahoma pipe line bill.' " [13]

The 1919-1920 campaign finally dwindled to two candidates—Frank P. Stubbs and John M. Parker.

A meeting was arranged between Mr. Parker and myself when he reached Shreveport in the early part of November, where he was to speak the next day. I urged that he should renew his declarations on the oil question in somewhat more specific language and rather assured him that if he did so, I would come to his support in the campaign.

I went over some of the hardships imposed on the independent oil men and farmers as a result of the freeze-out.

"I know how to sympathize with you fellows," Parker said. He looked very straight at me and continued:

"You know, once I had a patent that some big outfit decided to take away from me, and when I started to get into a fight with them I went to a lawyer and

---

[13] New Orleans States.

was told that I might win it, but that it would cost me more than I would ever get out of it."

He made sufficient pronouncement the next day to satisfy my mind. I declared in his favor.

There was no time to lose in North Louisiana. Because of our lack of newspaper support in some sections, I had many thousands of circulars printed for distribution. I took the stump for a period of approximately seventy days and went to many places where no other campaign orator had ever reached, traveling at times by horse-back to fill appointments.

We managed to break what our opponents called the "solid North Louisiana vote." It gave a slight majority for Parker. He was elected.[14]

Governor Parker immediately addressed me a few letters, taking occasion to thank me for the support which I had given to his candidacy.

Before his inauguration, however, I was shelved.

It was here I saw occur a phenomenon that has frequently presented itself in the after years. Those of us, zealous for reform and who had exhausted ourselves in the election, hied back to our work to give attention to our several neglected affairs. The crowd of wiseacres, skilled at flattery and repartee, surrounded our newly elected governor. Soon he was convinced that his insurmountable virtue alone had wrought the victory; before long he was made to see how much bigger his majority might have been but

---

[14] The North Louisiana districts were swung over to Parker by the narrow majority of 761 votes.

for the "hindrance" of such "objectionables" as myself.

The elements we had defeated, always in his easy view, broke into ecstasies of delight at which they had so lately found to be his words of wisdom. They had felt a divine spark. When the slaves of the campaign had the time to visit him, the element we had expected to oust were needed to introduce us to our late candidate.

He made his own program with the help of Standard Oil lawyers, who had been called in to write some of the laws affecting that Corporation. He appeared to desire only such legislation as was agreed to in compromise on all sides.

Cain became his own judge.

But the independent oil interests and I fostered our legislation none the less. The Governor had made too many promises to oppose us in the open, for the time being.

His floor leader, however, announced the Governor's opposition to the passage of our pipe line bill when it came up for a vote in the Lower House, in spite of which we won with the scant margin of two votes.

The bill went through the Senate, though considerably emasculated—as a result of the Governor's efforts.

We feared, and our enemies thought, that it had been so weakened that the pipeline companies could not be held as common carriers.

Some years later, however, as an attorney before the Supreme Court, I succeeded in getting a decision holding these lines to be common carriers under that statute.[15]

As a result of the fight over this pipe line legislation Governor Parker and I became openly hostile. He called a public hearing at which he presided, and requested me to explain certain statements I had made and caused to be published. I faced him with pledges he had made.

Though I do not presume to give the reason for Governor Parker's reticence, since that day he has never dared to offer himself for an office in Louisiana, and we have been bitter enemies.

### Political Reverses

A blow to whatever political ambitions I may have had soon came. My eldest brother, the District Attorney at Winnfield, became a candidate for judge.

I went back to the old territory to work among the people there. The result was that my brother was decisively defeated.

My brother continued to practice before the judge who defeated him. He came to Shreveport one Sunday, where we undertook to devise a means by which a case should be extracted from the court at Winnfield.

In a flash, I remembered somewhere I had read of a quick change of residence so as to give a Federal Court jurisdiction.

"Let's see," I said. "What we need to do is to get out of that court at Winnfield."

---

[15] Louisiana Public Service Commission v. Standard Oil Company of Louisiana, 154 Louisiana Reports, page 557.

"That's the first thing I think we will have to do," my brother replied.

"Where does our man live?" I asked.

"He lives in Arkansas."

"Where does the man live he is suing?"

"He lives in Arkansas too."

"Then let's move our man," I said.

"When?" he asked.

"Isn't he in Winnfield now with his family?"

"Yes."

"He's moved now."

Our client declared his change of residence. On Monday morning we were in court, with an action in rem. A few days thereafter a receiver was appointed.[16]

---

[16] Charles G. Gilstrap v. Matthews Stave Co., U. S. District Court, Western District of Louisiana, Shreveport Division. Diversity of citizenship was necessary to give a United States Court jurisdiction. By one man living in one state he could sue in the United States Court if the other lived in a different state.

# CHAPTER V

WE never stopped opposition to Governor Parker and the big oil interests after 1921. We kept the issues alive every minute, seeking to force the pipe lines to the common carrier status and to compel a severance tax more in line with what was needed by the State. The latter necessitated our upsetting what the Governor announced to be his "gentleman's agreement" with the Standard Oil Company.

Fuel was added to this fire when an application was made by the Cumberland Telephone & Telegraph Company for a heavy increase in its rates.

The original application failed to state any particular rates claimed at the individual exchanges.

I called on Chairman Taylor at his office on the day that this application was set to be heard in Baton Rouge, October 15, 1920, and asked him what he knew about the case.

"Seems like somebody else is being told more about it than me," he answered.

"Well, you and I are the majority of the commission," I said. "You're the chairman, and if these people are going to tell anybody anything, I would think you would have been the first man they would have seen."

"That's what most anybody else would think!" he exploded. "Here." He turned to his desk, produced a country newspaper which he handed to me, and continued: "Read this. That little paper has a big influence. They think this whole application is an outrage."

"The fact that they have dodged around you does not make it look any too good to me," I said. "Of course, being as far away as I am, I naturally have to rely upon you for preliminary information in these kind of cases."

At the conclusion of our conversation we had tentatively agreed, in the absence of some showing to justify the contrary, that we would postpone the hearing when the matter came up in the afternoon.

With the three members sitting en banc in the afternoon, the array of counsel and agents for the telephone company marched down the aisle of the State Senate, where we had assembled, headed by my old friend, Hunt Chipley of Atlanta, then Vice-President and General Counsel of the telephone company. He entered with his distinguished look and bearing that would well become an English duke, a cigarette in a decorated holder, nonchalantly poised between his teeth, ready to present the case of the company.

I whispered to my friend Taylor:

"Look at that pompous guy with that decorated cigarette holder—looks like he has taken charge now."

Chipley began to make his presentation before the commission.

"Your honors," he said . . .

Taylor broke in. "I am glad you found out who

is supposed to hear this case. What are you asking for?"

"Why, your honor," Chipley responded politely, "we are asking for a fair rate in this State for the telephone services we are furnishing."

"That don't mean anything to us," the chairman responded. "We hear this fair rate business every day of our lives, with everybody starving to death except these birds that are yelling 'Fair Rate! Fair Rate!' "

I broke in:

"I agree with the chairman. We would like to know something in dollars and cents, something about this application."

"Yes," yelled back the chairman. "Something tangible, something to the point."

"In line with that," I added, "just how much do you propose to raise the telephone rate in Winnfield, Louisiana?"

"It is not in our application," the telephone attorney responded, "but we have the figures here on what they should be."

"Yes, so you have got the figures there, but you didn't put them in your application. How did you expect these poor devils to know how much you were asking to raise their telephone rates? Why didn't you put it in your application or tell somebody," our Chairman ranted.

I interpolated:

"Seems at least that you might have informed the chairman of the commission and left it up to him to decide the kind of notice that should be given in this case."

The attorney for our Commission broke in at this point:

"Well, Mr. Chairman, I have understood what they were asking for."

"You have, have you!" the chairman roared. "Then they'd a dad-gummed better sight have told somebody that had something to do with it than to have told you about it."

Needing only one vote, and Taylor appearing ready to furnish that, I moved to defer the application and to require a more specific pleading showing what the company claimed to justify a hearing.

Eventually the telephone company's application was properly amended. At the conclusion of one of the hearings, the two other commissioners signed an order immediately, granting all of the demands made by the telephone company for its rate increase.[17]

I filed a dissenting opinion. I likewise issued a public protest against the Commission having granted the increase in rates within an hour after the termination of the hearing, which had taken days, and before briefs could even be filed.[18]

In the meantime, I had become involved in another legal fight in the City of Shreveport over the street railway fare. An ordinance had been passed calling an election to increase the car fare from five to six cents. Certain promises had been made by the company, which were not fulfilled. I contested the election and the ordinance in the courts, bringing the suit "Huey P. Long versus City of Shreveport and

[17] Order of February 26, 1920.
[18] See front page of Shreveport Times, February 27, 1920.

Shreveport Railways Company." In the lower court I was given judgment placing the fare back to five cents. An appeal was taken to the Supreme Court.

In such condition of public ferment, the Constitutional Convention, which had been voted, met in the capitol in Baton Rouge in the month of March, 1921, for the purpose of writing a new constitution for the State.

The office of Railroad Commissioner which I held was a constitutional office.

While I was out of the State, a supporter of the Parker administration introduced an ordinance, the effect of which was to take me off of the Railroad Commission. I drew amendments to save my right to continue as a Commissioner. We brought the amendments to a vote at the most propitious time.[19] My status as a member of the old Railroad and of the newly named Public Service Commission was thus preserved.

But the constitutional convention adjourned in a furor. Even former Governor Pleasant, whom Governor Parker had appointed a delegate to the convention, denounced the members in a speech which he made on the floor of the convention for having allowed the lobbyists and attorneys of the Standard Oil Company to dominate their official conduct.

"I was at a conference at the Governor's Mansion," the former governor said. "We discussed the three per cent severance tax and practically everyone there was in agreement for it to be written into the

---

[19] Journal of proceedings, Constitutional Convention of Louisiana, 1921, Palmer Amendments.

constitution. All of a sudden Governor Parker rang for the treasurer of the Standard Oil Company to come to the Mansion, and upon his coming there and peremptorily announcing that his company would not stand for the three per cent law, the Governor informed us that that ended the matter; that he could not tolerate the three per cent severance tax provision in the constitution." [20]

With its adjournment, the constitutional convention issued a call for a special session of the Legislature to meet on the first Tuesday of September, 1921. When that Legislature met, a draft of a new law on the severance taxes was to be submitted.

I issued a document to the members of the Legislature, which is a part of the court records of the District Court of East Baton Rouge Parish, Louisiana, which read in part:

> As a means of forcing upon the State legislation injurious to the people but highly profitable and beneficial to the Standard Oil trust and its allied corporate monopolies, you have seen an administration trade in offices which belong to the people and barter them away in a manner unbecoming an ancient ruler of a Turkish domain. Better to have taken the gold hoarded in the Standard Oil vaults at 26 Broadway and deliberately purchase the votes with which the administration has ruled this State for nearly two years than to have brow-beaten, bulldozed and intimi-

---

[20] Governor Pleasant would not sign the Constitution of 1921 on ground of improper influences having influenced the work of the body.

dated the Legislature for the benefit of the corporate interests through the free use of the peoples'
patronage.

Bold and amazing is the Governor's cry that he
has no bill to submit to you, for the reason that it
is at 26 Broadway for its final polish. Are you,
law makers of Louisiana, to return to your people
as fallen chattels who have been counted at the
behest of an administration which loudly pro-
claims the visible control vested in the hands of
the corporate interests by an administration which
has crept into office through false promises and
under pretenses which have shamed the best of
our citizens?

A storm broke loose in the Legislature, in which I
was severely condemned and threatened with impeachment or prosecution but at the conclusion of
which I issued another circular, headed:

"THEIR SINS HAVE FOUND THEM"

I followed later with a third circular.

I issued other statements to the newspapers, some
replying to an attack made on me.

I had scarcely returned to my home in Shreveport,
when I was telephoned by the Sheriff of our Parish:

"Huey, the Governor has had them issue warrants
for your arrest for libel. Say nothing about it. Come
to my office to see me."

No news of the matter had reached anyone up to
that time.

"Of course, Huey," the Sheriff said, when I called
at his office, "I am not going to arrest you. You take

these warrants and papers and go on to Baton Rouge as soon as you can and make bond. I will say nothing about it."

I returned to my law office and called my secretary to my desk. She was an elderly woman. I said to her:

"The Governor has had warrants issued for my arrest on charges of libel. It is not generally known yet, and I want to take as quick steps as I can before it is known. I must call some good friend as soon as possible."

"I would advise you to wait until they come," she answered.

Action was announced to result in specific process to bring me to impeachment. A caucus was called, composed of the members of the House of Representatives, either to start process to impeach or to address me out of office as Public Service Commissioner, also including the names of the other two members of the Commission.

The caucus of the members formally assembled at night. The air was heavy and the reek of tobacco would have resurrected Carrie Nation. Nerves were worn and tempers were out of bounds. It was a gathering in which loyalty was at a premium.

My opposition was in the majority, but a few clever parliamentary strategists aiding me kept the caucus in confusion.

Eventually, I suggested a motion that the three members of the Public Service Commission be requested to forthwith submit their resignations and to thereafter reappear before the people for reelection.

Some legislators seized upon the suggestion as being a fair and quick solution.

I immediately had it stated from the floor that I was there and then personally ready to tender my resignation and make my appearance before the people for reelection. One member shouted:

"Sure he will, but he is the only one that can be reelected!"

The opposition forces began to react.

We got a break. The floor leader of the House for the Parker administration arose.

"I am no Huey Long man, but apparently you are not willing for anything to be done here that is fair. I am taking my hat and walking out of this damned session."

Near pandemonium reigned. Any kind of a yell would result in a general confusion. Someone gave the yell.

That ended the impeachment effort in my career for eight years.

Before the legislature could adjourn I drafted a recall law for the State. It was passed.

I was soon to stand trial on the two criminal charges in the district court of East Baton Rouge Parish. Some kind of gesture or adroit action to end the trouble was urged. I wrote the following, viz:

> No doubt my friends, whose advice you communicate, are sincere in the belief that, for the present, I must adopt an adroit policy and play a safe situation. Quite probably their advice is inspired solely for the reason that they wish me to hazard no personal or political loss, in a fight

which has for its object the elimination of any corporate domination in any of our State affairs. I appreciate their advice and the sentiment which prompts their giving it, but fear that they are more than probably misled in the belief as to what is actually for my own personal betterment.

Good lawyer that you are, the following authority which I extract from the Saturday Evening Post will appear in point:

"There is real pathos about a certain class of politicians to be found in every capitol. They are men, public servants, of marked and acknowledged ability, whose inborn talents would have made them first-raters if they could have mustered a little more courage, a little sterner devotion to principle (rather than expediency), a sense of duty a little higher; *if they could only lose their heads at the right time and refuse to play it safe;* if, in short, *they could have brought themselves to pay the price* that the truest success exacts even of genius itself. Their status is not that of men who are naturally qualified to lead, but who deprive the world of their best services because *they grudge the price* that leadership costs. All the world over too much power is in the hands of the second-raters —not the force of inspired leadership, but the power that springs from patronage and political adroitness." (See Lost Leaders.)

Our past efforts to bring the Standard Oil Company and the allied corporate interests to where they exercise no greater control in affairs of State than the humble citizenship is now at its crucial stage where the slightest move forward or back-

ward may mean victory or defeat. If we hold our
ground, pay the price which circumstances may
require, lose our heads at the right time and refuse
to play it safe, just as we have done for the past
three years, past history and arithmetic alone will
assure the success of our efforts. It is now too late
for me to play it safe. Too much depends upon my
standing my ground, continuing the fight and
maintaining the position heretofore taken.

The trial in Baton Rouge was heard.

"Mr. Long," the judge said to me, "I think under
the circumstances we all understand it to be impetu-
ousness that persuades you to make some of the statements you have made. The sentence of this court is
that on the first charge you serve thirty days in prison,
but I will suspend that; and on the second charge my
sentence is that you pay us $1.00 or serve one hour."

He left the entire amount of the costs, amounting
to a large sum of money, to be paid by the State.

"Judge," I answered, "I am not going to pay that
dollar."

"Well, some of us will have to pay it," answered
the judge smilingly.

I had noticed that the judge had failed to add
the words "during good behavior" to his suspension
of sentence.

Judge Brunot declared a recess of court for five
minutes and came down from the bench. Of two of
the defense counsel he asked 25¢ each, which they
gave him. He then took 50¢ out of his own pocket
and handed the dollar to the Sheriff. Resuming the
bench, he said:

"Mr. Sheriff, Mr. Long's fine is paid. Adjourn court."

When, a few days later, I started the fight all over again and reiterated what I had been saying about the Standard Oil Company and the administration, I heard that Judge Brunot was asked to call me back to court on the suspended 30-day matter. According to report, Judge Brunot became angered and said:

"I've tried to save Governor Parker's face—now don't try it again."

## STREET RAILWAY FARES

My suit to reduce the street railway fare pended in the Supreme Court. On that hearing the Court gave me a complete victory. Thereupon the street railway fare went back to 5¢ per person.[21]

The old saying, "Once burned, twice shy," applies to governors as well as other mortals and Governor Parker never wanted to face the fire of our fight again. Before the Legislature met in the spring of 1922 he announced that he was "released" from the "gentlemen's agreement." [22] We thought we had been of some service to "release him," poor fellow! So our 3% severance tax on oil was introduced in the legislature without his opposition. It appeared headed for certain enactment.

But, lo and behold, from out of the woods came

---

[21] Huey P. Long v. City of Shreveport and Shreveport Railways Company, 151 La. Reports, page 423.

[22] A cartoon in the New Orleans Item described the governor as leaving the "Gentlemen's Agreement dog" to be stolen to relieve him of trouble.

former governor, J. Y. Sanders, who appeared before the Committee considering the bill to oppose it. The following news report is pertinent, viz:

### SANDERS ASSAILED FOR TAX BURDENS OF "POOR PEOPLE"

#### LONG'S DOCUMENT PLACED ON DESKS OF MEMBERS OF LEGISLATURE

Baton Rouge, La., June 8—Huey P. Long, chairman of the State Public Service Commission and member of the body from the North Louisiana District, broke into the limelight again here today with an attack on former Governor J. Y. Sanders. The document, which was in multigraph form, was placed on the desks of members of the Legislature. It follows:

"The bold and publicly discredited lobby of the Standard Oil Company and its associated corporate allies have been compelled to flee from the floor of the State House. Its methods, its demands and its plunder-grabbing policy which it forced upon the constitutional convention and the State administration during 1920 and 1921, so stirred this State that the people were about to rise in disgust and throw the institution from the border of our commonwealth as a measure of self-defense.

"If a yearling is born in December, they begin to tax him in January and the taxing continues until he dies. But if oil is brought to the ground, it is taxed only once and then ends the tax.

"As much as I regret, the necessity compels that I should tell you that some time ago Mr. J. Y. Sanders became interested in those properties or a concern covered in a deal made with the

Ohio Oil Company, a subsidiary of the Standard Oil Company of New Jersey. Mr. Sanders is now at Baton Rouge, purported to be rather, or somewhat, disinterested in the matter, doing all he can to defeat the 3 per cent severance tax, just as he did when he was in the constitutional convention.

"Mr. J. Y. Sanders is the author of our newest and latest tax addition of more than $5,000,000 a year on wagons, trucks, vehicles, buggies, etc., and this is on the people and on their property which had already been taxed. Mr. Sanders was a board of affairs advocate and the originator of the game wardens. He voted for every salary raise in the constitutional convention. Now, after adding these burdens on the poor people, is he going to be allowed to put through a proposition to prevent taxes on the oil trusts?"

Sanders issued a reply which I immediately answered. He never returned to the fight. The bill thereafter passed both houses and the Governor signed it.

# CHAPTER VI

WITH the Railroad Commission standing two to one against my general line of policy I remained a minority member until on November 22, 1921, when Commissioner John T. Michel died at his home in New Orleans. With the election of another member of the Commission to take his place, on platform pledges to stand as I had stood for a reduction in telephone rates, I was voted into the chairmanship of the commission.

We set the telephone case for argument. It was then nearly two years old, pending on application for rehearing. The Commission, with me presiding, met to hear arguments within four days.

Immediately upon the Commission session being called to order, with the calling of the telephone case, the company's counsel stepped forward with a motion.

"I wish to file a motion," he said, "to recuse the new member of the Commission who is sitting on this case. I file herewith a campaign election card on which is his photograph with the statement, 'I will vote to reduce the telephone rates.' The motion reads. . . ."

"Don't read the motion," I instructed, as the chairman. "We will not allow the motion to be read this time nor will we entertain it. There is no provision in the law to recuse a member of the Public Service

Commission, regardless of what kind of campaign pledge he makes."

"Let it be shown on the record," the telephone attorney undertook to instruct, "that the chairman overruled this motion without consulting the other members."

"Let nothing be shown on the record except what I say will be shown on the record," I instructed the reporter. "And now I instruct the counsel. . . ."

"I am going to have the record show . . ." the lawyer persisted.

"You are going to jail if you infringe upon the Commission's procedure another minute," I announced.

The bedlam was thereupon ended. Arguments on the record of the case were concluded within a few days.[23]

I returned to my home in Shreveport with the full record of proceedings in the case and began the preparation of an opinion and order. Upon their completion, I called the Commission into special session and handed down the same, annulling the increases in telephone rates, which had been granted by the old Commission, and ordering a reinstatement of the rates and charges prevailing prior to that increase.

The telephone company filed suit in the United States District Court at New Orleans. I caused myself to be placed in control of the litigation as chief counsel. Our Attorney General, Judge A. V. Coco,

---

[23] The argument before the United States Courts to recuse the new member of the Commission was not noticed in the opinions.

addressed me a letter bristling with the resentment of which he was quite capable.

Judge Coco was about 64 or 65 years of age, of strong physique, handsome and dignified in appearance. He had run for several offices, had been defeated several times, and had been elected several times.

In one of his races for Congress against Congressman Sam Robertson, of the Sixth Louisiana District, the Judge and Congressman Robertson engaged in a joint debate in a rice warehouse at Crowley, Louisiana. Judge Coco condemned the tariff on rice. Congressman Sam Robertson arose and propounded a question to the Judge, viz:

"Judge Coco, please tell the audience just how much the tariff on rice is that you are talking about."

The Judge halted for a moment, and appeared to think for just an instant.

"Ladies and gentlemen," he said, "This Congressman here has been sitting in the House of Representatives for fourteen years and he has not learned what the tariff on rice is yet. He wants me to tell him what it is. I will not do it. Let him get out of Congress and let somebody go there that knows something about it."

Immediately after the meeting, Judge Coco was informed at that time there was no tariff on rice.

I prepared the pleadings and briefs for the Commission in the telephone case and took the lead in the three-judge court. By a vote of two to one the three-judge court ruled that the order which I had written should stand.[24]

---

[24] Cumberland Telephone and Telegraph Company v. Louisiana Public Service Commission, 283 Federal Reporter, page 265.

The Company appealed on an order of one Judge, which I undertook to set aside, all resulting in a complicated legal situation before several courts.

The new Commissioner's term was about to end. In their common desire to bury me politically, once and forever, all political forces in Louisiana undertook to unite in support of the candidacy of the opponent to the new member of the Commission.[25] But complications made the union impossible. The new member was reelected.

My application to dissolve Judge Foster's appeal order, with injunction pending appeal, was argued and a decision rendered in our favor.[26]

The legal status of this case was such that the telephone company cried for peace. $467,000.00 was returned to the telephone users of Louisiana in cash and rates were reduced one million dollars per year.

[25] New Orleans Item, July 10, 1922.

[26] Huey P. Long, ex parte, and Cumberland Telephone and Telegraph Company v. Louisiana Public Service Commission, 260 U. S. 212; — 754 — 759.

# CHAPTER VII

PERHAPS I can qualify as a product of the melting pot for in my veins there flows the blood of English, Dutch, Welch, Irish, Scotch and French forebears. An eminent ethnologist has been at great pains to prove that such an admixture produces one capable of conflict.

I proceeded promptly against the Standard Oil Company, having issued Commission process to compel it to bring its books and records before our body. Litigation began. It was in process when matters were suspended for the summer vacation of the courts. Before they reconvened in the fall I had become a candidate for Governor. A writ of injunction had been issued out of the Court in Baton Rouge to stop our hearings. I took the chance of contempt, ignored the injunction, proceeded with hearings and applied for a writ to the Supreme Court. I was upheld.[27]

On my thirtieth birthday, August 30, 1923, I announced my candidacy for Governor in the primary election to be held in January, 1924.

I had neither newspaper nor organized political support, other than my own scattered faction.

Neither could I get favorable or complimentary mention by any of the newspapers, which gave me

---

[27] Louisiana Public Service Commission v. Standard Oil Company of Louisiana, 154 Louisiana Reports, 157.

less than no credit for anything I had done up to that time. They warned against the wild activities with which the people might be afflicted should I become the Governor.

Therefore I proceeded to condense a few of the editorials from these newspapers and publish them in circular form as follows:

### LEST WE FORGET!—EDITORIALS OF THE PAST

#### *Item*

Mr. Long has put action into the Commission. He would have it really regulate public service corporations in its jurisdiction. Commissioner Long has handled the case against the telephone company ably. He brought a new point of view into public utility practice in Louisiana, and galvanized the Commission with new life. A rebate from the telephone company is like manna from Heaven.—From editorials New Orleans Item on May 17, 1922, December 21, 1922, and January 19, 1923.

#### *Times-Picayune*

The State's victory (in the telephone case) lies in the fact that what might easily have become interminable litigation has been escaped, that refund will have been secured for a large sum exacted in error, and that a schedule of charges will have been put in force sufficiently near pre-war rates to harmonize with the average citizen's idea of reasonable advance.—From Times-Picayune editorial, January 17, 1923.

## Daily States

We have frequently commended Mr. Long's public services and especially his efforts to secure for the people a square deal in respect of their relations to the corporations of the State. In all controversies between the people and the corporations he has stood four square. . . . When the Cumberland went into Federal Court, as a very able attorney, Mr. Long asserted his right as of counsel for the Public Service Commission. It was his argument which won the decision from the Court of three, and it was his argument before the Supreme Court of the United States which lies at the base of Monday's decision. . . . He is entitled to the gratitude of the people for the fine fight he has made in this case in behalf of the public. . . . Business houses and residences are to have returned about $440,000 and the new rates. . . . The Public could not have got as much but for Mr. Long's persistent efforts in their behalf.—From editorials in New Orleans States, December 1, 1922, November 22, 1922, January 18, 1923.

## Oil World

We predict, too, that before Commissioner Long gets through with the Standard, there will be something doing, and old man John will know that Louisiana is on the map.—Oil World of May 19, 1923.

## Shreveport Times

The decision of the United States Court, dissolving the temporary restraining order of Fed-

eral Judge Rufus E. Foster in the Cumberland
Telephone Company case, is a victory for Huey
P. Long, chairman of the Louisiana Public Service Commission. Mr. Long personally argued the
case for the commission both in the district court
and the Supreme Court of the United States. And
now he has scored. The victory is not one of self-
interest but of public trust. It is a victory of a
public representative for the people. The Cumberland Company bows . . . The sum to be re-
funded is $440,000, and future savings to the
public will foot larger totals.—From editorials
Shreveport Times, November 1, 1922, and January 16, 1923.

### Baton Rouge State Times
### (Standard Oil Defender)
### (Huey P. Long's Sworn Enemy)

There h⁻ʒ been some unnecessary horn tooting
over who is to have credit for reduction in telephone rates. . . . But the credit for a reduction,
if any is to be secured, belongs to Huey P. Long.
We do not enroll ourselves as a champion for Mr.
Long, but we always want to be fair. . . . In the
meantime if there is any credit to any one for anything that has been accomplished in the telephone
rate case up to the present time, that credit belongs to Huey Long. It has been his fight from
first to last.—Editorial of State Times, November 23, 1922.

I pursued my campaign for Governor.

We issued many other circulars which I handed out
and which Mrs. Long and our children mailed from

my home and my office helpers mailed from my law office in Shreveport. Campaign posters were tacked up with my own hands, for I had been a sign tacker in the old days and that experience served me in good stead.

I drove my automobile and usually travelled alone, my car loaded with campaign literature and buttons which I handed out at my meetings before and after speaking.

In certain sections of southern Louisiana, following my speaking engagements I found it easy to secure permission from the merchants and from the business people to allow me to hang my posters in their show windows. The town usually was placarded following my meeting and as I departed.

If, however, I chanced to drive through the same place a few days following, I found the windows cleared of campaign posters altogether

I knew my only chance to keep a poster in the windows was to personally see that it had been placed there. On an occasion in the town of Eunice, Louisiana, two speakers assisting in my campaign were with me when I asked a store owner for permission to place a poster in his window.

"That will be all right," the store owner said. "You just leave the poster here, and I will put it up myself tomorrow morning."

I felt reasonably sure that the poster would be in the trash of the next morning rather than in the window.

"Well," I insisted, "I've got these two men hired to do nothing but hang these posters. They're experts in their line. No use to put you to that kind of trouble. Get in there, fellows, and put up a couple of posters!" I instructed.

They glued them in the window reasonably secure.

I found further that my posters were being taken down from old buildings and trees alongside the road. My sign-hanging experience came again into good use. I adopted the art of driving my automobile close to the tall trees. From the top I reached with a long hammer as far as possible, to hang my campaign poster beyond the reach of any hand.

Of my two opponents, one was the Lieutenant Governor serving under, and the other had been an appointee of, the same governor.

It had been arranged for the three of us to appear on the stump at the same meeting in Lafayette Square in New Orleans on Armistice Day.

I had planned a stroke for that day. I thought it would surely turn the tide of the campaign.

With the two on the platform with me, I planned to tell the following, which I originated:

A merchant finding business slackening, went into producing and selling eggs. He picked the guinea that was the most dependable laying fowl, but when his premises became covered with the guineas their cackle and cluck was such that he was unable to stand their constant racket. He therefore concluded to breed a cross between the guinea and some fowl not possessed of the objectionable cackle. So he took two eggs from the nest of a guinea; one of which he put under a turkey, the other of which he put under a setting

hen, expecting both to hatch, one with a cross between the guinea and the turkey, the other a cross
between the guinea and the hen, trusting that
through the cross breed of one or the other, he
would develop a fowl with the laying qualities of
the guinea and minus its cackle and cluck.

When the products of the hatch grew to full
size, they were guineas, still with the cackle and
cluck.

Now, ladies and gentlemen, gaze at my two opponents on this platform; both come from the
political nest of John M. Parker. One of them has
been put in the incubator of the New Orleans
Ring, the other has been put in the nest of the
Sullivan Ring. Both Parker eggs are to hatch.
One is supposed to breed a cross to lose the cackle
of Parker and the other is supposed to breed a
cross to lose the Parker strut. But, ladies and
gentlemen, before the day of inauguration shall
have arrived, from the hatch of these candidates
you will have nothing but two men with the same
cackle, cluck and strut as you had during the
last four years.

Both of the opposing candidates, who at no time
had appeared on the platform with me, learned that
I had planned some kind of faux pas for the occasion in Lafayette Square.

The largest crowd in the history of the campaign
assembled there to hear us; but, at the eleventh
hour, both opponents sent in the report that illness,
accident or something else prevented their appearance.

I went through with my illustration, but without

the two candidates there the loss of its effect failed to give me the hoped momentum.

During the last part of the campaign, there appeared a possibility of my being in the second primary. I had carefully surveyed the State. I was hoping to enter the second primary, as I had when I ran for Railroad Commissioner, by reason of a heavy country vote and in places where my strength was least suspected.

On the night preceding the election, a heavy downpour of rain fell in every part of the State.

The Ku Klux Klan issue was injected.

One of my opponents drew almost solid Klan support, and my other opponent a solid anti-Klan endorsement. The State, aroused and divided into bitter religious conflict, cleverly manipulated by the corporations and newspapers, left me out of the running in many places.

There was no need of full returns for me to know of my defeat. I knew it when the first box was reported. Some one said to me, late in the afternoon.

"Have you heard about the first box?"

"No," I said. "What is it?"

"It's the Clay box. 61 votes cast there and you got 60 of them."

"I'm beat," I replied. "There should have been 100 for me and 1 against me. Forty per cent of my country vote is lost in that box. It will be that great in the others."

It was a case of

> "Rise and shine,
> Stand up and take it!"

The vote was, in round numbers, Fuqua 81,000, Bouanchaud 84,000, Long 74,000. I carried the country over both opponents, but ran too bad a third in New Orleans to be second.

I settled down to my law office in Shreveport. There was considerable private litigation awaiting attention. I was seriously in need of money. I immediately delved into the preparation and trial of lawsuits, sometimes as many as two to three in one day.

Among these cases was a very important one involving the reorganization of the largest bank in North Louisiana. Representing one of the former directors of that bank, I brought suit against the bank and seven of its previous officials and directors. I succeeded in cancelling a guaranty of about $100,-000.00 and recovering $5,000.00 in damages.[28] Another suit on a promissory note, which I defended, resulted in such a settlement that I made a saving to my client of some hundred thousand dollars.[29] In another one of these suits judgment was rendered against us for some three hundred thousand dollars. The case was appealed, resulting in a complete reversal and absolving our client of all responsibility.[30]

[28] Bernstein v. Commercial National Bank et al., 153 Louisiana Reports 653, and 161 Louisiana Reports, 38. The case was decided against Bernstein on exception. It was appealed and reversed. The case was again decided against Bernstein on the merits. It was appealed and reversed and judgment rendered in favor of Bernstein.

[29] Commercial National Bank v. E. R. Bernstein and E. M. Brown, Jr., First District Court, Caddo Parish, Louisiana, Docket numbers 35,338, 35,339 and 37,710.

[30] William F. Smalley et al., Receiver for Tex-La-Homa Oil Company v. E. R. Bernstein and E. M. Brown, Jr., 165 Louisiana Reports, page 1.

In some of these suits my success was largely due to a very able associate counsel, Mr. Robert A. Hunter.

Right here I should acknowledge my indebtedness to some of my corporate opposition. If I possess any qualities or if I have acquired any particular learning in law or public affairs, I owe much of it to the opposition which the big interests have furnished and the intense research and exertion which they have at all times required me to make.

My fight with the Standard Oil Company continued until I was more or less vindicated. While the Court held we had no jurisdiction over its refinery, its pipe lines were nevertheless declared to be common carriers, and required to transport anybody's oil.[31]

I sought to prescribe a set of preliminary rates and orders for the oil company. It again sought an injunction, which was granted by the District Court at Baton Rouge.

My term as member of the Louisiana Public Service Commission expired.

The administration of Governor Fuqua, who had defeated me for Governor, heartily opposed me for re-election to the Public Service Commission. I paid little attention, however, to my campaign of that year, for I was more concerned with opposing the State administration's candidate for the United States Senate, my very bitter, personal enemy, Mr. L. E. Thomas, the Mayor of my home City of Shreveport.

---

[31] Louisiana Public Service Commission v. Standard Oil Co. of Louisiana, 154 Louisiana Reports, page 557.

If there has ever been a politician like unto the cat with nine lives, it has been L. E. Thomas. He has held office beginning with the 90's; despite who won in the political campaign for Governor, he never failed to show up with them as a leading supporter, though claimed by his opposition a great liability to every candidate.

I had opposed Thomas when he ran as one of four candidates for the minor office of member of the Democratic Party Committee for a congressional district. Three were to be elected out of the four candidates, and we so manipulated matters that Thomas ran fourth and was left out.

On the heels of that defeat he announced for Mayor of the City of Shreveport, and defeated five candidates by a clear majority of about two to one.

My effort to defeat him in his various campaigns was only equalled by the intense opposition he made to defeat me in several campaigns I made.

Mr. Thomas' repeated and vitriolic denunciations of my campaigning caused me to develop the following, which I told from the platform:

In the country where I came from, most every summer we held a religious revival called a camp meeting. People came from miles around, bringing their dinner baskets. Preaching lasted all day, with dinner on the ground at noon time. Of course, the weather was hot.

Now and then one of the babies would become hot and fretful, and finally begin to whimper and cry. To keep the preacher from being disturbed it was customary for the mothers to mix up a little substance of dry biscuit, butter and sugar, which they put in a rag and tied with a string, and called a sugar tit. When the young 'un made the first squall they put the sugar tit in his mouth. He would suck away, become quiet, and then go to sleep.

These were the days before we learned about the hygienic and germ theory. If another broke out, they would take the sugar "tit" out of the baby's mouth that was asleep and put it in the other young 'un's mouth. If still another began to squall, they would hand the same sugar "tit," until they put him to sleep, and on until the sugar "tit" was worn out.

But ladies and gentlemen, at birth the sugar "tit" of the State of Louisiana landed in L. E. Thomas's mouth. It's been there ever since. He's worn out a dozen of them. Now he's grabbing for more.

But L. E. Thomas was not being outdone if he could help it. He rejoined in kind. He said:

A man was passing through hell. The devil showed him a big, large iron box, with heavy weights on it, and a big lock. The man was curious. He took hold of the box.

"Let's take a look inside this box," he said to the devil.

"Oh, no!" said the devil. "That's Huey Long in there. We can't let him out. He'd take charge of hell if we did."

Senator Ransdell, the opponent of Mr. Thomas, was reelected by a large majority. I was thanked

by the Senator for my support, which he described
as being "invaluable."

I was returned to the office of Public Service Commissioner in the same election by a majority of about
eight to one, carrying twenty-eight out of the twenty-
eight parishes of my district, including the home parish of my opponent, in which I defeated him by a
majority of some seven to one.

### Broussard-Sanders Senatorial Contest

Two years later, in 1926, the State administration,
with the support of the New Orleans City administration, advanced its "warhorse," J. Y. Sanders, former Governor, as a candidate for the United States
Senate against Edwin S. Broussard. I took the stump
for Senator Broussard. The campaign that followed
was very heated.

Practically all, if not all, of the speeches which
Senator Broussard made in the campaign were from
the platform with me. It was almost impossible to get
him to break away from politicians and go to bed at
night, or to get him up in the morning as the result
of such late hours.

We made from four to six speeches per day. The
Senator was unable to speak more than a few minutes
at each meeting, on such a difficult and extended
speaking tour, but I was able to speak for as long as
an hour or more each time. We covered the State in
twenty-one days.

On Saturday, September 11, 1926, preceding the
Tuesday of the election, the North Louisiana District, which I represented, was conceded by the Brous-

sard campaign management, in a public announcement, in favor of Sanders by several thousand
votes.

On the night of the election, with disappointments
in early returns from South Louisiana, some of the
Broussard faction were about to concede defeat. I
telephoned from Shreveport and gave them the news
that even their publicly conceded figures for North
Louisiana, could be reduced several thousand. Thereupon, they announced that there was a possibility of
their winning.

Senator Broussard was reelected by a majority of
3479 votes.

## MORE POLITICAL MISFORTUNES

But the 1926 campaign was generally disastrous
to my political·fortunes. The brother of the new member of the Public Service Commission had been given
a raise in salary by the Fuqua administration. Both
had pledged their support to the administration's candidate, ex-Governor Sanders, for the United States
Senate.

Supporters of Sanders for the Senate backed a
candidate for Railroad Commissioner in the South
Louisiana District, who declared himself for Senator Broussard for the Senate.

They were out to eliminate Huey Long from running the Public Service Commission.

My hands were tied because I was occupied with
trying to save the Broussard election and because of
the previously known unfriendliness between Taylor
and me. Therefore, I could do little of value by any

remark in Taylor's behalf in opposition to the effort being made against me.

At last, a candidate was elected to the Public Service Commission who promptly voted with the other member to remove me from the chairmanship.

"I have skated on thin ice for six years to remain the head of this Commission," I announced to the public. "With two members always ready to vote against me for Chairman, it is only now that any two have ever been able to assemble where one would vote for the other."

Soon after I had been displaced as Chairman of the Commission I went to the capital to attend what I understood to be a meeting of the Commission. When the hearing was called I took my seat. The new Chairman announced:

"You're welcome to sit here as a spectator, but this hearing of the Commission is under a resolution of the Commission signed by two of us, which authorizes me to hold it."

"Do I understand," I asked, "that a Commission resolution has put you in charge of the hearing, and as a member of the Commission, I am not supposed to sit on it?"

"That's right," he answered.

"All right," I announced publicly. "I will not remain here for such a proceeding."

On the very first day of the new Commission organization, all orders which I had issued against the Standard Oil Company and many other interests were immediately set aside and annulled without hearing, and many suits which I had pending in the courts for years to establish jurisprudence and public rights were ordered dismissed.[32] At last no corporation lawyer or officer subject to regulation by that Commission need pay me further note, and none did.

I had, however, taken early advantage of opportunity to provide for transportation of oil by rail at low costs and orders I issued to that effect materially protected independent oil operators of the future.[33]

The oil companies in which I had been interested

[32] Order of Louisiana Public Service Commission, signed by Williams and LeBlanc, dismissing Standard Oil litigation:

Order No. 123, signed by Chairman Huey P. Long, concurred in by the other two commissioners, dated May 5, 1923, struck off $9,120,180.64 of the value claimed on pipe lines by the Standard Pipeline Co.; also required oil to be accepted by common carrier lines in quantities of 1,000 barrels or more, and further that oil should be stored for 48 hours after reaching destination free, with a charge of 10c per barrel each ten days thereafter. See Louisiana Public Service Commission, Volume 1923-24-25, pages 41 to 45, inclusive.

Order No. 433 of the Louisiana Public Service Commission, signed by Commissioners Francis Williams and Dudley LeBlanc, December 16, 1928, without hearing, stipulated "that Order No. 123 of the Louisiana Public Service Commission of date May 5, 1923, issued in case 197 on the docket of the Louisiana Public Service Commission, be and the same is hereby revoked, annulled, rescinded, and set aside and voided in all respects."

In connection with the last order, the Louisiana Public Service Commission approved Standard Pipeline Co. of Louisiana local tariff No. 4, among other things stipulating that concerns should forward through its lines oil at certain rates "not less than 100,000 barrels." This provision, coupled with the provisions cancelling out the right of the shipper to have 48 hours within which to move his oil, made it impossible for the pipelines to be used as common carriers. An oil operator strong enough to retain 100,000 barrels of oil at one time does not need a pipe line law or rate.

[33] Order 72 of Louisiana Public Service Commission.

had long since been "frozen out." The oil produced on our leases which we sold for $1.55 per barrel until it was declared "worthless" by the oil trust companies, rose in price to about as much as $3.00 per barrel when the trust concerns took the field.[34]

Following my removal as chairman of the Public Service Commission, I was provided with more time to pursue my private law practice. It had grown by leaps and bounds. I worked through the nights to take advantage of the opportunities.

I pause here to say that my wife and children paid a rather dear price for the fights I made against the entrenched powers of the State. With the exception of some few big cases, I had generally represented only the poorer class of clients. My fees were many but small. It required continuous work to earn them.

I had persisted in a course to take no business that might require me to act against any poor man.

We now had three brilliant children who had learned almost by the time they could walk to fold and mail literature for campaigns. The eldest of my children was a little girl named Rose, after her mother. The next child was a boy, whom we named Russell Billiu after my wife's favorite cousin. The youngest child was another boy named Palmer Reed, who was born the day I was indicted in Baton Rouge and given the name of two of my lawyers in the case.

If the loyalty of a wife and children could have elevated anyone in public life, I had that for complete success. The thing that hurt me at heart in

---

[34] The quoted pipeline rate may have been somewhat less, but a premium above the quoted price was frequently paid.

losing a political campaign was the disappointment of our children, who could not seem to understand how the people could fail to elect me.

When the millionaires and corporations of Louisiana fell out with each other, I was able to accept highly remunerative employment from one of the powerful to fight several others which were even more powerful. Then I made some big fees with which I built a modern home in the best residential section of the City of Shreveport at a cost of $40,000.00.

My family was happy and content in their new surroundings. Encouraged by the peace and quiet of a less active political life, I had considered settling down entirely to my law business and pursuing no further political ambitions.

While carrying on my law practice at home, I had also formed a partnership in the State of Arkansas. I devoted a considerable part of my time to practice in the southern part of that State.

Further cause for my attitude toward having less to do with politics came with the death of Governor Henry L. Fuqua, who was succeeded by Lieutenant Governor O. H. Simpson. Governor Simpson had supported the re-election of Senator Broussard. It was known that he would be a candidate to succeed himself.

# CHAPTER VIII

## THE TOLL BRIDGE OUTRAGE

NEW ORLEANS is largely surrounded by water to the north, east and west, with the Gulf to the South. With the coming of the automobile the necessity for bridges into the City was accentuated. It therefore became a question as to when, how, and in what manner bridges would be provided for motoring to and from that City. The policy to be adopted regarding New Orleans would no doubt control the building of other bridges throughout the State, in which there are many streams, bayous and large rivers, some of them, in several places, more than a mile in width.

In 1918, an amendment to the Constitution of Louisiana had been adopted, providing that a free bridge should be constructed by the State over Lake Pontchartrain north of the City of New Orleans.[35] But the Sanders-Fuqua administration, upon coming into power in 1924, fought to annul or at least to render nugatory that provision of the Constitution and to adopt a toll bridge policy for the State.[36]

Therefore, on February 26, 1925, the Highway Commission of that administration made a contract with what was known as the Watson-Williams Syndicate, providing for a toll bridge over Lake Pontchartrain. In the negotiations with the Highway

---

[35] Act 18 of the Extra Session of 1918, Louisiana.
[36] Act 141 of 1924, Louisiana.

Commission, the Syndicate to whom this franchise was granted, was represented by former Governor Sanders as its attorney. It had been understood that Mr. Sanders had other personal interest in the success of the venture.

Another concern competing for a franchise across Lake Pontchartrain complained that it had offered a more satisfactory proposition to the Highway Commission which had been rejected.

Former Governor Sanders, the controlling factor of the Fuqua administration, and former Governor Pleasant had been close political allies, opposed to me and for the election of Governor Fuqua. Their falling out as to whose clients should have been granted the franchise for a toll bridge gave us the opportunity to make use of the one for the exposure of the other. In the final end I had in mind that neither of their clients should profit, but that a free bridge should be built by the State.

"Which side shall we help?" I was asked by some of my friends in New Orleans.

"Help Pleasant to show up Sanders; then help Sanders to show up Pleasant. One is worse than the other," I replied.

"But where will we finally land?"

"We'll land against them both, in time, for a free bridge owned by the State. In the meantime, let's help them cut each other to the ground, if we can."

I was the Chairman of the Louisiana Public Service Commission at the time. Declaring that the contentions of neither company should have been recognized, but that a free bridge should have been

provided as the law stipulated, I gave wide currency
to my statements. In time, those protesting the
granting of the franchise to their competitors, joined
in favor of free bridges as the most feasible form of
opposition to the Watson-Williams contract.

Under the "J. Y. Sanders-Watson-Williams
franchise," as it was termed, the operators of the toll
bridge were to be allowed to charge as much as $3.60
for an automobile crossing the bridge each way, plus
15c per passenger, which meant that a car with five
occupants coming to and leaving the City of New
Orleans would pay toll charges of $8.40 to cross the
bridge.[37]

In my capacity as a citizen and taxpayer of the
State, as a holder of a bond under the law of 1918
and as Chairman of and in behalf of the Louisiana
Public Service Commission, I filed suit to annul the
franchise granted for the toll bridge to the Sanders-
Watson-Williams syndicate.[38] My suit, and others
like it, all tried at the same time, were finally lost in
the Supreme Court of Louisiana. But the Supreme
Court upheld the right of the State to build a free
bridge under the law of 1918 at the point specified,
but at none other.[39] Otherwise the toll contract prevented a bridge at any other place across the lake.

---

[37] Minutes of Louisiana Highway Commission, February 26,
1925.

[38] Louisiana Public Service Commission v. Louisiana Highway
Commission et al, 159 Louisiana Reports 932, 106 Southern 385;
Talbot v. Louisiana Highway Commission, 159 Louisiana 909,
106 Southern 377.

[39] Report of mass meeting called by Huey P. Long held in
Baton Rouge, Louisiana, for free bridges, in all newspapers of

Fuqua's administration had greatly depleted the fund out of which such free bridges should be built. Moreover, there was a means by which such administration might forever prevent any fund being accumulated sufficient to build any free bridges. Therefore, the holders of this toll bridge franchise, which had organized into the Pontchartrain Bridge Company, proceeded with plans to build the private toll bridge and advertised bonds for sale throughout the United States. In none of their advertisements, however, did they say that the courts had upheld the right of the State to build a free bridge paralleling the toll bridge.

In my undertaking to prevent this toll bridge from being built, and to warn the people generally (not only in Louisiana but outside the State) who might be led into the purchase of the toll bridge bonds, I drafted an order for the Louisiana Public Service Commission, declaring this proposed bridge to be a public utility, ordering the rates set in the franchise by the Highway Commission to be annulled and citing the company to show cause why reasonably low rates and charges for automobiles to travel over it should not be prescribed by the Commission. An injunction was immediately sought against me in the District Court in Baton Rouge, which was granted. An appeal was taken to the Supreme Court of Louisiana and that Court held that I could take no jurisdiction over the toll bridge before it was built.[40]

New Orleans on June 2, 1926. See front page of Times-Picayune of that date.

[40] New Orleans Pontchartrain Bridge Company v. Louisiana Public Service Commission et al, 162 Louisiana 874, 111 Southern 265.

In the Broussard campaign for the Senate in 1926, we made "free bridges" an issue against Governor Sanders. Over in Texas at that time "Ma" Ferguson was serving her first term as Governor. Mr. Sanders had such recognized influence over Governor Fuqua, that we referred to that administration as the "Pa" and "Ma" regime in Louisiana. The Watson-Williams franchise made it possible for us to defeat Sanders for the United States Senate.

The private toll bridge interest proceeded with construction, bonds having been readily purchased by the unsuspecting public who were never made aware in any of the advertisements that a State-owned free bridge was required by law to be built parallel to it.

"Go build that bridge," I said, "and before you finish it I will be elected governor and will have free bridges right beside it. You are building the most expensive buzzard roost that has ever been constructed in the United States."

It was not meant that the State would ever be permitted to exercise its right to build a free bridge, particularly if the toll bridge was constructed before the free bridge was undertaken. The administration of the State would see to that!

On October 11, 1926, some few days after Mr. Sanders' defeat for the Senate, Governor Fuqua died and was succeeded by Governor O. H. Simpson, who had supported Broussard in his election for the United States Senate.

While Governor Simpson had held aloof in the free bridge fight, and had taken no hand in it one way or the other, he had none the less appeared unfriendly to Sanders. Some few months after he became governor he announced that he would proceed with work to carry out the law of the State on free bridges.

"They have stolen Huey Long's clothes while he went in swimming," some of my opponents began to remark as Governor Simpson made known his intention to build free bridges.

"I will lay all my plans on my front porch," I replied, "and I will never holler 'Stop Thief' when they make their getaway if they want them."

Governor Simpson removed the Highway Commission serving under the Sanders-Fuqua administration and appointed one acceptable to himself. That Commission did not let full bridge contracts for the free bridges, but did let contracts for the construction of some piers on which free bridges could be rested. Such was the condition of the toll and free bridge fight at the time of the gubernatorial campaign of 1927-28.

# CHAPTER IX

CAMPAIGN FOR GOVERNOR, 1928

MY disinclination to enter a second race for Governor soon melted away, and I found myself actively campaigning as a candidate. A legion of political supporters counted heavily upon my making the campaign of 1928, the issues which I had urged four years before became so much the topic of Louisiana's political circles, that it was practically impossible for me not to be moved into the sea of that fight.

I designated an organization force in charge of Mr. Harvey E. Ellis, at Covington, Louisiana. Then I sought to secure some kind of organization in the City of New Orleans and some newspaper support. Colonel Robert E. Ewing, at that time the Publisher of the Daily States of New Orleans and of the Shreveport Times in Shreveport, who was aligned with Colonel John P. Sullivan in New Orleans, early appeared as about ready to espouse my candidacy.

But complications were not long in developing. Colonel Ewing had a son by the name of John D. Ewing, who was operating the Shreveport Times in Shreveport, where I was living. In his newspaper he frequently attacked the Police Department, under the jurisdiction of one of my friends, and then gave causes for arrest which no department, friendly or unfriendly, could ignore.

On one occasion he had been arrested and I had

persuaded my friend in charge of the Police Department to assist him. A few days later the young Ewing published a severe attack on the Police Department. The very next day he was arrested by a policeman who claimed he was driving through the streets of the city at a rate of speed in excess of seventy miles per hour, considerably possessed of liquor on his breath.

While seated in my office, my telephone rang.

"Huey, this is John Ewing. They have arrested me again for speeding. You've got to get me out of it."

My heart sank. I knew I had a task. I·saw a situation. But I braved the storm and called my friend, Tom Dawkins, over the telephone. Immediately upon my mentioning the name of Ewing he slammed up the receiver. Thereupon I took off afoot to his office.

"Don't come in here!——don't come in here," he stormed as I tried to enter.

I, of course, went in anyway. The presiding municipal judge had announced from the bench when young Ewing had been released on the previous case that, from that time on, anyone coming before him, and found to have speeded through the streets at a rate in excess of forty miles per hour, would be sent to jail. After considerable labor I managed to persuade my friend Dawkins to postpone the case until that judge took a vacation. Then young Ewing appeared before a substitute judge, plead guilty, and was fined, but was given a very severe lecture by the temporary court.

I had thought that the young man was satisfied. He should have been, for he had escaped the jail. In the meantime, however, I had seen his father in New

Orleans, and had told him that he should take steps to correct his son's recklessness for fear of future consequences. Hearing of my mentioning the matter to his father, and also blaming me for the lecture he received from the bench, the young man blew into a rage. His father became equally as vicious.

I finally went to the young man's office, sat down and reasoned with him as best I could. He agreed that he could not see where I had intentionally done him wrong. I can recall that he at no time expressed his thanks for my help in that or any other matter.

Eventually, Sullivan announced his support for me. Colonel Ewing was soon to follow. We wanted the support of Ewing's newspaper in New Orleans. It developed that to get Ewing we would have to take Sullivan first. Our forces argued pro and con on whether we would lose more to take Sullivan than we would gain in getting Ewing. The campaign manager was adamant against taking Sullivan to get Ewing or anyone else.

I finally settled the issue to try to get everybody.

Immediately upon Sullivan announcing for me, my campaign manager, Mr. Ellis, publicly resigned as my campaign manager, issuing a blistering statement that he would not tolerate the Sullivan support. He declared that Sullivan's name was a synonym for vice of various forms, particularly gambling.

I little dreamed at the time that final returns of the election would show the percentage of my votes in the area affected by Sullivan's organization and Ewing's newspapers to be less than I had received in the campaign four years before when I ran without political organization or newspaper help.

On July 8, 1927, a political conclave was held in the City of Alexandria, composed of all groups opposed to my becoming Governor, for the purpose of drafting some candidate possessing outstanding qualifications, the principal requirement being his probable ability to beat me. It was declared that Governor Simpson was not strong enough to make the grade, and that another and stronger man must be had. With considerable glamor, newspaper headlines, trumpeteering and barbecues, all participants unanimously went on record as calling for the candidacy of Congressman Riley J. Wilson to save the State from Huey P. Long.

Mr. Wilson, like myself, had been born in the Parish of Winn, and raised a country boy. He had moved to the eastern part of our parish where he taught school, became judge, ran for and was elected to Congress. He was then serving his fourteenth consecutive year. His friends claimed he had put forth great effort to secure flood control, which was at that time quite a lively issue among the people of the State. It was announced that his candidacy would largely be based upon what he had done and what he proposed to do in the work of flood control.

Our forces waited about one month after this conclave in Alexandria and advertised a meeting to be held in the same city to open my campaign for Governor. Our rally was attended by an even larger crowd than the meeting of our opposition.

The newspapers and interests behind the calling of

the Alexandria gathering against us had generally announced that the meeting would be composed of men of affairs in the business and politics of the State. They heralded their gathering as a meeting of "the better element."

We thereupon paraded throughout the State the announcement of our meeting to be held in Alexandria with a display of banners reading:

"EVERY MAN A KING, BUT NO ONE WEARS A CROWN"

Mr. John H. Overton, our keynote orator, described the opposition conclave as a "rump convention," wherein the dukes, earls and lords of the State's politics had gathered to witness the heralded birth of a new Crown Prince to preside over the destinies of the commonwealth. He pictured the political stork arriving, placing the political babe, Congressman Wilson, in the cradle, from which he was handed from dignitary to dignitary.

Mr. Overton followed with the satire that the babe thus presented was in swaddling clothes, had not yet become old enough to stand alone, much less to walk, and that by election time it would know not "how to run."

In answering the clamor that Congressman Wilson should be elected Governor by reason of his flood relief work, I said:

"So they seek to elect the gentleman because of his flood record! What is that flood record? Why he has been in Congress for fourteen years and this year (1927) the water went fourteen feet higher than ever before, giving him a flood record of one foot of high water to the year, if that's what he's claiming credit for."

The satire and ridicule of the meeting spread throughout the State and almost destroyed the Wilson candidacy. It was months before it could be revived. For some time it appeared that Governor Simpson would be the second candidate in the race.

It was in the speech that I delivered under the historic oak where Evangeline waited for her lover Gabriel, as described by Longfellow, that I said:

> And it is here under this oak where Evangeline waited for her lover, Gabriel, who never came. This oak is an immortal spot, made so by Longfellow's poem, but Evangeline is not the only one who has waited here in disappointment.
>
> Where are the schools that you have waited for your children to have, that have never come? Where are the roads and the highways that you send your money to build, that are no nearer now than ever before? Where are the institutions to care for the sick and disabled? Evangeline wept bitter tears in her disappointment, but it lasted through only one lifetime. Your tears in this country, around this oak, have lasted for generations. Give me the chance to dry the eyes of those who still weep here!

My political opposition pointed out early in the campaign that even if I were elected Governor the Legislature would be 3 to 1 of men opposed to me.

"Those men will never stand for what Huey Long is advocating. They will impeach him before he is Governor a year," they said frequently.

War broke out between L. E. Thomas, the Mayor of Shreveport, and myself again.

The Mayor, in an especially advertised meeting, accused me of what vices there remained (if any) of which he had not already accused me in previous campaigns.

I announced a special meeting to reply to his attack. After accusing him of exaggerations and other things I said:

> Why ladies and gentlemen, a Chinaman, a Fiji Islander and Thomas made a bet as to which one could stand to stay locked up the longest with a pole cat.
>
> The Chinaman went in the room with the animal and stayed ten minutes. Then he had to come out. He couldn't stand it any longer.
>
> Then the Fiji Islander went in and stayed fifteen minutes with the pole cat and came out a very sick man.
>
> Thomas's time came. He went in and stayed five minutes, and the pole cat ran out.

This and other things were too much for the Mayor of my home city. He had me arrested the next day. Later the district attorney filed bills of information.

By accident the charges against me failed to specify that the Mayor was a man "of good repute," a necessary allegation to prosecute one for slander in Louisiana.

The court dismissed the charge on that account. Mayor Thomas was disgusted at this technical failure

to have left out the words that he was "of good repute." He had cooled off and declined to refile the
charges.

But we soon learned that a combination of interests
had been effected between much of the support behind
Governor Simpson and that behind Congressman
Wilson so that, if I failed to secure a majority over
both of them in the first primary, common cause
would be made by both the Simpson and Wilson
forces behind whichever candidate was in the second
contest.

I discussed this situation with my campaign leaders
and workers. I said to them:

"With the big vote that will be registered against
me in the City of New Orleans, it is a matter of practical impossibility to beat both these candidates in the
first primary; the leaders in these two camps are
friendly and are determined to be together if there is
a second race, regardless of which one has to run it
off with me."

"There is no way to separate those leaders," said
one of my workers.

"Now, there is a way," I answered. "We must keep
tab on how they are running, one as against the other
and direct our fire always against the strongest opponent until he becomes the weaker of the two, and
then switch and direct our fire against the other, and
keep those two bullies neck and neck for the next
several weeks. Fire will break out between them as
sure as lightning, if we can do that."

We followed that course persistently for several
months. It looked like it was doomed to failure when

one Sunday evening one of our forces came to me and said:

"The Wilson newspapers want our dope on Simpson. They have agreed to play up any remark you make on him."

"We will give it to them," I said. "Now see if we can't find some traitor in our camp who will be willing to go to the Simpson crowd and advise them that this other gang is working to ruin their candidate. We will have them fighting like cats and dogs by next Monday."

We found a volunteer who "betrayed" the information. It didn't take until the next Monday for them to be at each other's throats.

The two candidates began to attack each other, one calling the other "unknown," and the other retaliating with the statement that the attacker was "thus known." We poured all the oil on the fire that we could.

In the first primary election, occurring January 20, 1928, the vote was as follows: Long 126,842; Wilson 81,747; Simpson 80,326.

I had defeated both of my opponents together in the country outside New Orleans by 7,518 votes. Each of them had defeated me in New Orleans, Congressman Wilson leading me in that City by 20,425 and Governor Simpson leading me by 4,505.

The Sullivan-Ewing support in New Orleans meant little.

My ex-Campaign Manager sent me word:

"What did I tell you?"

I led Congressman Wilson by 45,095 votes and

lacked but a few thousand votes of defeating both opponents in the first primary.

The animosity which had grown up between Wilson and Simpson and Simpson's defeat was too much for the Simpsonites. They were further aroused by the fact that Governor Simpson had beaten Congressman Wilson outside the City by 14,499 votes. Some claimed Wilson had been counted into the second primary in New Orleans.

I have lost New Orleans in all my campaigns, but I think I am one of the very few candidates who has never claimed to have been counted out there.

Despite the effort of the Simpson State campaign managers, and whatever pledges they had made, the Simpson City Organization and a large majority of the country workers would not countenance their support going to Congressman Wilson.

They early announced that if a second primary were held between Congressman Wilson and me that they would support me in the run-off.

I was too near victory for any kind of combination to have beaten me.

My running mate for Lieutenant Governor was Dr. Paul N. Cyr, of Jeanerette. He was elected.

All three of the candidates for governor, however, Wilson, Simpson and I, declared in favor of letting the final contracts for the free bridges over Lake Pontchartrain.

"You will have to take me on my record in this matter," I said, in speaking of this and other issues.

"I had an uncle," I continued, "who late in life started to join the Baptist Church of which many of

my family are members. On the day my uncle was to
be baptized, his wife and small boy sat on the bank
of the creek happy over his conversion. As my uncle
was led out into the water by the preacher, there
floated out of his pocket face up, the ace of spades,
and a few moments later, the king of spades. As the
preacher was just getting ready to take hold of him,
there floated behind those cards the queen and jack of
spades, and then out came the ten of spades. His wife
saw the situation and screamed:

" 'Don't baptize him, parson, my husband is lost
. . . my husband is lost!'

"But the young boy on the bank yelled out excitedly:

" 'No he ain't ma! if pa can't win with that hand,
he can't win at all!'

"So if my record will not win on this point, there is
nothing I can give you."

There were prominent leaders in the campaigns of
both Wilson and Simpson either friendly to or en-
twined with the toll bridge owners whose influence
was feared to be such as to thwart the building of
free bridges by either of them should they be elected,
regardless of their good intentions. It is significant
that the interests behind this toll bridge fought only
my election.

Under Governor Simpson the Highway Commission had drifted into rather bad repute and there
were misgivings as to what might be expected from
that body insofar as letting final contracts for "free
bridges" over Lake Pontchartrain were concerned.

When my election as the next Governor of Louisiana was conceded, I was given a banquet by the business interests of the City of New Orleans.

My friend Judge Foster was one of the speakers. He said:

"I first looked upon Huey Long as a bad boy making faces at authority, but I later learned he knew his cases and studied the law."

There were other equally complimentary remarks. A few presents were tendered me, including a chest of silver, on which my wife's initials were engraved. The interests behind the toll bridges were among those present, and they expressed the wish that my administration would be successful.

I did not wait to become Governor, but asked Governor Simpson to begin the operation of free ferries parallel to the toll bridge immediately. Governor Simpson was later to become part of my administration. He ordered the free ferries. The bridge company went into the hands of a receiver soon after I became Governor. It is in such a situation today. Its possible $8.40 charge has since fallen to 60c.

# CHAPTER X

## A LEGISLATIVE STRUGGLE

THE Legislature of Louisiana met in the Capitol at Baton Rouge May 14, 1928.

Before the meeting of the Legislature and my inauguration, I had made every effort to conciliate my political opponents. Even when it was certain that I would organize both houses of the Legislature, I still appealed to my opponents to make the session one of harmony, good will and progress for the State.

I met two of the important leaders of the opposition in a private conference.

"I would like to have peace to carry out the program for the State," I said.

"How much peace did you give us when we were in power?" they asked.

"I was against what you were doing. I advocated other things which the people have now approved and you ought to support them."

"That is the way we felt," they answered.

"Well, let me be generous. I have no objection to some of your leaders having important chairmanships of the committees."

"Who is going to control the committees? Will you turn them over to us?" they asked.

"Not hardly," I answered.

"In other words, you will let our men write up what you want instead of letting somebody else do it. Do you call that a compromise? How about the patronage of the State; is that the basis of compromise?"

"You lost that as the spoils of war," I answered.

Finally one of them rose and said:

"We think we will let you run this State for about a year."

"Do you mean after that, that you will be with me?" I asked.

"Why don't you ask us if we mean that you will be with us, or whoever we have got running things then?" they answered good naturedly.

"Sounds like you mean impeachment," I said.

"Brother, you said it," one of them replied and waved his departure.

They were not far wrong, as events later proved.

I faced a very queer and difficult situation in the first session of the legislature. There were 100 members of the House of Representatives and 39 members of the Senate. Of that number, only 18 members of the House and only 9 members of the Senate had supported me for Governor.

To pass any legislation I had to recruit my support from legislators who had not favored me for Governor.

The first test came in the election of the Speaker. My candidate was John B. Fournet, who won by a vote of 72 to 27. In the Senate, Senator Philip H. Gilbert was our candidate for President Pro Tempore. He was also elected.

My program for the legislature was to supply additional funds to the schools of the State, and to furnish the children with free school books. To secure revenues for that purpose it was necessary to change the severance taxes on oil, gas, timber and other natural resources to a quantity basis, resulting in a considerable increase from the corporations pursuing such businesses. Coupled with such was a tax on the business of manufacturing carbon black in the State.

We avoided complications in the free school book law. The Constitution of the State prevented any State donations to private or sectarian schools. I drew a law providing that the books should be furnished children, thereby enabling us to provide all children attending schools with the text books required.

Our highway system had so deteriorated that some of our roads were nearly impassable. The Department owed more than five million dollars, and had no money to improve old roads or build new ones. We proposed a Constitutional amendment (which had to be submitted to the people for a vote) to secure funds for the debts of our predecessors and to begin a program of paved highways and free bridges in the State.

We sought to increase the appropriations for the schools for the blind and deaf and dumb; also for the two hospitals for mental diseases and our two general charity hospitals. The school for the blind had been conducted in an old building which had been abandoned as unfit for use as a public schoolhouse in the '90's; the patients furnished treatment for mental diseases had been held in cells or locked beds at night and chained to hoes and plow stocks to work in the day time. The charity hospitals had been forced to allow some of their patients to lie on the bare floor.

We also proposed legislation needed to strengthen the hand of the administration, such as giving the Governor the power to remove the old and appoint new boards to control the levees and manage the State Board of Health.

We were faced by an opposition composed of good parliamentarians and clever strategists. In the House they introduced bills in great number and persuaded other members of the legislature, men who were inclined to be friendly to us, to introduce bills to cover their pet schemes.

Eventually we were faced with a clogged calendar and were unable to force consideration of our important proposals. Every effort we devised failed to clear the way. We met on several occasions to devise plans to extricate ourselves from the dilemma. At one of them a little French representative stammered out excitedly:

"What would happen if you passed all those bills?"

I thought a moment and said:

"Well, it would take just as long to pass them, wouldn't it?"

"No," he shouted. "Why you don't move to pass every bill quick as you reach it? No man can complain because you pass his bill whether he speak or not!"

I saw the light. After a little discussion I said:

"Tomorrow morning as fast as a number is read on a bill, allow as little talk as possible and let the Speaker recognize our floor leader and let him move the final passage and previous question. You can clear the calendar in a day in that way. I will veto every bill after it is passed that I don't want."

The next morning the legislature opened early. The first numbered bill was called. Our floor leader rose.

"I move to final passage of the bill and move the previous question."

The bill was passed instantly. With only occasional speaking every man's bill was passed. The calendar was cleared by noon. The opposition had been unable to figure a way to prevent it.

In the rush of so many bills passing, one member of the opposition, somewhat intoxicated, sought to halt the proceedings. He rose and shouted:

"Mr. Speaker! A point of order!"

"The pint is well taken," replied the chair. "Sit down!"

I later vetoed the objectionable bills by the score.

Our fights were severe in both houses. To secure Constitutional amendments we were required to have two-thirds of the votes of the membership of both the House and the Senate. On the fourth of July we could count only sixty-five members present who would vote for the road amendment. Two of the number on which we depended were absent. The Sergeant at Arms came to me.

"I can't find those two men."

"Call the floor leader out here," I said.

When the floor leader walked into the hall outside the House chamber I said:

"Keep the speaking going until I can find those two representatives. It may take several hours."

"We'll do that," he said, "but I think we can keep the opposition doing most of the talking."

Eventually we located the two absent members. They were brought to the House chamber. Then the vote was taken, and we received the bare 67.

The law had provided that one claiming a public office must bring suit against any intruder holding the same through a petition to be filed by the attorney general. We feared that in the future the attorney general would fail to bring the necessary suits. We secured the passage of legislation, over the ruling of the attorney general that the same was unconstitutional, giving to any person the right to bring suit for any office which he claimed.

The demonstration staged by the friends of the Standard Oil Company and its allies against the additional tax on oil resulted in a frenzied session before the Finance Committee of the Senate, necessitating my appearing before that Committee to insure securing a favorable report for the bill. We had the combined opposition of the public press, of the chambers of commerce and boards of trade, aided and abetted by the corporation lobbyists.

When John M. Parker was a candidate for governor in 1923, his chief promise was to bring natural gas to the City of New Orleans. Such promise was made by other governors who had been elected. None had performed. I made the same promise to bring natural gas to New Orleans and all other principal places in the State in both of my campaigns for governor, particularly in the one of 1928. I proposed before the legislature to create a franchise commission so that I might use it to force natural gas into the City of New Orleans. Very heated legislative argument ensued over the natural gas question until the electric power concern controlling the artificial gas distribution system in the city accepted terms which I proposed to place natural gas in the City of New Orleans. Despite the mild weather which discourages the use of any gas for heating purposes in South Louisiana, the natural gas delivered has almost double the heat units of the artificial gas then being sold, with the natural gas being furnished at a considerably lower rate. Sufficiently low rates were secured for its practical use in the industries of the city. No agitation has ever developed over the arrangements on either side since the acceptance of the rates and terms which I enforced.

The adjournment of the legislature, however, was not the end to the fight for our new laws. Every statute was contested before the courts, particularly including those seeking to dismiss one set of officials so that I might appoint others. All such contests over public offices, however, finally resulted in our being sustained by the courts.

Then the time arrived for the public schools to open in the early fall of 1928.

Suits were filed to set aside the statute and to prevent the free school books being given to the children of the State. Such suits against the free school books were companions of other suits brought to annul the taxes imposed on the oil and gas interests to pay for them and other school work.

My enemies took every advantage of the school term beginning. On the day when all the schools were to open, I had been unable to secure the funds with which to pay for the school books already sent to the State but awaiting payment for same before delivery to us.

I had called a session of the Board of Liquidation of the State to borrow $500,000.00 to pay for the books until we could collect the taxes in contest. When I called upon the fiscal agency bankers of the State at New Orleans to negotiate such a loan, they hesitated and informed me that their attorneys doubted the legality of such loans. I was present at some of their meetings with their lawyers.

The matter could not be longer delayed. The schools had to open one way or the other. I took my last chance.

"I understand you bankers to hold that you doubt the legality of such loans made to the Board of Liquidation of the State," I said to the bankers.

"Our attorneys feel that way about it. We must be guided by their advice."

"Then I will be guided by your attorneys' advice, too. Did you know that the State owes you $935,-000.00 on these Board of Liquidation loans now?" I asked.

"Oh, that has been ordered paid by the appropriation bill of the last legislature," one of them responded.

"Yes, but it hasn't been paid yet," I rejoined. "And what's more, it ain't going to be paid. Your attorneys ruled those loans illegal, and if it's illegal to make them it's illegal to pay them. We'll keep the $935,-000.00 and buy the books and have $435,000.00 to spare, under the ruling of your lawyers."

I waited for no reply. I immediately left the bank.

I was somewhat outdone. I walked to the hotel, where I was staying, sat down to a table and instructed the waiter to bring me a thin sandwich. While I was waiting for the waiter to return, one of the bankers entered the dining room.

"Governor," he said hurriedly, "let's stop this talk where it is. We voted to make you the loan."

"When can I have it?" I asked.

"Right now," he replied.

The waiter was returning with the sandwich.

"Take back the sandwich," I said to the waiter. "Fry me a steak!"

The schools opened with free school books for the children.

My enemies were outraged. They had counted strongly on paralyzing the schools until I was forced to relent on certain plans. They threatened that the banks would never get back the money loaned. But they did.

The hope for free school books which had become a dream of the children of the State, particularly in the poor families, was at last a reality. Never in my life have I witnessed the pleasure to as many children and families. No accomplishment of my career has given me such satisfaction.

But in the Parish of Caddo, my home parish, the opposition was so furious that it would not relent even after the books were sent to them free.

"This is a rich section of the state," said Mayor Thomas of Shreveport. "We are not going to be humiliated or disgraced by having it advertised that our children had to be given the books free."

Their school board and public bodies pronounced the whole idea of free school books one of corruption and ordered suit. Even the church of which I was a member, holding a statewide convention in Shreveport, passed a resolution condemning the law.

At about that time, it so happened that an airport was to be built by the U. S. Government, the Third Attack Wing, immediately adjacent to the City of Shreveport. It was a fine and needed improvement for the City of Shreveport and Parish of Caddo. By some act of Providence, it developed that the State of Louisiana owned 80 acres of the ground needed for its construction. The Government would not finally award the airport unless the State would make a deed for that 80 acres to it. I was requested to make the deed.

"You have decided here," I sent word to the boards of Caddo, "that your children can't have free school books. People so well off don't need an airport. Whenever you get ready to allow these free school books to be handed out to the children, then I will be ready to talk to you about the State deeding 80 acres of land to the government."

The newspapers, with one voice, criticized such action on my part. Col. Ewing called me to New Orleans and stormed. I had no intention of relenting.

The Caddo Parish authorities finally consented to distribute free school books in their schools. I deeded the 80 acres to the Government.

In the meantime the injunction to prevent the

State from buying school books had been refused by the Supreme Court, but in a preliminary order only, by the narrow vote of 4 to 3.

The term of office of Judge Land, one of the four justices of the Supreme Court who had refused the injunction against the free school book law, was about to expire. He came from the Shreveport District.

There was a strong opposition candidate. The defeat of Justice Land would have meant the change of one vote and therefore the defeat of the free school book law. The suit was pending in that Court awaiting hearing on appeal.

I moved back to my home in Shreveport to take charge of the campaign of Justice Land for re-election to the Supreme Court. We had hard work ahead to save the day. Though beaten in Shreveport, Justice Land was re-elected by a majority of 5193 votes.

The severance tax lawsuit came up for trial in the United States Court at Shreveport. On the day preceding the time for hearing, I called on the Attorney General in New Orleans to find out if he was prepared to defend the State's interests. I discovered that he had done nothing. Less than 24 hours remained when the case was to be heard 300 miles away.

"I know you are busy here," I said to the Attorney General, upon my arrival in his office. "If you have no objection, I will take one of your boys and we will delve into this little matter and get up some pleadings."

He consented. I immediately commenced, with the

help of a young lawyer in the office, to prepare the proper pleadings.

We all boarded the train for Shreveport that night and argued the case before the three Federal judges the next day. I took the lead in the matter before the Court. The result was a decision favorable to us.[41] An appeal was taken by the oil companies to the Supreme Court of the United States.

I returned to Baton Rouge and proceeded with my work as Governor of the State, prosecuting the campaign for the ratification of the constitutional amendments in the month of November.

Our enemies were in position to go before the people, pleading the fact that when others (themselves) were in power they had wasted the public bond funds amounting to millions of dollars, and that the people might expect us to do likewise.

"Suggest any means on the face of the earth to safeguard the expenditure of the funds that I am asking you to vote," I said to the people, "and I will comply with it."

I already had caused to be written into the constitutional amendment the provision that the funds acquired from the sale of the bonds could not be expended except by and with the consent of the Board of Liquidation of the State Debt, which was composed of the seven principal office holders. That was claimed to be insufficient.

Someone suggested that if a non-partisan and non-political board would be appointed, whose consent

---

[41] Ohio Oil Company v. Conway, 28 Federal (2nd) 441.

would be required before action was taken by the Board of Liquidation for the expenditure, that opposition would not be made to the passage of the amendment by the people. I seized upon that suggestion and asked that they suggest the name of such a committee.

Such names were suggested and thereupon, I caused the Board of Liquidation of the State Debt to pass a resolution providing that until the committee composed of the names suggested had sanctioned each and every transaction, not a dime of the public funds voted by the people would be spent.[42]

But that was not enough to satisfy my opposition. The newspapers contended that the board should have been legalized in the constitutional amendment. Thereupon I proposed that, if the majority of members of the legislature who had voted against the amendment would pledge themselves to legalize that committee, I would immediately call the legislature into extra session and submit a new constitutional amendment. They declined to do so.

We were in position of high respect by our offer and the enemies' refusal. We stood our ground. The constitutional amendments were ratified by majorities of some 5 to 1.

My floor leader in the State Senate was my old friend Oscar K. Allen, of Winnfield. He had been my law client and political associate for life. He had never served in a Legislature, but, none the less, took the floor leadership in the Senate the day he was

---

[42] New Orleans Item, Wednesday, August 2, 1928.

sworn in. While I was scanning the State to find
someone to run the Highway Commission, I saw my
friend Senator Allen's picture in the newspaper with
the announcement from him that he would head the
Highway Commission when the Legislature adjourned. I met Allen that afternoon.

"Oscar," I said, "did you give out that statement
you were going to head the Highway Commission?"

"Yes," he confessed, without embarrassment.

"Well, suppose I had promised it to someone else;
I didn't say I was going to appoint you."

"If you have promised it to anybody else, you'll
have to break your promise," he replied. "There are
too many things dead up the creek in this business to
suit me. The only way they can ruin this administration is a bad management of that Commission. I'll
take charge and save that situation."

A few more words and I was convinced that Senator Allen had made the proper selection.

Matters had begun to develop in my combination
with Colonel Bob Ewing and Colonel Sullivan in
New Orleans. Soon after my election I had occasion
to call and talk general matters with Col. Ewing at
his newspaper offices at the Daily States.

"Colonel," I said, "I don't want you to think I am
not appreciative of the effort that has been made for
me. I know you did everything you could in the City
of New Orleans and I will say the same thing for
Sullivan, but did you ever stop to realize I didn't
receive any better percentage of the vote of the City
of New Orleans in 1928 than I did in 1924 when I

had no newspaper or organization whatever and less than no money?"

"Yes," the Colonel replied. "I have thought of that."

"Now, Colonel, let me tell you how bad it was. Ninety-five per cent of the money we raised for my campaign for Governor was spent through Mr. Sullivan in New Orleans, including all of the money we raised in the country, and yet I ran a poor third in this city. One candidate beat me more than 20,000 votes and another candidate beat me by about 5,000 votes, and with no money to carry on our work in the country, I had to hit the line of the city 70,000 votes ahead of my nearest opponent to get the office. Now what is our answer?"

"Well, I will ask you," replied the Colonel.

"Well, Colonel, you know and I know the people of this city will not stand for Sullivan and his business as a gambler. We had to get him to get your help. Now if we want to be his friend, had we not better tell him the truth and give him to understand that while we can be of help to him, he should locate himself in something besides politics? He cannot help anybody and can only hurt himself."

The Colonel agreed.

"Now, Colonel," I said, "I want to tell you something about your newspaper in Shreveport. In 1924 I carried the Parish of Caddo without any newspaper supporting me there. Now with your paper supporting me there, in this last election, I was badly beaten in the parish."

"You don't mean to say my son running the news-

Cartoon Published by the New Orleans Item on Break Between
Long and Ewing.

Spectators Packed in Galleries for Trial of Gov. Huey P. Long before State Senate Sitting as a Court of Impeachment. Gov. Long is Shown in Foreground With His Legal Staff of Nine Attorneys at His Left.

paper there didn't help you, do you?" the Colonel asked.

"I don't mean to say he didn't try to help me, Colonel, but I just want you to read the sign that it is bad luck to have your son running the newspaper in Shreveport if you expect anybody you are supporting to get many votes."

I realized I had discussed a delicate subject in mentioning the Colonel's son, and I quickly turned the conversation back regarding Sullivan.

"What would you advise me to say to Sullivan?" I inquired.

"I would say to him just what you have said to me. If he has made any political promises, then fill them and make it easier for Sullivan to get out of politics."

"Well, now, Colonel, fortunately I had an understanding with Sullivan that whatever promises he made were to be communicated to me and I was to agree to them as we went along. I am prepared to fill every promise."

I left the Colonel and returned to the hotel. I immediately met John P. Sullivan. He came to my room.

"John," I said, "I have got something to tell you. Colonel Ewing doesn't know I am going to tell you we had a conversation, but we have," I continued. "I want to tell you what occurred."

Thereupon I repeated the conversation.

Thereafter, however, efforts of what was left of the Sullivan faction to amalgamate with the Regular Organization of the City of New Orleans began to

bear fruit. I was asked to consent to the proposition
and declined to be a party to the merger. When the
merger was affected, despite Colonel Ewing's approval, I publicly denounced it and declared I would
not accept its support or give it support.[43]

The break between Colonel Ewing and myself became open. It had been smothered for a long time and
several breaches only narrowly averted. At last the
break was an acknowledged fact.

The New Orleans Item gloating over the break
after Colonel Ewing and myself had exchanged certain notes in the public press, published a cartoon
labeled "Dropping the Pilot" in the form of a corruption on the cartoon when the young Emperor of
Germany discarded Bismarck.[44]

In the spring of 1929, the Supreme Court of the
United States temporarily reversed the opinion of
the three-judge Federal Court in the severance tax
cases.[45] We had calculated upon a favorable decision
at an early date, and such a victory in favor of the
big oil companies was alarming.

We had immediate problems on hand that could
not be deferred. Need for the severance tax money
was evident.

My friends and I were outraged at the persistence
with which the big oil companies resisted the payment

---

[43] Times-Picayune, February 24, 1929; New Orleans Item,
February 24, 1929; March 7, 1929; Morning Tribune, March 6,
1929.

[44] Cartoon reproduced in this volume.

[45] Ohio Oil Co. v. Conway, 279 U. S. 813.

of taxes and with the political opposition they continued to give us.

I immediately called the Legislature into session for the purpose of imposing a tax of 5 cents per barrel on oil refined in the State. That was my gauge of battle to the "Oil Trust" for all the fight they wanted. It was, in one respect, a rather insignificant tax, but sufficient to yield the schools nearly $5,000.00 per day, or more than $1,500,000.00 per year, which they badly needed.

The spirit of my political opposition had risen with the decision of the United States Supreme Court. Things blazed and turned to a white heat. Baton Rouge swarmed with strange faces. Chambers of Commerce, boards of trade, newspapers, corporation lobbyists, all ex-office holders and the New Orleans organization with everything that could be raked or scraped came to the Capitol for the legislative session on Monday morning of March 3, 1929.

This first show of opposition did not disconcert me. I had overcome it before. Furthermore, I had taken nothing for granted. I had secured the pledge of nearly two-thirds the membership of both houses in favor of my proposed bill before I issued my call.

Of all the newspapers, only the Times-Picayune had spoken well of me for some time before the extra session.[46]

The combined "Oil and Gas Trusts" which had lashed at me with clubs in preceding days, now struck with hammers of iron; pens of the publications that

---

[46] Times-Picayune, February 17, 1929.

had been dipped in gall to write of me, were now dipped in vitriol. In the Capitol City, the apparent free use of money exceeded anything I had ever seen.

I began to lose support in the Legislature. Many newspapers, printed daily, weekly or monthly, abounded with unusual advertisements displaying popular brands of the oil companies. The "Oil Trust" knew how to fight. Even the Times-Picayune opposed the tax on refining oil, but did not, for a time, otherwise attack me or my administration.

A member of our administration called me late at night to come at once to his home. Upon reaching there he told me that a certain member of the legislature who had been extremely friendly to our organization, had knocked on the back door of his house and was then hiding in the kitchen, waiting to see me. I walked through the dwelling and into the kitchen.

"They're going to impeach you," he said.

"Well, that's news, sure enough!" I replied, "are you going to vote for them to do it?"

"Every member of my family has been looked up. They have all been to me. Everyone of them loses his job now if I don't swing into line. The Standard Oil Company will fire them all. They can't live without their jobs."

"Then why are you worrying?" I asked. "If all you have got to do is to vote for the impeachment to keep them from being bothered, go ahead and vote."

"If it will do any good, Huey," he said, "I will vote against your impeachment. But they are going to have enough votes without me. I hate to put myself on record before you in that kind of a scheme. I want you to tell me what to do."

"No," I answered, "with all the folks that you have, I don't see how you can do anything else, and I don't want you to do anything else if it will hurt them. But let me ask you this: If I see that your vote is material, can I have it?"

"If it will save you, I will give you the vote when you want it."

"Now," I said to him, "we've got to fight the devil with fire. They are using the bread and butter of your family to make you cast an improper vote. You can be of help to me. Turn now and be vicious; don't ever pay me another compliment. Get in their camp. Vote with them for everything. Where they say damn, you say double damn. Keep me lined up on the incidents. I will never expose you unless the time comes when your vote will save the day."

He gave me his word.

A mass meeting was called by my combined opponents to meet in Baton Rouge. The call was heard. It was the largest gathering by far ever held by my opponents in the State of Louisiana up to that time.

My ground had begun to slip from under me. Rats began to leave the apparently sinking ship. I had to draw back to find out where I stood.

# CHAPTER XI

## *The Dreher-LeBoeuf Case*

IF the opposition were to succeed it was necessary that they have the Lieutenant Governor with them. He had been elected on my ticket. During the 1928 session of the Legislature he remained faithful, even in our fight with the "oil trust." He had, however, made some inquiry as to who might be the next Governor.

A reason or an excuse arose to give him grounds for announcing a break. It was the Dreher-LeBoeuf matter.

James LeBoeuf, a man of about 45 years of age, was an electrician in the town of Morgan City, Louisiana. One night his wife and himself, on his wife's suggestion, went boating near the city. They were met by two men, Dr. Thomas E. Dreher and Jim Beadle, riding in another boat. One of these men shouted:

"Is that you, Jim?"

LeBoeuf answered that it was. He was immediately shot down.

Previously, in order to avoid being shot also, the wife, luring her husband to his death and murder, took the precaution to ride in a separate boat from that in which her husband rode.

LeBoeuf's body, removed from the scene of the

126

tragedy by Dreher, Beadle and Mrs. LeBoeuf, was slashed open and all precautions taken against gas forming. Weights were attached to the head and feet. The body was then lowered into apparently very deep water.

Mrs. LeBoeuf, Dr. Dreher and Beadle returned to the even tenor of their ways as though nothing had happened. LeBoeuf failed to be seen around the streets. A search was instituted for his whereabouts. Mrs. LeBoeuf could give no information and Dr. Dreher gave less.

By an act of Providence, when the body was sunk it rested at a point where there was a slight elevation in the bottom of the lake. Due to this situation the body was discovered and taken from the water. Mrs. LeBoeuf and Dr. Dreher were arrested immediately and Jim Beadle was taken into custody a few days later. When arrested, Dr. Dreher, after making a motion with a pistol as though to take his life, confessed to the murder.

Mrs. LeBoeuf's statement showed that beyond question the affair was premeditated; that she, the wife of James LeBoeuf and the mother of his children, agreed to lead her husband to the lone and solitary spot of his death.

Never had a more conscienceless murder been known.

The trial was held in the district court at Franklin, Louisiana. Before that time Mrs. LeBoeuf and Dr. Dreher changed their story somewhat. The Jury found Dr. Dreher and Mrs. LeBoeuf guilty of murder in the first degree. They were sentenced to hang.

Jim Beadle, the hired hand of Dr. Dreher, who had turned state's evidence, was given life imprisonment.

The foregoing happened before I became Governor of the State.

Beadle accepted his sentence and entered the penitentiary. Dr. Dreher and Mrs. LeBoeuf took the case to the Supreme Court.

After I became Governor the Supreme Court affirmed the conviction and sentence against Mrs. LeBoeuf and Dr. Dreher. An appeal was then made to the Board of Pardons, seeking a commutation of their sentence to life imprisonment. On the vote of the Attorney General, Percy Saint, and the trial Judge, James Simon, as against the vote of the Lieutenant Governor, Dr. Paul N. Cyr, the Board of Pardons declined to recommend a commutation of sentence.[47] I immediately signed the warrants under the law to carry out the sentence of the Court.

It happened that the execution would have fallen during the Christmas holidays. I was asked to extend the time for the execution beyond the holiday season and the request was granted.

Later efforts were made to save the couple from hanging due to two facts; first, Dr. Dreher was connected with one of the leading and most influential families of the State; second, no white woman had ever been hanged in the State.

Maudlin sentiment was fanned to a fever heat by some of the newspapers and by misguided organizations.

---

[47] See New Orleans Item of February 1, 1929.

Another session of the Board of Pardons was called. With the vote of the Attorney General and the Lieutenant Governor, that time the Board recommended commutation.[48] The trial judge declared the matter to be ridiculous and dissented.

I rejected the recommendation of the Board of Pardons and agreed with the trial judge. I ordered the sentence of the Court executed.

The leading newspaper of the State at the time, the Times-Picayune, endorsed the position which I took in the following editorial:

### SOUND AND COURAGEOUS

Denying clemency to the murderers of James LeBoeuf, Governor Long sets forth at length the facts and reason compelling his decision. After recalling the crime and its attendant circumstances, and reviewing and analyzing the evidence, the governor fails to find "one single condition or extenuating circumstance which would justify" his "thwarting the course of the law as it has prevailed for centuries past." Capital punishment, he points out, "is the law of the land. I am an officer sworn to enforce that law. . . . I cannot, under my oath as governor, disrupt the process of law, hold out an example that murder shall be given punishment contrary to the statutes, or that clemency should make this land one in which human life shall not have a reasonable degree of sanctity."

Those who have joined in the cry for clemency in this case should read the governor's statement

---

[48] See Associated Press summaries of Louisiana newspapers February 1, 1929.

entire. It reminds the public of what many seemingly have forgotten—that the murder of James LeBoeuf was popularly accounted at the time of its gruesome revelation one of the foulest crimes ever committed in Louisiana. It should be remembered also that the defendants under sentence have had their day in the highest courts of the state and nation, and that all these tribunals uniformly have sustained the fairness of their trial and the validity of their conviction.

We think the governor's reasoning and decision are alike sound. We honor him for the courage he displays.

The Lieutenant Governor, Paul N. Cyr, was frantic.

He declared, in the course of his effort to release the couple, that in the event of the absence of the Governor of the State, he would become Governor himself; that if the State could be rid of me, he would sign proper credentials to commute the sentence of Dr. Dreher and Mrs. LeBoeuf, and a pardon for the man ridding the State of me.[49] The couple were hanged as ordered by the Court.

Dr. Cyr's first speech contained:—

"How long have I been humiliated by having to deal with this man? When two lives were at stake the

---

[49] New Orleans Item dispatch of January 11, 1929, page 3, says: "FRANKLIN, LA., JAN. 10—'I'd not only settle the LeBoeuf-Dreher case, but I would pardon the kidnappers,' Lieutenant Governor Paul Cyr remarked here this afternoon, upon his return from a futile visit to Baton Rouge, in response to a suggestion that Governor Huey P. Long might have been kidnapped."

Governor blocked me!" etc. He further attacked the efforts I was making to tax the business of refining oil. The public press declared his address "immortal."

Then a great attack was made because I had commuted the sentence of one Pleasant Harris.

The Harris case was one in which a man and woman, illegally living together, constantly fighting, finally ended by the woman being killed. The woman, however, as it was shown, had shot the man on a couple of occasions, failing to kill him. They were reconciled from time to time and were living together again.

In some kind of a drunken brawl, the woman was shot. Harris was tried before Judge Charbonnet of the Criminal District Court of Orleans Parish, and sentenced to be hanged. He appealed to the Board of Pardons for a commutation of sentence. The Board of Pardons by unanimous vote, in an opinion rendered by the trial judge, declared that the judge had made a mistake in failing to notice the facts that the discharge of the gun was accidental. The judge, the Attorney General, and the Lieutenant Governor, said there should be a commutation of sentence. The judge who tried the case especially asked it by writing the plea.[50]

I approved the finding of the Board of Pardons in that case for commutation to life imprisonment.

---

[50] Records of Pardon Board of 1928, contain decision of Judge Charbonnet, concurred in by the Attorney General and Lieutenant Governor, unanimously recommending clemency for Pleasant Harris on the grounds of Judge's error in charge to the Jury.

No attack or criticism was made either of the Board of Pardons or of me until the impeachment when I alone received the brunt of the attack. The Attorney General and the Lieutenant Governor who were trying to impeach me were not mentioned.

# CHAPTER XII

## THE IMPEACHMENT PROCEEDINGS

I T was not possible that we should be able to hold a majority of either house in favor of imposing a tax on oil refined by the Standard Oil Company or on any of its associates in that Special Session of the Legislature of 1929. Starting with what appeared to be pledges of more than two-thirds of both Houses in favor of the legislation, our strength withered to the point where we could not command a majority in either House.

Even the floor leader of the lower House had deserted us, declaring, however, that except for the tax on refining oil, he would support the administration. We sought a way out. The opposition was gathering strength to begin impeachment proceedings.

The Times-Picayune, in its issue of March 24, 1929, pointed that way. It published a front page editorial, saying in part:

### ADJOURN AND GO HOME

The best service Louisiana's Legislature can render this people and State under present conditions, is by way of immediate adjournment without date. When the first of the current special sessions was opened last Monday this newspaper had hoped the opportunity might be used for passage of some constructive laws that would justify the call. It speedily became apparent that such work would be difficult. . . . Add to this frenzied factional turmoil, the political "whoopee" that had bred an atmosphere of excitement and sensation in which there can be neither clear nor straight thinking and you have at Baton Rouge a condition of chaos which can only be cured by immediate adjournment.

. . . . . . .

Gentlemen of the General Assembly, when your houses resume, offer and carry the motion for final adjournment. That is the best service you can render Louisiana and her people in this troubled and delirious time.

So, when the Legislature assembled on Monday, March 25, a resolution to adjourn was offered. The member offering the resolution shouted in a vain effort to make his voice heard above the roar that rose and welled around him on every side. No one was seated; rather, the assemblage was like unto a few hundred highly intelligent animals temporarily bereft of reason and milling wildly about.

Blood and fire shone from every pair of eyes and the most trivial untoward incident might have caused them to run amuck. Finally the mob, augmented by outsiders, entered upon one of those brief phases of calmness so common to mass hysteria. Then, in this lull, began shouts, "No vote! No vote!" No one could seat the members, but the Speaker ordered a vote.

The voting machine, operated by and under the control of a Clerk of the House of Representatives (who was affiliated with the opposition) in some manner failed to function properly after the roll call had been taken. This was without the knowledge of the

Clerk who directed it. The Speaker had no access to the machine whatsoever except to cast his own vote. The machine showed practically all of the members of the House voting for the adjournment.

We had expected only about sixty-five votes out of the hundred, but the machine showed more of them voting for the resolution to adjourn. The Speaker rose. He looked calmly into the faces of the opposition and found only pent up hatred and emotions aflame. After a pause he descended to be immediately surrounded by friends endeavoring to give counsel and enemies shouting epithets in their denunciations.

In the midst of this uproar, which no pen can adequately describe, and while all interest was centered on the Speaker, another member quietly slid around the milling horde and took the Speaker's seat. Seizing the gavel he began pounding for order. After some minutes he caught their attention.

"The house will come to order!" he shouted.

And though the members did not "come to order" somehow the proceedings continued. Eventually the matter was ended by the Senate rejecting a motion to concur by reason of the Clerk's certificate declaring the house not to have voted to adjourn.

The opposition forces and newspapers of the State, saying nothing whatever about their own clerk, a nephew of Senator Ransdell, who operated the machine, and who tabulated and handed the vote to the Speaker, undertook to have it appear that the Speaker had in some way arranged the device so as to have an adjournment shown which was not voted.

It was here that I felt the hand of Fate in more

ways than one. To begin with, my principal friend in politics, Colonel Swords R. Lee, of Alexandria, had died. He was my most powerful supporter in all my campaigns.

In one of my serious battles, when many of my friends had declared I had made a mistake, it was Colonel Swords Lee who shouted to them:

"Damn it, this man don't need friends when he's right; he needs them when he's wrong. Shut your mouths!"

He was possessed of considerable wealth, and spent most of his time fighting the Huey Long battles. He contributed large sums of money to help me. He had been a powerful factor in all the campaigns of the State for forty years.

Only such help as I had previously had from him could have quelled the tide and ended the desertions that I was suffering.

The forces of impeachment had gathered.

The opposition, followed by the newspapers, the next morning wildly clamored for the removal of Fournet as Speaker of the House, accusing him of having manipulated the machine to misrepresent the vote. The opposition's strength was such that we instantly saw he was almost certain to be removed.

We played for time to cool the situation.

My first move was to take three members of the House loyal to me, to have them to suggest to three different members of the opposition that they should be made Speaker to succeed Fournet. Three candidates of the opposition developed immediately.

I knew it would take some time for them to smooth

out that difficulty; then we set to work. Fournet made a speech from the chair showing how impossible it was that he could have understood the situation better than he did. This calmed some of the opposition, but not enough of it.

The plans went forward from day to day to remove the Speaker. We continued to develop candidates in quantities for the opposition. Never were they able to get together. Finally we had a majority against the removal. The motion to remove the Speaker was not made at that session.

On Tuesday night I was called over telephone by members of my political organization in New Orleans.

"We have just been talking to the Times-Picayune," they said.

"I hope you have some good news from them," I said.

"It is very good, they are going to come out denouncing all this impeachment fiasco. They are going to stand by you to the limit now."

"When are they coming out?" I asked.

"Maybe in tomorrow morning's paper, but not later than the next day at the worst," they answered.

"Well, the sooner the better, I sure am in need of a breath of life."

I slept well that night. I was much eased by the report from New Orleans. I needed the rest very badly. On the next morning when I passed through the hotel lobby I was not at all surprised to notice an editorial on the front page of the Times-Picayune.

"They rushed the matter up," I thought to myself. "That will be a life saver to me."

I took a copy of the paper, folded it and walked toward the Capitol. As I was about to cross the street from the sidewalk opposite the Capitol, I glanced at the paper. I could not believe my eyes. To my amazement, I read:

### THE PEOPLE VS. GOVERNOR LONG

This newspaper will support any properly organized movement to compel Governor Long to vacate his office as chief executive of the State of Louisiana. The reason for this is that he is temperamentally and otherwise unfit to hold the office.

I read no further. I had seen so many changes occur, so mysteriously in favor of the big oil companies, that I was prepared for anything. As in the other newspapers, the big advertisements of the "Oil Trust" began in the Times-Picayune. Sometimes these advertisements from one company were for as much as $500.00 per day. This had not occurred before this newspaper's change of attitude.

Only those who could resist the tom-toms of the mighty or the lure of their "courtesies" came to me. My mail on the subject was scant. Few callers knocked on my doors. At last I had the peace of quiet and solitude for which I had so often longed.

I barricaded myself in my rooms in the Heidelberg Hotel overlooking the Mississippi River. The water was rising. It looked as if another flood might come. Maybe — surely — I would hear from some of the mighty ones who remembered what I had done for them. I pondered, I wondered and reflected. Perhaps the writer was right who said:

"When misfortunes come, they come not in single files, but in battalions."

Where was Senator Ransdell, to whose relief I had gone in 1928? Where was Senator Broussard, whose own organization conceded his defeat until I stemmed the tide? L. E. Thomas, who had opposed Ransdell and J. Y. Sanders, who had opposed Broussard, were on the ground helping to direct my impeachment. I had gone to the aid of Ransdell and Broussard in their hours of distress against these men. There must be some mistake! I waited for a time and called for one of them. He could not be reached. I understood,—

"That's gratitude!"

Later I learned it was more than that.

## *The Mass Meeting*

The opposition called a mass meeting in the Capital City to start the fireworks for my impeachment. It was held March 26, 1929. Headlines of the Times-Picayune, on its front page of March 27, 1929, give a synopsis of that story, to-wit:

6000 AT MEETING CALL FOR INQUIRY INTO LONG'S ACTS

PROTEST GATHERING AGAINST TAX TURNS TO
SCAN MISDEEDS

The resolution of that meeting, like that of the tailors of Tooley Street, began,

"We the people of the State of Louisiana, in mass meeting assembled, etc."

The first and most prominently displayed cause for urging my impeachment by this mass meeting was stated:

> 1. That for the purpose of satisfying a personal grudge and getting personal revenge for a real or imaginary personal grievance against the oil industry of Louisiana, and in pursuance of his boast often shamelessly publicly announced, he has proposed and used the power of his great office to have enacted a so-called occupational tax on oil refineries and other manufacturing industries of the State, etc.

In other words, I had dared to propose to tax the Standard Oil Company!

Further along in the resolution were pronouncements of such statements as:

> 13. That he has attempted to intimidate and browbeat capital honestly and worthily invested, etc.

That was an answer to my program to shift taxes from the small man to the flourishing corporate interests operating in the State, so that the wealth gathered from the top might be used to build up the citizenship from the bottom.

When the resolution had reached the "Be it resolved" part, among other things the following was contained:

> Be it further resolved, That we condemn as being vicious, dangerous and utterly without merit, any and all systems of taxation, whether they be

called an occupational, a license or a manufacture
tax, which directly or indirectly seek to impose
tax burdens upon industries within the State of
Louisiana.

From the above it appeared that the opposition element was about ready to tax nobody but the one-
horse farmer and small business man in the State.

The Baton Rouge mass meeting, presided over by
our political enemies, was furnished music by a very
fine brass band of sixty pieces of the Standard Oil
Company, known as the "Stanacola Musicians,"
without cost to the meeting. Quite appropriate!

While this band had always theretofore paraded
in splendid Standard Oil uniforms tailored to fit each
of its members, on the night of this particular mass
meeting, they were supplied with new and well-fitted
blue serge suits. Only two mistakes were made in the
disguise. No masks were on the faces of the musicians
and someone forgot to rub off the sign on the drum
—"Stanacola Band."

Simultaneous with the meeting, resolutions were
proposed in the House of Representatives to impeach
me as Governor of the State. I had the distinct privilege personally to listen to some of the speakers from
a door of the balcony where I was not seen by many
persons. I heard one say:

"Our best people up in Caddo Parish have been
outraged. He held the gun on them and made them
put free school books in the schools there, because he
would not let us have the government's airport unless
we agreed to do it."

I saw others beat their breasts, lift their eyes heavenward, as in holy enchantment, over the dire distress that was about to afflict the suffering big interests of the State. The taxes levied upon them by my administration were described as blood drawn from a sickening indigent in its last throes of life.

Some speakers declared me too weak and unlearned to give the courage and talent necessary to the Executive Department of the State, while others pictured me as a dictator, with scheming motives and designs. Charges in the legislature were not entirely similar to those urged by the mass meeting. On the contrary, the following were the principal ones.

1. That I had carried a pistol at times, particularly during the Dreher-LeBoeuf hanging; this, notwithstanding the fact that the laws and Constitution of the State of Louisiana not only make the Governor the chief peace officer of the State but make him the head of the National Guard.

2. That I had illegally paroled a convict by the name of Elmer Dunnington; this, in the face of the fact that the Attorney General, Percy Saint, and the Lieutenant Governor, Paul N. Cyr, my political enemies, had signed and recommended in writing the granting of the parole and it had passed through my office almost as a matter of form.

3. That as Governor, I had bought some law books, to-wit: Reports of the United States Supreme Court; statutes of the United States and Reports of the Supreme Court of the State of Louisiana and Revised Statutes of the State of Louisiana. It appeared to be the view that the Governor need not consult the

statutes of the United States, nor the decisions of any courts.

4. That I had torn down the old mansion; this, notwithstanding the fact that the Board of Liquidation, by unanimous vote, and the Legislature of the State, by an overwhelming majority vote, had authorized the building of a new mansion on the old mansion site. The Attorney General had taken the position that authority to build a new mansion on the ground whereon sat the old mansion did not authorize tearing down the old building.

5. That in using the militia to raid gambling houses and to seize their funds and to otherwise maintain law and order, I had acted without authority.

6. That when the Legislature allowed me $6,000.00 to entertain the Governors of the States, either all the money was not spent for entertainment or else that part of the same might have been spent for liquor; this, notwithstanding the fact that I held a receipt for the expenditures made in the full amount from the member of the entertainment committee placed in charge of the matter, and that certain additional costs had been paid by friends and people anxious to have the best of entertainment.

7. That one Battling Bozeman had been asked by me to kill a member of the Legislature; on this charge the testimony of the said Bozeman was accepted without allowing any testimony to be introduced to the contrary. Yet the opposition did not allow that charge to be voted upon in its own controlled House of Representatives because of its ridiculousness.

8. That a publisher of a newspaper had a brother

who was in the hospital for the mentally sick (which brother was subsequently cured), and that I had told the newspaper publisher that I was going to tell the public about it; this, notwithstanding the fact that all persons in public hospitals of the State are enrolled on several records subject to the public's general inspection.

9. That during the Mardi Gras season in New Orleans, I had attended a Little Theatre where some actresses hired for the show danced scantily clad, and that some of the persons had taken a drink of liquor during the performance.

10. That I had fired some people and appointed others in their places, among whom was a telephone operator who failed to secure a telephone connection soon enough to satisfy my extreme haste.

11. That a cousin of mine had been hired and paid money to act as a chauffeur.

12. That I had walked into a committee of the Legislature and asked it to adjourn, and that upon the chairman refusing to do so, I persuaded the members to adjourn and leave any way.

13. That I had undertaken to impose my views upon the Legislature, the condition being that the Legislature could operate better without the Governor.

14. That I had recommended that the Highway Commission pay for some culverts which had been built, which some thought to be defective; this, notwithstanding the fact that the culverts had been paid for before I became Governor of the State and the Highway Commission under me had held up some

other money belonging to the contractors until they made some deduction on the same. The culverts are in use to this date.

15. That members of the Legislature who helped put through programs of the administration, were favored by patronage, but that those who voted the other way were not favored so well.

16. That when visitors from the City of Shreveport (where they refused to hand out the free school books), called upon me that I used some "cuss words" in expressing the way I felt over their actions.

The foregoing include a great many things upon which even the House of Representatives d'd not vote impeachment. It likewise includes everything upon which they did vote to impeach me.

Be that as it may, the law of impeachment is such that if the legislative body impeaches a man for walking the streets and the Senate will vote guilty on the charge, it is an impeachment nonetheless.

The Memphis Commercial Appeal of April 27, 1928, came to our aid. It said, in part:—

### A Charge Not Yet Made

The Lower House is still considering evidence, and it may be that some legislator will discover that Governor Long has been guilty of the heinous offense of having at one time played the saxophone.

This was an outside paper, with not much circulation in Louisiana. Later it turned against me. Such happened to some few other outside papers with some scant circulation throughout Louisiana. Let one favorable word of me come in their column and soon either their silence was ominous or their course reversed.

The truth was not to be had from the daily newspapers. They made all manner of displays, distorting every kind of fact. If we gave them a reply to a charge it was generally ignored altogether, or else distorted, deleted or hidden away so as to be worse than no publicity at all.

On one occasion the Superintendent of Education gave a statement showing the requirements of public schools for revenue which was not even printed. On another occasion the greatest publicity was given to a charge made by Lieutenant Governor Cyr that I had performed a swindle worse than that of Tea Pot Dome in the execution of an oil lease.[51] Upon our preparing a statement to show that the oil lease in question had been made by Governor Parker, and that no act had been taken by me, except to permit the holder to enter into a drilling contract, our reply was practically buried by most of the newspapers.

We saw immediate necessity to institute a campaign to undo the malice of the mass meeting of our opposition held in Baton Rouge and the constant newspaper publicity.

My friend Robert Maestri came to my room at Baton Rouge.

"Do you need some money?" he asked.

---

[51] See front page of Times-Picayune of March 2, 1929, streamlines reporting: "State swindled says Cyr in fiery attack on Long."

"All the silver in India and all the tea in China,"
I replied.

"How fast do you need it?" he inquired.

"Just as fast as a printing office can turn out circulars and the government can sell stamps."

"I will take care of that," he said.

## SINEWS OF WAR AND THE CIRCULAR CAMPAIGN

We had been without the money necessary for such
a constant and wide distribution of circulars as was
then required. The printing alone would cost at least
$3,000.00 for an issue of 1,000,000 copies. The cost
of distribution by mail and from hand to hand was
even more serious. It was a proposition of involving
a cost of from $20,000.00 to $40,000.00. Where was
the money? Some had already begun to come. People
in no manner connected with the State administration
came into the office, contributing from one dollar up
to one hundred dollars. This amounted to probably
as much as $6,000.00 or $7,000.00. But a more substantial sum had to be found.

My more conservative friends and advisors took the
position that our defense must be judicial, strictly
made before the Senate, and that we should
not undertake to counter-attack the propaganda of
our enemies but rely upon the presentation of the cold
facts made before the Senate. This was particularly
the lawyer-type view.

"You are not being tried before the people," said
one of our leading counsel, "but before the Senate.

It will injure your case to do anything else. However much you may influence the people does not mean votes in the Senate."

"But I feel," I replied, "that we have got to do something to acquaint the people with the facts. They'll never be given the truth that will come before this Senate."

At about this point O. K. Allen entered my bedroom and listened to the conversation.

"Hell!" he broke in. "You've got to fight fire with fire in this thing. I know what some of those senators will do. They'll do anything to you they dare do. Start out over the country. Get those circulars going. You'll sit here and be ruined. Get up a mass meeting! Get it up quick!"

In that instance, as I have many times of my life, I took the advice of O. K. Allen. All the others were persuaded to take that course.

Immediately we set forth to call a mass meeting in the hostile center of Baton Rouge, calling upon people from all parts of the State to attend our first gathering to formulate plans to resist the impeachment.

The city was swamped. Even the streets could hardly hold the crowds. People gathered in and about the Capitol and around in various public places. Hurriedly as the meeting was called, it was a panic, and very few of the laborers or farmers had taken time to change from their working clothes to come to the capital.

They were a determined-looking set of people. There was some rumor that public authorities of the city might undertake to prevent the meeting from being held in one of the public squares, but lucky for us all, no interference was put in the way of the meeting.

No quarters could be had large enough to accommodate the crowd undertaking to hear the speeches. Through loudspeakers' apparatuses we addressed the crowd gathered for considerable distances. John H. Overton was our principal speaker. In the course of his address he said:

"I've supported every Governor that has been elected in Louisiana for twenty-five years, all on promises that they have made to the people. Not one of them has been able or, if able, willing to carry out what was expected of him. The present Governor is throwing out of office the clique that all other governors promised to throw out.

"He is backed to the wall in his efforts to redeem his campaign pledges.

"As I see him there now, with his rapier flashing, fencing off the enemies to the left, to the front and to the right, when this smoke of battle shall have cleared, as in the beginning, I will be standing or lying by the side of Huey P. Long."

That night I spoke for more than two hours, giving the complete details of every public quarrel which I had had, recounting the laws which I had passed, and the necessity for revenues for the schools and other eleemosynary institutions of the State. I said:

"It may be that other governors before me would have desired to carry out their pledges, but saw what I now see; that the man who dares to undertake the destruction of these entrenched forces and the taxation of the powerful interests of this State, faces an impeachment. They probably were wiser than I have been."

It was nearing midnight when I closed my speech:

*Out of the night that covers me,*
  *Black as the Pit from pole to pole,*
*I thank whatever gods may be*
  *𝔉or my unconquerable soul.*

*In the fell clutch of circumstance*
  *I have not winced nor cried aloud:*
*Under the bludgeonings of chance*
  *My head is bloody, but unbowed.*

*Beyond this place of wrath and tears*
  *Looms but the horror of the shade;*
*And yet the menace of the years*
  *Finds, and shall find, me unafraid.*

*It matters not how strait the gate,*
  *How charged with punishment the scroll,*
*I am the master of my fate:*
  *I am the captain of my soul.*

After the meeting it appeared that, where the Huey Long voters of the past had been enthusiastic supporters, they scattered to the four corners of the State as zealots.

In the distribution of circulars, I needed to cause myself no worry. I had fought the organized politicians of the State in battle after battle when they were backed by all the newspapers. Through the years a system had been perfected for the mailing, and thereafter a hand to hand distribution, of circulars which almost took care of itself.

In the impeachment, however, my Secretary was able to call on volunteers ready to speed the circulars in large bundles to central distributing points. It was all so perfectly coordinated that if necessary, a document prepared by me in the evening could be printed and placed on the porch of practically every home in the State of Louisiana during the morning of the following day.

Thus were the farmers at the forks of the creek, the merchants at the cross roads, the laborers on the railroads and in the factories brought into perfect coordination.

The newspapers have ever since been rendered powerless in politics in Louisiana.

With no reward except that of serving the cause of public good, these people then and ever since have labored zealously through the day and oft times through the night, to protect benefits accomplished for them by my administration. They have spread the truth to the people.

This organization was later pronounced by our enemies as a marvel.

At least we had the newspapers beaten to death so long as the money held out. Maestri, the greatest of all friends in foul weather, stayed at hand to see that this didn't happen.

We began to distribute circulars throughout the State. The first one of them was signed by me. Including the headlines, it read in part:

### THE SAME FIGHT AGAIN!

## THE STANDARD OIL COMPANY VS. HUEY P. LONG

*Has It Become a Crime for a Governor to Fight
for the School Children and the Cause of
Suffering and Destitute Humanity?*

### Newspapers of Standard Oil Company Battle to Keep This Nefarious Corporation (Thrown Out of Texas), from Paying Any Reasonable Tax at All

People of Louisiana:

I had rather go down to a thousand impeachments than to admit that I am the Governor of the State that does not dare to call the Standard Oil Company to account so that we can educate our children and care for destitute, sick and afflicted. If this State is still to be ruled by the power of the money of this corporation, I am too weak for its governor.

This is the third time in my yet young life in which this nefarious combination has been able to drag me before the bar to fight for my own liberty and political preservation, all just because I fought down the line until they were compelled to submit to right. . . .

"Hell is not hot enough for the man who tackles us" is the warning this nefarious corporation gives to public officials.

Ever since I took my first public office in 1918, have I stood every form and manner of attack, every low down accusation, every kind of persecution, but for it all, I am having my own reward; I'm standing for the vituperation, for the

slander, and now I want to stand for the insult
that has been heaped upon others who honorably
sought to help me in a fight for the children and
the afflicted of this State; let it all be blamed upon
me. I am alone responsible.

They've fought me harder this time than ever
before. Where they poured out hundreds in other
fights, they have poured out ten thousand in this
one. They have covered their newspapers, front,
inside and out with every imaginable lie and villi-
fication; they have stormed the State House to
where the weak-hearted feared even for the life
and safety of my supporters and myself. By a
process known only to them they have been able
to either "take over, to beat over or to buy over"
some in whom I had reposed respect and confidence
and for whom I yet indulge a charity.

. . . . . . . .

. . . I asked that on a gallon of lubricating oil
manufactured in Louisiana and selling for $1.40,
that the State be paid $\frac{1}{7}$ of 1 cent (out of the
$1.40), and that the same tax be paid on the gaso-
line, benzine, kerosene, etc. The bill which I drew
distributed the money thus raised to the school
children and to the various hospitals and colleges
of the State.

. . . . . . . .

Why, today we make such things as cotton seed
oil mills pay this tax to refine our own cotton seed
oil; but the Standard Oil Company is to be allowed to tear the State wide open and to remove
the Governor from office who dares to mention that
anything can be done with them.

The impeachment proceeding was highly illegal and improper on its face. An extra session of the Legislature in Louisiana has to have a definite date for its expiration fixed by the Governor calling such session. I had fixed that date of expiration on the 6th day of April, 1929. The session had no life or existence after that time, but none the less (with the exception of one charge thrown out of the Senate on first argument), all charges of impeachment were voted by the so-called House of Representatives after the date for the expiration of the extra session.

In no State had it ever been held that there could be a session of the Legislature for impeachment or anything else unless assembled in the form prescribed by law. Even the impeachment expert whom my enemies paid and brought from Oklahoma, where they had impeached three governors, had given a public statement to that effect.

There was a Louisiana law prescribing the procedure for impeachments.[52] Such an act had been aimed at preventing anything except impeachments in accordance with well-prescribed rules followed in the courts. But the rump House of Representatives, unable to follow such procedure, would not allow even public records presented which would have made the charges farcical.

They ignored the act which prescribed the procedure as if it had never been written. The ever-ready-to-rule Attorney General, Percy Saint, was on hand. He "ruled" laws off the books or back on the books

---

[52] Revised Statutes of Louisiana, Section 1738 to 1745, inclusive.

as fast as the occasion required. The combination of elements and their interests required that they should not be affected by such a thing as law or propriety in their undertaking.

But the opposition to bolster their forces began to make it known that votes, not crimes committed or law thereon, was all that it took to secure a man's impeachment and removal from office. They pointed out that originally less than one-fifth the members of the legislature had wanted me for Governor any-way.

They were like unto a man who studied law a few days in the course of his work of running a livery stable for a lifetime, who later took it upon himself to run against a distinguished jurist who had served on the bench at Opelousas for many years. When the two met on the platform the old jurist said:

"My friends, my opponent never had a lawsuit in his life. He hasn't seen the inside of a law book in thirty years and very little then."

Whereupon, the opposing candidate said:

"It's not the law what will make this judge,—it's the votes."

He was elected.

So it was with the impeachers who in order to bolster their forces, boldly began to assert in advance of any trial in the Senate, that they had about lined up the votes of enough Senators to remove me from office.

Colonel Ewing's paper, the Shreveport Times, may be taken as a fair sample for proof of that matter. In the issue of that paper on April 16, 1929, it said:

With one Senator absent, the anti-administrationists were Monday night within three Senators of a sufficient number to impeach. The absentee is Senator Sidney Cain, of New Orleans, and an adherent of Colonel John P. Sullivan. At least four of the fifteen Senators who voted for the Governor are expected to cast their votes with a majority when the question of impeachment is actually before the Senate. They are Boone of Claiborne; Oser of Orleans; Fisher of Jefferson, and Larcade of St. Landry.

So much for the high-minded "honesty of purpose" guiding the press of the State, displaying the votes already committed to impeach before a witness was heard!

By that time Colonel Ewing was in the lead of all those directing the impeachment.

I opened up a speaking campaign, while the impeachment proceedings were being carried on in the House of Representatives and during the time before trial was to start in the Senate. The crowds which came to hear me were immense.

I had made any number of political campaigns in my lifetime. Like other candidates and public men, I know what it is to be presented with flowers and bouquets and words of encouragement from strangers and friends. But there was a new kind of reception in the meetings which I held in the impeachment days.

Here and there a straggling child would bring me flowers which no hot house or florist had ever seen. I was made to realize that we were at grips with the problem of the common people.

No such thing as a meeting inside a building for such throngs was remotely possible. I was making seven speeches per day.

"God give me the voice and weather for open meetings, and the people will know my side," was my wish.

Other circulars went to the people. One contained the following:

### THE STANDARD OIL REGULARS

THE PAID-OFF NEWSPAPERS; PAID HENCHMEN OF THE OIL TRUST; WATSON-WILLIAMS BRIDGE SCHEMERS; J. Y. SANDERS; JOHN P. SULLIVAN; THE OLD NEW ORLEANS RING—THE WHOLE GANG THAT IS OUT TO SCUTTLE THE STATE

*Standard Oil Regulars vs. The People's Government. How the Impeachment Charges Began*

I called a session of the Legislature for the principal purpose of collecting a license of 5 cents per barrel off the oil refined by the Standard Oil Company and its allies in the State of Louisiana; the same kind of license that is paid by all other businesses and professions in the State, including cotton seed oil mills. The politicians and the newspapers and the lobbyists of the Standard Oil Company openly threatened that unless this effort of mine to tax the Standard Oil Company should be abandoned that I would be impeached as Governor. Later a mass meeting was called in Baton Rouge, the Standard Oil domicile, where music was furnished by the Standard Oil Company's brass band, dressed in plain clothes, and resolutions were adopted against taxing this concern and my im-

peachment was urged. The Standard Oil Company went out to take control.

.    .    .    .    .    .    .

And, back of that, the old gang is trying to get
back in power to gobble up the funds belonging
to the people. They want to load the Watson-Williams bridge on the State for $5,500,000.00, and
they are all set to do it. My administration will
complete free bridges right beside the Watson-
Williams bridge by Thanksgiving Day at a cost
of only $1,500,000.00. So they hurry to slaughter
me before it is too late and before I can build the
free bridges, because it will be hard to put over
this scheme once the free bridges are built and in
use. The newspapers are in on this deal. Something has happened to them, too. Why have these
newspapers stopped their opposition to this
scheme to have the State take over the Watson-
Williams bridge? Let Echo answer!

.    .    .    .    .    .    .

The gang cannot get back in power by an election of the people; they must get back some other
way. So they now try to get twenty-six men in
the Senate to remove me and do what they know
hundreds of thousands of people in the State will
not do. That's their game. The Lieutenant Governor, who rode in to his office on the Long ticket,
is now trying to get into the Governor's office by
this impeachment move. He could never be elected
to the office. I make the prediction that he can
never again be elected to any kind of office anywhere in this State, at any time after this is over,
or now.

Another side to the impeachment was beginning to develop. After it was publicly known for months that the Standard Oil Combination of interests was the principal moving force for my impeachment, that concern saw fit to publish full page newspaper advertisements in defense of itself, purporting to say that it was not to blame for my trouble, but that I had brought it on myself.

But the leadership of Colonel Ewing undertook no such distinction. On April 30, 1929, his New Orleans States editorial said:

> If he had not called the Special Session last month, ostensibly to meet a decision of the United States Supreme Court, but in reality to punish the Standard Oil Company, against which he has a private grievance dating long before he became governor, he would not today be facing trial for high crimes and misdemeanors before the bar of the Senate.

The quest for votes went on. It was apparent that quick action was necessary to hold my friends together.

There were thirty-nine members of the Senate; fourteen of them could prevent impeachment. It took twenty-six votes in the Senate to find me guilty on the charges. I waited until the week-end. Nearly every member of the Senate had gone to his home. Baton Rouge was quiet and deserted.

The opposition was busy in New Orleans making up a slate of appointments for the "New Governor" when I was impeached. They had already begun to wrangle over the spoils. To hold some of their men in line they had promised the same job to more than one.

The hour had arrived when I had built my power to strike to the maximum.

I had prepared a document, generally referred to as a "round robin," containing, among other things, the following:

> Therefore, we, the members of the Louisiana State Senate, do respectfully announce and petition:
>
> 1. That by reason of the legal irregularities and the circumstances bearing upon the procedure as above outlined, we cannot conscientiously and will not approve the impeachment proceedings and charges preferred against the Governor by the present extra session of the Legislature, or to be preferred under the purported and illegal continuance of said session.

I kept my plans to myself.

Suddenly I arranged for an automobile to be at the premises of each of fifteen Senators whom I telephoned and asked to come immediately to Baton Rouge. All of them came. I asked them to sign the "round robin."

Some of them signed without quibble. With some of them I argued and discussed the law until I had secured the signatures of thirteen Senators. I needed but one more to have more than one-third of the membership of the Senate.

The fourteenth Senator reached my office a short

Eastern Outlet to New Orleans, Old Spanish Trail, before Long.

Same Eastern Outlet to New Orleans Built During Long Administration.

New Orleans—Ponchartrain Road, Built Before the Long
Administration, 16 ft. wide—Asphalt Type—
Cost $80,000 per Mile.

New Orleans—Ponchartrain Road, Built by Long Administration, 41 ft. wide—Solid Concrete—Cost $40,000 per Mile.

time before midnight. He read the document which I had drawn. He was unequivocally against impeachment but was not convinced on the propriety of the round robin.

"When you sign this," I said, "I have one member more than the one-third."

"But," he rejoined, "you are asking me to say here that regardless of what may be shown, I will not vote to impeach?"

"You are a lawyer," I answered. "I am asking you as a lawyer to say that charges which, in law amount to nothing, cannot be the basis of impeaching me. None of these charges, even if true, can legally be the basis of an impeachment."

"I admit that, but is this not a funny way to do it?"

"Haven't you filed many a demurrer to an indictment?" I asked.

"Yes," he answered.

"Didn't your demurrer to the court say that even though your client was guilty of all that which he was charged with, still he should not be tried on a defective charge?"

"That is right," he answered.

"Now let me talk to you from a practical standpoint. I am exhausted; I have not a dime financially. This fight has cost me all I had; all I can rake, scrape and borrow. It is taking one thousand dollars a day to get the truth to the people. How long can we stand it?

"Is all that necessary?" he asked.

"It is necessary for you. If you were to vote to free me from this impeachment, it would be dangerous unless your people have been given the facts so that they noted the propriety of your vote," I answered.

But still my friend hesitated. We argued back and forth, hour after hour. Soon the sun would be throwing its light across the earth. He said,

"What would you think if I asked my law partner for his advice on the law in this case?"

"Fine," I answered.

Immediately we called over the telephone to his law partner in New Orleans. He agreed to leave immediately for Baton Rouge. We awaited his arrival. He came just at good daylight.

Again we went over the proposition. The law partner read the petition and left with the Senator whose signature I was then requesting. Within about one hour they returned.

"Governor," said the law partner, "this is the right thing to do."

The fourteenth senator's name was signed to the round robin.

Later in the day, a fifteenth member affixed his signature. I had one more than necessary. We tried to keep that document's existence a closed secret.

I had the assurance of a few other members of the Senate that they agreed on the law, but considered it best not to sign the resolution. Nevertheless I continued my speaking tours and the distribution of circulars throughout the State.

The people were becoming aroused to a white heat. In crowds of ten to fifteen thousand a vote would be taken, never more than one or two failing to hold their hand up in my favor.

But the impeachers and the newspapers pursued their efforts furiously. The Senators who had signed the "round robin" were being approached; offers to them were immense.

In glancing at a newspaper, while on a speaking tour, I noted a statement by one of the Senators who had signed the round robin. He stated that I had been quoted as saying that fifteen members of the Senate had signed a document declaring that they would not vote to impeach, and that he wanted it understood that he was not one of the signers.

I thought it best to say nothing of that denial since I had given no statement about the round robin. I did not see that particular Senator for several days.

But on passing through a certain town on my way to speak in Shreveport, I met another Senator who told me that he had been to one place when I had reason to believe he had been somewhere else.

I was in that Senator's home late at night, sitting on the side of his bed, when I began to question him.

"Now, weren't you in Shreveport today?" I asked.

"No. I was in Alexandria."

"Didn't you go to both places today, Shreveport and Alexandria?"

He looked at me without answering. After a pause he said:

"—— is sick in Shreveport. He's an old friend of mine. I have agreed to try to go up there tomorrow to see him."

The party he mentioned was a business associate of one of the millionaires whom I had sued in the Bernstein case. The Supreme Court had forced them to pay over considerable money, and had judicially declared them to have been engaged in a scheme to swindle my client.

Their hate for me was as great, if it did not exceed, that of any other men in the State at the time. I pressed my first question for answer:

"But didn't you go to Shreveport today?" I again asked.

"Well," he blurted without explanation, "—— had nothing to do with that. He is just an old friend I knew over in Texas. He has done me and my family many favors. He just wants to see me because he is sick."

"All right," I said, "if you are going to Shreveport tomorrow I will get you to speak with me there to-morrow night. We have a meeting."

He reluctantly promised he would speak at the meeting.

I undertook to dissuade the Senator from calling on the "sick friend," but without avail. On the follow-ing night I spoke in Shreveport. The senator did not appear. He could not be found. We closed the meet-ing without him. I later learned that he stood by a radio some fifty miles south of Shreveport and listened to my speech, in which I said:

"Certain gentlemen in this city have been calling senators to this town, to pay them off to vote for my impeachment. I may give the names, the dates and the places."

The next day the particular senator in question issued a statement rebuking my comment. He issued some further statements in the few days that followed.

In the meantime, however, his name was signed to the round robin that he would not vote for the impeachment.

On a certain night when I spoke in Monroe, Louisiana, I learned that this Senator was spending the night in Baton Rouge. I was determined to see him before the morning. Following my speech in Monroe, I went to the hotel, entered my room and turned out the light as if to retire. Later, I came down and departed through a side door unnoticed.

I drove in an automobile the entire night, crossing the Mississippi River into Baton Rouge at first sunrise, after travelling a distance of 250 miles.

My friend Maestri was on hand. He had seen the Senator and had boldly accused him of undertaking to "cash in" on my impeachment. I met Maestri.

"Where is the senator now?" I asked.

"He is in his bed. But I can tell you he hasn't slept any."

"Come with me, and he won't sleep any," I said.

We went to the Senator's room and knocked on the door. He invited us in.

"Well," he confessed, "here's the situation. I was to go to New Orleans today to be paid off by Big John. I've tried to keep you off of me. The more real I could make this the better. I have thought every day I could bring you the money to blow the impeachment out of the water. But they have hesitated. Now shall I try further?"

We decided to draw an affidavit that the Senator was on his way to New Orleans to be paid the bribe money, which he would return and publicly hand over for exposure.

Thereupon we called a stenographer and notary public, whom we all met in an office building, after which the Senator left for New Orleans to receive the bribe money.

The same night the Senator returned.

"The son of a gun was as white as a sheet. Some one tipped them off I saw you," he declared.

It became almost a known secret that the opposition, desperate as it was, realized that to make certain of my impeachment it needed the votes of three more senators. They had hit on the scheme of securing three senators at one stroke, fearing to undertake separate negotiations in view of disclosures we had already made. Other senators had given us the information of propositions made to them.

The air was surcharged with the information. Accordingly, three senators were selected by them as most likely to yield to the persuasion of purchase. One of the three was told to call the others into session. He immediately reported to me.

"They have asked me to call these two other senators," he said, "and offered $250,000.00 for the three votes. I told them where to go."

"We've been trying to land them on that," I said. "Go back and try to get $250,000.00; if you can't get that much, get them to give you $80,000.00 for one."

He left me. That night he returned.

"They have dodged me coming back," he said.

I had feared that result.

We remained quiet, awaiting an opportunity for developments. News reached me that another of the signers of the round robin had been offered a large sum of money. I undertook to secure his consent to accept it.

"Governor," he said to me, "the man they sent to offer me that money is closer to me than you have been or will ever be. I can't uncover this friend."

We were never able to get hold of the cash to make a real exposure.

On returning from one of my speaking engagements near daylight I sat at my desk in the governor's office. I dropped off to sleep and slept until after daybreak. I was awakened by the noise of handsaws cutting lumber and the ringing of hammers.

I immediately raced up the stairway to find out the cause for the unusual racket. I located it in the Senate Chamber. A number of carpenters were at work there. High seats and benches were being built. The whole inside of the Senate Chamber was being made over. It seemed like preparations for a pre-revolution French hanging.

"What's this going on?" I asked the foreman. "Looks like you're fixing up a scaffold or something. Who's this for?"

"Governor, they're fixing it for you, but I hope they don't get by with it."

"Who told you to do this? The building is under me. They have no right to come in here and do this."

"They gave the orders to us. Mr. Booth, the Secretary, is having it done."

I looked at the ceilings, and found them to be

freshly painted. The chandeliers had been gilded. I concluded to say nothing further.

Judge Philip H. Gilbert of Napoleonville had been the Acting Lieutenant Governor under the administration of Governor Simpson. Upon my becoming governor he was our candidate for President Pro Tempore of the Senate and was elected. In the case of a vacancy in the office of Lieutenant Governor, he would have taken that office, and in case of a further vacancy he would have become Governor.

Senator Gilbert was a splendid scholar and parliamentarian. He had been a candidate for Lieutenant Governor when Parker was elected Governor.

My friend in the legislature, who was voting with the opposition in the House of Representatives and sitting in their caucus, ran to me early one morning.

"Huey, they are going to pull a fast one. They have decided that they have got to have Philip Gilbert to impeach you. They are going to make Gilbert Governor to get him."

Men in whom I had placed as much, if not more, trust than I had ever reposed in Judge Philip Gilbert, had left me for far less chance of gain.

"Run back," I said, "Get me the very latest you can on what has happened on that line."

Within less than an hour he ran into the room.

"Gilbert's turned 'em down!" he shouted.

I waited for some information to come from Gilbert. He never vouchsafed any. I concluded to broach the matter.

"Philip," I asked him that night, "did anybody say anything to you about being Governor?"

"What's that got to do with it?" he asked, with a shrug of the shoulders—full blooded Acadian French that he was.

The intense hate of my enemies toward me has been a matter of frequent comment. It is more than offset, however, by the loyalty of friends.

### IMPEACHMENT TRIAL

Eventually the day for the trial of the impeachment charges came. My attorneys filed demurrers and answers denying all charges. By a vote of nineteen to twenty, we failed by a scant one vote to throw out all the charges excepting one; by a vote of twenty-one to eighteen we threw out the other one.

With the Senate recessing, the only charges remaining for trial were those which had been voted after the time for expiration of the session of the Legislature, those which we had failed to throw out by one vote.

We prepared during the night a condensed resolution along the lines of the round robin. The same fifteen Senators who had previously signed that paper signed the resolution.

Coupled with that resolution was a motion for the Court of Impeachment to adjourn sine die. This later document was also commonly called the "round robin."

On the morning of May 16, 1929, Senator Philip H. Gilbert, the President Pro Tempore of the Senate, arose and filed the document, viz.:

On motion of the undersigned Senators of the
State of Louisiana, and on suggesting to this Honorable Senate, sitting as a court of impeachment,
that:

1. This Senate organized itself under the law,
as a court of impeachment, on the 6th day of
April, 1929, by virtue of the filing with it, on said
date, by the House of Representatives of the State
of Louisiana, of a certain impeachment charge
preferred against Huey P. Long, Governor, which
charge is referred to as No. 1 and is commonly
known as the Manship charge;

2. The said Senate, sitting as a court of impeachment, did, on the 15th day of May, 1929,
sustain a demurrer to said charge and thereby
declare it to be null and void, and of no effect ab
initio;

3. Prior to sustaining said demurrer on the
said Manship charge, nineteen members of the
Senate, sitting as a court of impeachment, did, on
the 15th day of May, 1929, vote in favor of an
exception declaring that all charges of impeachment preferred against the said Huey P. Long,
Governor, after April 6, 1929, were unconstitutional, illegal, null and void;

4. The undersigned, constituting more than
one-third of the membership of this Senate, sitting as a court of impeachment, do now officially
announce that by reason of the unconstitutionality
and invalidity of all impeachment charges remaining against Huey P. Long, Governor, they will
not vote to convict thereon;

5. Further proceeding in this Senate, sitting as
a court of impeachment, therefore, becomes inef-

fectual, vain and will incur a useless cost and expense to the State of Louisiana and will only serve to prolong the turmoil that now exists and will continue to disrupt the ordinary affairs and businesses of our State;

Now, therefore, we move that the Senate, sitting as a court of impeachment, do now adjourn sine die.

PHILIP H. GILBERT
J. HUGO DORE
W. C. BOONE
BENJAMIN H. DUCROS
THOMAS C. WINGATE
F. E. DELAHOUSSAYE
FRED W. OSER
JULES G. FISHER
R. B. KNOTT
E. B. ROBINSON
HOMER BAROUSSE
T. A. McCONNELL
H. L. HUGHES
JAS. L. ANDERSON
HENRY D. LARCADE, JR.

Our opposition had already smelled a mouse. The leaders had begun to flee the capitol. They were the rats leaving another sinking ship. Quarters had been vacated during the night time. Even the Lieutenant Governor had arranged for an early departure.

Upon the "round robin" being filed, the Senate took a short recess, but upon reconvening thirty-nine out of the thirty-nine voted to adjourn sine die.

I sent a crew of carpenters into the Senate Chambers where they began to tear down what I had termed the scaffolding arrangement made for my trial.

The newspapers, ever vicious over my victory in the impeachment, never ceased to call attention to any favor I did one of those fifteen men.

"Theirs is the earth and the fullness thereof," the papers proclaimed.

It became a matter of considerable mirth among the fifteen senators and myself.

On one occasion one of these senators, a full blooded Frenchman with a great sense of humor, Hugo Dore, called to see me in my bedroom in New Orleans.

"Governor," he said, "we want to get a little road gravelled leading out east of Mamou."

"My gracious, Hugo!" I exclaimed. "Won't you ever get through asking for roads for that country? There isn't room to plow there now, we've got so much pavement and gravel in that country."

"Now, Governor," shot back the senator, "don't get too strong now; remember what we've done for you."

Several of our friends seated in the room laughed at his remark.

### THE CASE OF LEJEUNE

"Keep your seat, Hugo," I said. "You fifteen bullies are always reminding me of what you did for me. The time has come to tell you of something that happened over in your neck of the woods. Close to where you live is a creek called Bayou Niggerfoot."

"Yes, yes," chirped the senator. "I know the bayou."

"Well, now, Hugo," I continued, "when you were very young a traveling man used to make that territory out of New Orleans. He was the kind of a man that sold goods to the stores, bought their cotton, made up their accounts, advanced them money and collected at the end of the year. This drummer reached Opelousas on his route every Thursday.

"In the middle of December he left Opelousas and drove out to cross Niggerfoot Bayou. It was a cold day. There had been a great deal of rain.

"When he reached the bayou he found that it had overflowed. Icicles were hanging on the logs and limbs in the woods. So the drummer said to his driver, 'George, drive up about one mile from here and there is a bridge where you can cross. Then drive down on the other side and I will be at that house over yonder. I'll walk the foot-log across the bayou.' The driver departed.

"When he had gone, the drummer started to cross the bayou on the foot-log. It was partly covered with ice and when he reached the middle of the bayou he slipped and fell.

" 'Help! Help!' he yelled.

"The man in the house on the other side heard him. He ran to the bank, reached the drummer a rail and pulled him to the shore. Then he took the drummer to his home, pulled off his clothes, put him to bed while he dried them; and when they were dried, the drummer dressed and the man's wife sat him in front of a table prepared with good fried ham, biscuits and hot coffee. The drummer ate heartily. When he had finished, the driver having returned with the buggy, he made ready to continue his journey.

"The man of the house was named LeJeune. The drummer turned to him and said: 'Mr. LeJeune, you have saved my life. I would have drowned but for your help. Your kind wife and yourself have done more for me than I can ever do for you. I reach Opelousas every Thursday. I would like to meet you there on one of those days to show you my appreciation in a more material way.'

"The drummer took his leave. LeJeune had promised to see him in Opelousas.

"On the following Thursday the drummer reached Opelousas. LeJeune was standing in front of a saloon. The drummer greeted him. He hugged him. Then LeJeune spoke up:

" 'I am glad to see you, ma fren'. You is ze man what I pull from ze Bayou Niggerfoot. Ah, ma fren', bot for me you would not be alive today.'

"The drummer hastily said, 'I know that, Mr. LeJeune. Let's have a drink.'

" 'You could do dat,' said LeJeune.

"While the two stood at the bar sipping their drink, LeJeune began to speak again. 'Ah, ma fren', ze log was froze' over, you slip, you fall; I hear you holler.'

"The drummer broke in again: 'Mr. LeJeune, can't I do anything else for you?'

"LeJeune felt of his hat and looked at his shoes.

" 'Come with me,' said the drummer. 'Let me buy you a new hat and a pair of shoes.'

" 'You could do dat,' said LeJeune.

"So the two left the saloon for a store, where the

drummer bought LeJeune a good hat and a good pair of shoes, and bade him goodbye.

"On the next Thursday the drummer returned. LeJeune was standing in front of the saloon where the drummer had met him on the previous week. The drummer approached him again.

" 'Howdy, Mr. LeJeune. How you do today?'

"Ah, ma fren', I am all right. It makes me feel good to see you today. You remembah, ma fren', ze cold day when I pull you from ze Bayou Niggerfoot? Ze crawfish would have eat you long ago but for LeJeune.'

" 'Right you are, Mr. LeJeune,' said the drummer. 'Let's have a drink.'

" 'Ah, you could do dat,' said LeJeune.

"So the two entered the saloon, where they sipped a drink.

"Half way through, LeJeune stopped and began again. 'You recolleck, ma fren', ze Bayou was deep, you holler 'Help!' I——'

"The drummer broke in:

" 'I know, Mr. LeJeune,' he said. 'Isn't there something else I can do for you besides a hat and a pair of shoes I bought last Thursday?'

"LeJeune felt of his coat and brushed his trousers a bit.

" 'Come,' said the drummer, 'let me get you a suit of clothes.'

"So they left for the store again, where the drummer presented LeJeune with a new suit of clothes and again bade him the time of day.

"Thursday another week later, the drummer on his

usual round again came to Opelousas. LeJeune was standing in front of the same saloon. The drummer, seeing him from afar, crossed to the opposite side of the street, pretending that his attention was engaged on something immediately ahead as he passed on the other side by the saloon. But when he was a few steps beyond the corner, LeJeune shouted:

" 'Oh, ma fren'!'

"The drummer turned. LeJeune, patting himself on the breast, yelled:

" 'You recolleck LeJeune, whot pull' you from ze Bayou Niggerfoot?'

"Immediately the drummer crossed to the saloon.

" 'Yes, Mr. LeJeune; I shall always remember you,' he said.

" 'Ah, ma fren', I was 'fraid you forget LeJeune. You remembah, but for me you would not be alive today.'

" 'Come on,' said the drummer to LeJeune, 'let's have a drink.'

" 'Well, you could do dat,' LeJeune answered.

"The two stood at the bar and sipped a drink. When they had finished, the drummer said:

" 'Well, let's have another one.'

"LeJeune replied: 'Well, you could do dat. But for me, ma fren', ze crabs and crawfish would have pick your bones long ago.'

"When they had finished the second drink, the drummer turned to LeJeune. LeJeune met his glance.

" 'Ze bayou was deep, ze log was slick; you slip——'

"The drummer broke in:

" 'I know, Mr. LeJeune, I remember. Mr. Le-Jeune, have you got anything in which you could take something to the folks back home?'

"Le Jeune paused, shrugged his shoulders.

" 'I got ze wagon,' he said.

" 'Pull it around to Haas' store,' said the drummer, 'and let us get a few things to take to the folks back home.'

"LeJeune willingly complied. He backed up the wagon. They loaded in three barrels of flour, a barrel of meal, several slabs of side meat, hams, suits of clothes for the boys, dresses for his girls and his wife. They loaded in new harness for the horses, bolts of calico, gingham and silk; they put everything on the wagon it would hold. The drummer wrote out his check to the store for the full amount. Then he turned to LeJeune.

" 'Mr. LeJeune,' he said, 'would you like to have another drink before you go?'

" 'You could do dat,' replied LeJeune.

"So the two stepped next door to another saloon.

"Half way through the drink LeJeune turned to the drummer again.

" 'Ma fren',' he said, 'it was a cold day when I pull you from dat Bayou Niggerfoot. . . .'

" 'Yes,' interrupted the drummer. 'Mr. LeJeune, I want to mention that matter to you. You pulled me from Niggerfoot Bayou when I was about to drown. I give you credit for saving my life. I am under obligations to you deeper than I can ever discharge. But I want to make one more request of you, Mr. Le-

LeJeune backed up the wagon.

Jeune. If ever again you find me drowning in that damn Niggerfoot Bayou, damn it, let me drown!' "

I looked at Senator Doré:

"If ever again you fifteen round-robineers find me drowning, for Heaven's sake, let me drown!"

Senator Doré repeated that story until it became famous.

While I was tied hand and foot in the impeachment, my enemies made further moves to lessen my chances.

In the severance tax suits I had drawn the laws and the pleadings for the State and presented the case before the Federal Court in Shreveport. The Supreme Court had returned it for a final trial. The Attorney General, in the midst of the impeachment, announced he would try the case. And despite my protest, he persisted in "trying" it for the State.

I sent a lawyer and the Supervisor of Public Accounts, against whom the suit was technically filed, before the Court the morning when the case was called. They protested against the case being taken up for trial at a time when I could not be present.

The "Oil Trust's" attorneys insisted that the case should proceed with trial; so did the Attorney General. One of the Judges, sensing the situation, asked the Attorney General if his witnesses were present. He answered he had none. The judges would not allow the travesty. They postponed it until I could be present.

After the impeachment was over the postponed case came on for trial. In due course the three judges again handed down an opinion favorable to the State of Louisiana. The case was again appealed to the Supreme Court of the United States.

Shortly after the impeachment session had adjourned, a final decision of the Supreme Court of Louisiana was handed down by the same four to three votes upholding the validity of the free school book law. Judge Land's re-election had saved the day. This case was appealed to the United States Supreme Court.

In the meantime I hastened to the Third Congressional District to participate in a campaign that was going on for Congressman between a nominee of the Democratic Party and a candidate of the Republican Party. All newspapers and my political enemies, supposed to be Democratic, were either for the Republican nominee or else were rendering no help to our party nominee, because of his being an employee of my administration.

Well known National figures were touring the district advocating a Republican as best for a sugar tariff for that cane sugar district.

We had only a few days to overcome the Republican lead, but we sent the Democratic nominee to Congress by a substantial majority.

### The Never Relenting Impeachers

Impeachment would have been over anywhere except in Louisiana, and over in Louisiana with anybody except the kind of opposition which I had aroused. With any thread of hope, they would pursue their efforts.

They early took the position that the impeachment

charges, when started, remained in the Senate and were subject to trial by that body at any time.

The controlling political factor of the Times-Picayune newspaper was a railroad, telegraph and power company lawyer by the name of Esmond Phelps. He was also the head of the Board of Supervisors of Tulane University, on which sat others affiliated with such interests. The institution was largely supported by the Rockefeller Foundation.

A professor of that school led off the line of propaganda to continue my impeachment by delivering a speech at a professors' meeting as being on "an interesting legal question." The fact that the impeachment of President Andrew Johnson ended on the exact same motion "to adjourn sine die" mattered not. They made the law as they went, as they had been doing in Louisiana until 1928.

The professor's speech, declaring that charges were still pending against me, was widely published. There were reasons why these impeachers pursued their efforts:

We had advertised and secured bids for the actual building of the free bridges over Lake Pontchartrain, to parallel the toll bridge of the Sanders-Watson-Williams syndicate. Soon the toll bridge would become "a roost for the buzzards."

The severance tax suits against the oil companies would soon be decided, and, a favorable decision would force the big oil companies to pay the State millions of dollars.

We had an extra $20,000,000.00 realized from bonds to spend.

Our enemies feared our renewing the effort to impose a tax on the business of refining oil.

We were proceeding toward removal of all persons and boards proven to be unfriendly during the impeachment.

I had prepared recall petitions against a number of the members of the Legislature, who had undertaken to secure my impeachment against the wishes of their people.

### THE LAST INVESTIGATION

Cartoon on Constitutional League Investigations.

# CHAPTER XIII

## LEAGUE OF NOTIONS

FOLLOWING adjournment of the impeachment on May 16, 1929, I pursued the work of paving highways and building of farm gravel roads.

I delved closely into the affairs of education; I worked to improve the institutions of the State.

I gave a few days to the effort to recall some of the persons prominent in my impeachment.

All the opposition forces were called to meet in the City of New Orleans for the purpose of resurrecting efforts for my extermination. This meeting occurred Tuesday, June 11, 1929. I quote, beginning with the 8 column stream line, from Colonel Ewing's New Orleans States:

FORM LEAGUE TO SAVE STATE—PARKER HEADS LEAGUE TO SAVE STATE FROM LONG—LEADERS GATHER FROM ALL SECTIONS TO BATTLE POLITICAL LAWLESSNESS.

Organization of the Constitutional League of Louisiana, dedicated to the restoration of constitutional government in the State, was perfected at a statewide meeting of about 300 citizens at the St. Charles Hotel today, with former Governor John M. Parker, of New Orleans, as President, Senator Norris C. Williamson of East Carroll as Vice-President, George K. Perrault of St. Landry as Chairman of the Executive Committee, Paul A. Chasez of New Orleans as Secretary, and

Charles Farrell of New Orleans as Sergeant-at-Arms.

The meeting, which convened on short notice, was classed as the most representative gathering of citizens that has been held in Louisiana within a decade.

The purpose of the League, it was explained, in the propositions before the meeting, is to take any steps that may be necessary to enforce and to carry out the provisions of the constitution to prevent Governor Huey P. Long from treating the organic law of the State as a scrap of paper, and to stand by members of the legislature threatened with recall by the Governor.

"It takes money to fight any battle," President Parker said, after members of the Legislature who were threatened with recall were introduced. "We will begin now by calling on those who can do so to contribute . . ."

Contributions then came thick and fast. A considerable number of business men in the meeting announced subscriptions of one thousand dollars each. New Orleans pledged a minimum of $25,000, Caddo Parish $20,000, East Baton Rouge $20,000, and others in varying smaller amounts. When the subscriptions were closed, the total was estimated at around $100,000. This was done in less than fifteen minutes.

Before the Constitutional League could be formed, however, General Campbell B. Hodges, whose brother was so prominent in the formation of the Constitutional League had been told that he need not come to Louisiana to take charge of the State

Type of Bridge Near Shreveport, Louisiana on Dixie-Overland
Highway Before Long Days.

Same Bridge Site on Dixie-Overland Highway Built by Long
Administration.

Crossing at Waggoner Below New Orleans by Ferry Before
Long Days.

Same Crossing at Waggoner Built by Long Administration.

Pro-Long cartoon published in Louisiana Progress

University. Instead, a person of the highest collegiate standing was selected for that purpose. This added fury to the flames.

An editorial of the Times-Picayune commending this league, said:

### MEETING AN EMERGENCY

Shocked and aroused by the Governor's excesses and the demoralization that results from them, they have enlisted for the defense of Louisiana's general welfare, reputation and credit. . . . This newspaper long ago avowed its belief that Governor Long by his own acts had revealed his unfitness for the office he holds. . . . All State factions are represented in its membership.

The backbone of the organization, as usual, was the Standard Oil Company and the old New Orleans regular organization.

Necessity required that I locate in New Orleans to perfect an organization to give battle in that City. Amid clamor and the denunciation of the newspapers, I had the things in the Governor's office placed in a truck and moved to New Orleans. The newspapers labelled our administration the "Government on Wheels."

My friend and ally, O. K. Allen, then the Chairman of the Highway Commission, performed most functions required of me in Baton Rouge.

I took charge of the political situation in New Orleans as my major battle.

We knew that, at the session of the Legislature to convene in May, 1930, we faced the fight of our lives.

### REFUSING A RESIGNATION

District Judge H. C. Drew, prominent in the Constitutional League, had been elected to the Court of Appeal. His term of office as District Judge would have had less than one year to run if he had held it until his position on that Court began.

Judge Drew conceived the idea that he did not wish me to appoint the District Judge for the unexpired portion of his term, so he sent in his resignation on September 10, 1929, more than two and one-half months before his term of office would begin on the Court of Appeal. Where more than a year was to run on a term the law required an election. I declined to accept his resignation and thereupon, determined to create a vacancy, he walked off from the District Court. The Supreme Court, under the conflicting situation, designated a judge to serve in that District in the meantime.

I allowed enough time to expire so that the unexpired term of the office had less than one year to run, and then I issued a commission to Judge J. F. McInnis for the unexpired term of less than one year.

The Supreme Court withdrew the appointment of the other judge and Judge McInnis was seated in his position. Nine months later, the people re-elected Judge McInnis. It was the first time in the history of Louisiana that a Governor had ever declined to accept a resignation.

### STARTING A NEWSPAPER

It became apparent that we would have to issue some kind of newspaper, at least once a week. There was a specially noted cartoonist serving on the staff of one of the large newspapers of the city. I called him to my office one Sunday afternoon.

"Trist," I said (his full name was Trist Wood)—"how much money are you making?"

"I am making about forty-five dollars per week, only working half time."

"How long would it take you to decide to sign a contract for the next year at a hundred per week?"

"Right now!" he said.

I shoved the contract over for him to sign. I had already prepared it.

"Now," I said, "go get the best drawings that you can of the hi-moguls of these newspapers. I am going to start a newspaper."

I employed an editor and a staff of reporters and thereupon was begun the Louisiana Progress.

Our friends throughout the State voluntarily solicited subscriptions for the Progress. We begun to make life merry for our enemies with cartoons, statistics and comparisons.

The Times-Picayune newspaper, from the day it secured its large increase in oil company advertising, carried the fight against us most persistently. To my amazement I learned that a lawyer by the name of Arthur Hammond was listed on two State payrolls. In each position he was drawing $400.00 per month, or a total of $9,600.00 per year. He was the brother-in-law of the vested interest's lawyer, Esmond Phelps,

BEFORE LONG

The Kind of Recreation and Mind Relief Furnished Patients in the Central Hospital for the Insane; note the Barbarous Locked Chairs of the Dark Ages.

UNDER LONG ADMINISTRATION

Occupational Therapy for the Patients; Their Mardi Gras Ball, Showing Accomplishment in Patients' Operated Amusements, Beauty Parlors, etc.

BEFORE LONG
Tubercular Wards at Central Hospital for Mental Diseases.

UNDER LONG ADMINISTRATION
Modern Tubercular Wards at Central Hospital for Mental
Diseases.

The Lawsuits Can't Stop Him

Cartoon on Gov. Long's Victory for Free School Books.

who dictated the politics of the Times-Picayune newspaper which had originally been the official organ of the Louisiana Lottery.

Mr. Hammond was discharged from both boards and the following headlines, including an eight column streamer, appeared in the Louisiana Progress:

### *Times Pic. Dictator's Man Pried From Two Swill Tubs—*

Esmond Phelps' brother-in-law on two payrolls —Double salary collected while Times-Picayune held up hands aghast at dual office-holding—Governor Long, catching the spirit of the Times-Picayune to job propaganda, examines payrolls and finds the Mussolini of the Times-Picayune has his relative modestly taking State pay in New Orleans with both hands at the same time.

In the midst of this continued confusion and excitement, the Supreme Court of the United States handed down two opinions in my favor.

By unanimous votes they held the free school book law of the State of Louisiana valid and constitutional, and also upheld the validity of my new severance tax law. The State was supplied with considerable money. It eased things all around for my administration.

These were heavy blows to our opposition.

Within a few weeks another blow fell for our enemies. The free bridges across Lake Pontchartrain were completed and opened to the public.

This march of progress was more than contrary newspaper headlines could overcome.

My opposition was heavily supported by the management and employees of the Port of New Orleans.

I struck my first lick to take that Board from their hands. A Governor could not remove the members. But the term of one member was expiring. Another member of the board was friendly to me. Just one more member and I would have a majority of three out of the five to favor my administration.

I selected the one of that three whom I thought would probably be most ready to resign upon my request. He consented to resign. I appointed the fifth member. We held a special meeting of the board. By a vote of 3 to 2 such an organization was perfected as was friendly to the new and progressive policies of the State.

The newspapers yelled "bloody murder!" We had removed Marcel Garsaud as General Manager. Later I opposed this same man being confirmed by the United States Senate as a member of the Federal Power Commission.

All along matters were nip and tuck. In our efforts to pursue the recall elections, injunctions from the courts flew in every direction. The Secretary of State was affiliated with the Constitutional League. To aid my opponents he readily let judgment be rendered against himself, so that no ballots could be printed for and no promulgation made of recall elections. We had held two recall elections, one of which we had lost and one of which we had won.

Tied up in court, we agreed to a form of compromise between the Standard Oil Company and certain ones of the Constitutional League on the one hand and our group on the other, providing that recall elections would be suspended for certain concessions made to us.

# CHAPTER XIV

## THE GERMAN COMMANDER CALLS—THE GREEN PAJAMAS

WHILE in New Orleans carrying on the work of the Governor's office and undertaking to perfect a political organization, the Mardi Gras season arrived. I here reproduce an article which the Times-Picayune of Tuesday, March 4, 1930, saw fit to print:

### LONG IN REGALIA, MINUS STOVE-PIPE HAT, APOLOGIZES

#### GOVERNOR CALLS ON COMMANDER EMDEN IN ALMOST FULL DRESS

*Rex*[53] *Will Reign Today in Peace*

Possible international complications threatening the friendly relations of the United States and the German republic were dissipated with Metternichian eclat Monday morning when Governor Huey P. Long boarded the German cruiser Emden to apologize for having received Commander Lothar von Arnald de la Periere and Rolf L. Jaeger, German Consul in New Orleans,

---

[53] Rex is the annual ruler appointed for the gaieties of the Mardi Gras Carnival in New Orleans. He is supposed to be a jovial king, who arrives for the season of mirth and joy ending just before the Lent season. He arrives by steamer, is handed the keys to the city, and the celebration of various forms and kinds, including music, dancing, floats, and masking, pervade the city of New Orleans for several days. There is no carnival to compare to it in the whole world. It has existed for scores of years.

in a pair of green pajamas, a blue and red lounging robe and blue bedroom slippers when they
called upon the Governor Sunday.

A salute of 21 guns fired by the Emden in
honor of the governor blasted the diplomatic con-
tretemps that had existed for 24 hours.

The governor was in formal morning attire,
most of the accessories of which he had borrowed
from friends. Because a good friend failed to furnish a silk hat in time Governor Long carried a
snappy gray fedora in his hand. He never wore it,
however. He was accompanied by Colonel Sey-
mour Weiss, attired in the full dress uniform of
the governor's staff officers of his rank.

They made the trip to the Emden in the Dock
Board's boat, the "Hugh McCloskey," which
dipped the American flag from its stern as the
governor and Mr. Weiss started aboard the
cruiser.

Sunday morning the commander and the consul called at the governor's suite in the Roosevelt
to pay their official respects to Mr. Long. Colonel Weiss escorted them into the parlor of the
gubernatorial quarters and informed Governor
Long of the visit.

The governor was reading the Scriptures and
also listening to a sermon over his radio. He hastily threw a red and blue lounging robe over his
green pajamas, slid into his blue bedroom slippers
and went into the parlor to shake hands with his
guests. Colonel Weiss stood at attention at the
handclasps. They chatted freely for a few minutes
and the consul and the commander took their
leave.

Immediately afterwards the consul called on Mr. Weiss in the latter's office and demanded that he be ushered into the governor's presence to require an apology due to the commander and himself because of the Governor's attire.

The consul said: "The Governor's raiment to receive the commander is an insult to the German government and I demand an apology immediately. If the apology is given then the matter ends right here, otherwise——!"

Mr. Weiss persuaded the consul to await him in his office until he could see the governor. He hurried to the executive bedroom, explained the case and requested the governor to immediately see the consul and arrange to make the proper apology.

### Governor Surprised

"What's the matter with 'em?" the governor asked. "I had on a pair of green pajamas, took the time to put on a pair of bedroom slippers, a $35 lounging robe given to me by the State Banking Department for Christmas—what more do they want?"

"But, Governor," importuned Mr. Weiss, "this is a serious matter, regardless of how you feel about it. It is international. You must not let the matter go further. Whatever amends are required you must make them. It might be serious."

W. Lyle Richeson and John McKay of the Dock Board, who were present, came to the aid of Mr. Weiss and convinced the governor that he should make an apology.

"All right, bring them up," the governor acquiesced. Mr. Weiss returned with Mr. Jaeger.

Again the governor stepped into the parlor to meet the consul, still dressed in the pajamas, the robe and wearing the bedroom slippers.

### Begs Pardon

"I beg your pardon, sir," the governor said to Mr. Jaeger. "I am much embarrassed and humiliated for having given you and the commander umbrage. I have been up late, and I have been not at all well for the past several weeks. I hope you will excuse my failure to properly bedeck myself for the occasion of meeting the commander and yourself. I am indeed sorry. It is not my fault that this has occurred. I left a great deal to the colonel on my staff. I felt he would have informed me or, at least, have warned me against such unbecoming raiment, but he didn't.

"You see," the governor continued, "I come from Winnfield up in the hills of Winn Parish, in this State. I know little of diplomacy and much less of the international courtesies and exchanges that are indulged in by nations. In fact, I only happened to be governor of the State by accident, anyway. There was no royal heritage but simply by chance I happened to receive more votes than the other men aspiring to the same office. What can I do to right this matter?"

### Formal Call Arranged

"If you will come tomorrow to the cruiser Emden and call on the commander and make apology to him then the matter will be settled," the consul replied.

"Very well," responded the governor, "I will be there at 10:30 o'clock Monday morning."

After the consul left it began to dawn on the governor, the colonel and confreres that complications and international discourtesies might be charged against the executive.

A conference was called immediately to devise relief for the situation. The governor and his aides spent the remainder of the day in obtaining the proper apparel for the governor and Mr. Weiss, as his staff officer, in their scheduled courtesy call. When the proper procedure in punctilio had been decided upon, the governor borrowed a pair of striped gray trousers from one friend and Mr. Weiss found a black, silk-edged morning coat with tails. The governor extricated a dress shirt from his own armoire and another friend lent him a gray four-in-hand morning tie. A pair of black patent leather shoes were found deep in the gubernatorial closet.

### Everything But Hat

All that was needed now was a silk stove-pipe hat. Alfred D. Danziger, formerly president of the Association of Commerce and an attorney, was called into the conference and he volunteered to furnish the hat he had worn when with a group of lawyers representing the American Bar Association, he had called on King George in Buckingham Palace a year ago.

At sunup Monday the Governor and his aides were preparing for the forthcoming visit to the Emden. The governor rose ahead of them all. He had forgotten where he put the dress shirt. It was found after an hour of intensive search. Then he prepared for the call. Carefully he donned the

BEFORE LONG

Treatment Room at Central Hospital for Mental Diseases (no Sterilizer or Trained Nurses).

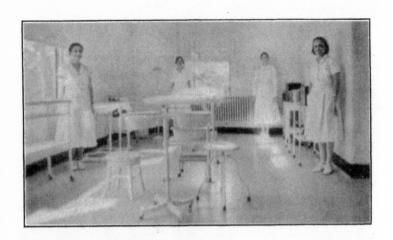

UNDER LONG ADMINISTRATION
Treatment Room and Sterilizing Equipment for Central Hospital, With Trained Nurses for Handling.

selected clothes. But there was no silk hat. Time wore on apace. Mr. Danziger arrived—without the hat. The governor was impeccably arrayed. He was ready—except for the hat. He could wait no longer and when the clock registered 9:30 a.m. he grabbed a snappy gray fedora and started for the boat at the foot of Canal Street. "If this isn't all right," he said, "I can keep it in my hand." Mr. Weiss and Mr. Danziger assured him that the hat was entirely correct.

The party boarded the Hugh McCloskey and she steamed up the river with an American flag whipping the breeze from her stern. As she came alongside the cruiser, the McCloskey dipped the flag in salute.

### Board Cruiser

Governor Long and Mr. Weiss went aboard the Emden after the gangplank had been lowered. They were met by the commander and the consul and escorted to the former's cabin. Then the governor addressed himself to the commander:

"I was hoping that this morning I might have the opportunity here to apologize for the indecorous raiment in which I was attired when you called to see me yesterday morning. I am really very much hurt over the incident. There is a great deal I might say, I undertook to explain to the consul."

The commander assured the governor that everything was all right. They had a friendly chat and the commander showed the visitors some of the relics of his work during the World War. They talked over some interesting points of modern history, the career of the commander and then began to take their leave.

### Salute Booms

The commander expressed a desire to fire a salute in the governor's honor. And while the governor and his party stood on the gangplank, a salute of 21 guns was fired.

The members of the governor's party all bowed.

There was now no rift in relations to mar Carnival.

But——

When the governor and his friend returned to the Roosevelt one of the hotel executives rushed into the dining room where the governor sat at breakfast, morning attire and all, and said, "We've had something terrible happen here. One of the city delegates, assigned to entertain the delegation here from Canada, declined to drink a toast to the king last night, and all is discord."

### Settles Another One

"Send them to me," the governor promptly replied. "We've settled one dispute this morning and I think we can settle another."

The Canadian party was assembled, led by the Scottish bagpipers in full regalia.

The governor made an official address of welcome. Alderman Wilkerson of the Canadian delegation responded. Greetings were exchanged. The governor and Mr. Weiss retired to their rooms where the governor arranged to return the several clothing accessories he had borrowed for his formal courtesy call.

And in the afternoon, attired in a double-breasted business suit of dark gray, a blue shirt and contrasting tie—all his own clothes—the governor received a courtesy call from Captain Adolphus Andrews, commander of the U. S. S. Texas.

They talked about parades and balls. "I have never seen such beautiful queens before in my life," the captain said. The governor laughed and agreed, too, that the parades were good.

Rex can reign today in peace.

# CHAPTER XV

THE enemy newspapers may have thought that all of the propaganda carried in their columns would do me less than good; on the contrary it redounded to my advantage and greatly pleased the folks of both city and country.

Our opposition was forced to resort to taking advantage of weak spots they had created in the State's armor when they were in power.

Bonds had been issued against the Port of New Orleans under governors who had preceded me and who spent the money realized, amounting to over $42,-000,000.00. Most of them were issued by Parker or Pleasant. They had been sold to the public on a ruling that they were State obligations. The people of Louisiana had been told that they were mere obligations of the Port.

My enemies knew the maturities would become serious in 1929 and 1930. They were wise enough to postpone the maturities in their day.

The Governors issuing these bonds and the amounts were as follows:

| | |
|---|---:|
| Blanchard .................... | $ 3,500,000.00 |
| Hall ......................... | 4,250,000.00 |
| Pleasant ..................... | 25,500,000.00 |
| Parker ....................... | 6,500,000.00 |
| Simpson ...................... | 3,000,000.00 |
| Long ......................... | None |
| Total ........................ | $42,750,000.00 |

The enemies were waiting the time for the bonds to default. Then their Public Press would be ready to picture the sad situation "due to the orgy of extravagance of Huey P. Long."

When I discovered the situation one year ahead of time, I undertook to secure help of those who sold the bonds, and spent the money, to establish some fund to pay the debts which they had created. Nobody home!

As they had done in the case when they left the Highway Commission in debt they left me to the ravages of time, preferring to bring the State to disaster in order to accomplish my ruin.

We exposed the conditions to the people; we showed who had issued the bonds on the Port of New Orleans, who had spent the money and how some of it had been spent.

By that time the Louisiana Progress was read and believed. It was serving the situation well.

We had started on the paved road system by scattering the work through the parishes, putting five, ten or fifteen miles to the parish. When the people once knew the pleasure of travelling over paved highways their support for a program to connect up the links was certain. Our enemies were quick to see the plan and attacked us bitterly for it. We persisted in our plan. None ever worked better.

Before the Legislature met in 1930, we began to agitate, through the columns of our Louisiana Progress and circulars, and through a speaking tour, for a continued plan of improvements to be presented to the regular session of the Legislature in May, 1930.

Louisiana Progress Cartoon.

This program included the completion of the paved roads, more farmers' gravelled roads, more free bridges, the building of a new State capitol, and a tax of one cent per gallon on gasoline, to be partially devoted to retiring the bonds of the Port of New Orleans and to help the Port of Lake Charles.

But the opposition had other plans afoot. Their last chance to attain the control of the State lay in the possibilities of the 1930 regular session of the Legislature. They had never, for a moment, ceased their activity to renew the impeachment proceedings.

Their first move was to undertake the removal of my faithful friend and ally, the Speaker of the House of Representatives, Mr. John B. Fournet.

A member of the House made the motion that the Speaker's chair be declared vacant. A vote was taken resulting in fifty-six votes in favor of Fournet and only forty-one against him. The enemy was not prepared for such a showing. They had lost twenty-one votes in the House during the interim between the extra session of 1929 and the regular session of 1930. It was "the blow that killed father," so far as undertaking to start trouble in the house went. In the Senate our administration elected the President pro tempore, Senator A. O. King, Judge Gilbert having been elected to the bench.

We immediately reorganized the House of Representatives taking out of some responsible positions those who had voted to remove the Speaker. All committees were placed in the hands of our friends.

We gave these enemies no quarter although

"They were as mild-mannered men as ever scuttled a ship or cut a throat."

In a last vain effort the opposition called another mass meeting. We called another for the same night, in the same city.

The two were held a few blocks apart. The crowds of the two sides mingled in Baton Rouge for the day. Many fights occurred.

Our meeting was so much larger than the meeting of our opposition that, on the following morning, the Times-Picayune displayed a picture of our crowd, under a caption indicating that it was the crowd of our opposition.

The photographer had undertaken to disguise the faces of the attendants. Unfortunately, the Irish countenance of my leader of the 11th Ward in New Orleans, R. H. (Pat) McGill, could not be disfigured. Severe ridicule was heaped upon them. They never denied the switch of photographs.

The administration of the city of New Orleans, the cornerstone of my political opposition, filed suit against the State Highway Commission, claiming an indebtedness to the City, made by my predecessors in office. The court was asked to enjoin the Highway Commission from using any of its several millions of dollars either to build, maintain or operate public highways and bridges until that indebtedness was paid. The District Court of Baton Rouge rendered the injunction, the effect of which was to paralyze the improvement work in progress by the Highway

Commission, and practically suspend such a thing as a public highway in the State.

I was in the midst of several embroilments in both houses of the legislature when I entered the Governor's office early one night and was informed of what had been done by the court. I immediately dictated to my secretary an application for writ of prohibition and mandamus and returned to the Legislative Halls, leaving it to the secretary to put the document in proper form as a suggestion to the attorneys for the Commission.

The following day I glanced at a newspaper of the opposition, to read that the application had been filed and that we were sustained by the higher court.

We went into the 1930 session of the Legislature with proposals for Constitutional amendments by which we were to submit to the people our entire program for improvements, and to make sound the bonds on the Port of New Orleans issued by my predecessors in office. The proposals were favored by the people.

The bills continued to gain so much support in the Legislature that it appeared barely possible we might secure the two-thirds vote of both houses necessary to submit them to the people.

When we were within sight of such a number in the lower house, two of the members upon whom we had relied died. The newspapers publicly gloated over our misfortune.

We changed our plans. We introduced a bill providing for the calling of a Constitutional Convention. A majority vote instead of two-thirds of both houses in favor of that bill would have submitted to the people the proposal for the calling of the Convention. If favored, the Convention could have adopted our program.

The bill to call the Convention came up in the House of Representatives.

"It's a damnable outrage," one of our opponents said on the floor. "What you are trying to do here is submit a constitutional amendment to the people to vote on without a two-thirds vote of this legislature. It is a subterfuge to have a majority vote to do what it takes two-thirds to do."

Our floor leader was quick to reply.

"You have taken the advantage that the hand of Death gave you to make it impossible to get a two-thirds vote of this legislature. You're using that to try to keep the people from having the right to pass on this program whether they want it or not. Any course we pursue is fair, if it contemplates no more than giving the people the right to decide. You have newspapers; you have the political rings. If you are right, the people will be most certain to see your side of the case."

We brought the question to a vote. We polled fifty-six in favor of the convention, five more than a majority.

The enemy was again on the run. Only one year before I had barely escaped impeachment by the same members of the Legislature.

When our bill for a Constitutional Convention reached the Senate, a well designed filibuster was organized to be carried out largely through the conduct of the Lieutenant Governor. At the beginning of

every morning session, some opposition Senator rose
to the point of personal privilege and spoke throughout the day.

No member of the Senate, not a party to that filibuster, could secure recognition from the presiding
officer, the Lieutenant Governor. For days and days
the filibuster persisted. We finally concluded our position would be best served to have the session end that
way.

Eventually the sixty day time limit of the Legislature expired, with the filibusterers in complete control
of the floor of the State Senate. The Lieutenant Governor had refused to recognize anyone else.

We were unable to account for the attitude of
some few senators who would not join us to overrule
the chair and take the floor away from the filibusterers. Somewhere there was an influence we could not
locate.

What was this influence?

When the Legislature had adjourned a plain enve-
lope containing a copy of a letter came to my office.
The original had been written by R. C. Watkins,
manager of the Southern Pacific Railway Lines. It
read:

New Orleans, July 13, 1930.

Personal
Mr. J. H. Tallichet,
Care Baker, Potts, Parker and Garwood,
Houston, Texas.

Dear Tallichet:

I take pleasure in advising you that Governor
Long's proposal for a Constitutional Convention
failed before the State Senate.

The Governor says he was defeated by a minority insisting upon observing the rules of procedure, but he knows, as do others properly informed, his defeat was by a clear majority. The Governor and his followers feared to force the issue to a vote before adjournment.

I write this to thank you for your kind and effective aid. You will be interested to know that the party you undertook to *reach*, though previously with the administration, came out strong for, and stood consistently with, the opposition until adjournment.

Very truly yours,<br>R. C. WATKINS.

Personal
Care Mr. H. M. Lull,
Executive Vice-President
Houston, Texas.

All the parties addressed were connected with the Southern Pacific interests. The writer of the letter had been for some time and is now engaged in an effort to cause a return to private interests of certain valuable oil and gas lands of many thousand acres now held by the State.

I was convinced the copy of the letter I had received was genuine, but how could I prove it?

To make no mistake, I called over the long distance telephone to the office of the law firm addressed in the letter.

"I have a copy of the letter here," I said, "that we want to trace to see if you have received it. Will you let me read it to you so that you can tell me?"

"That'll be all right; read us the letter," the answer came back.

I read the letter.

"Just wait a minute," I was told.

Within a few minutes an answer came through "We received that letter. Who is this talking?"

### CHARGE OF THE LIGHT HEADS

Louisiana Progress' ridicule on the League.

I hung up the phone. Thereupon we printed the letter on the front page of the Louisiana Progress in three separate issues. The authenticity thereof was never questioned.

Such were the influences operating in the dark which we often managed to overcome.

Copies of letters and documents sent to me by undisclosed persons have made it possible for us to defeat our more powerful financial opponents on other occasions.

When the 1930 Regular Session passed into history, among bills left for me to consider were the appropriations. After vetoing some of my own, I found $6,400.00 worth of appropriations for unnecessary expenses of the Lieutenant Governor, Dr. Cyr, and the unnecessary sum of $28,980.00 for the office of the Attorney General, Percy Saint.

I vetoed this latter item on the ground that his department had become counsel to the Constitutional League and not the Governor and the State departments, and that therefore his department did not need such amounts. I likewise passed the axe over Brother Cyr's unnecessary allowances.

A squall went up from both Cyr and Saint, but they had been alleging "extravagances" so much that their clamor met the "horse laugh" of the public.

In the impeachment proceeding of 1929, there came a time when, in order to carry on the illegal affair, money had to be borrowed to pay the expenses. The Legislature passed a resolution authorizing the Board of Liquidation to borrow $100,000.00 for that purpose. As a member of the Board I voted against the approval of such loan. I warned the banks against making it. There was, in fact, no authority for anyone else to have signed such a note for the Board.

The banks made the loan. The 1930 Regular Session of the Legislature appropriated the $100,000.00 to repay it.

I vetoed it.

# CHAPTER XVI

## CAMPAIGN FOR THE UNITED STATES SENATE

IT was necessary that the program which I had outlined be completed or that the State come to a standstill. There was no middle ground. Time was not far distant when the bonds of the State, issued by my predecessors for the Port of New Orleans, would require money. The State could not supply it. I preferred to retire if the people could not see the need of rescuing the State.

In the beginning of the formation of the Constitutional League, my old friend, Senator Joseph E. Ransdell whom I had consistently supported, had joined and issued a strong letter commending the cause and purpose of the anti-Long movement.

When the 1930 Regular Session of the Legislature passed into history, I immediately announced that I would carry my program before the people as a candidate for the United States Senate. I made no secret of the fact that if the people saw fit to stand with me in the election, I would expect them to back up the processes necessary to bring about a fulfillment of administration purposes; but that, should the people see fit to express themselves as not favoring me, that I would accept that verdict and allow Dr. Cyr to take the post of Governor.

A newspaper said:

"Huey Long has piled all his chips on the table to

Campaign cartoon in U. S. Senate race.

bet on one throw of the dice. Win this time and we are through with him."

It was the battle of Louisiana's history. For once the public press was united—all against me.

Our opposition undertook to form a coalition of practically every political element in the City of New Orleans to overcome whatever lead I might have in the country outside of that city.

The opposition was well on its way toward effecting such alignment, when I discovered the power behind the throne. We issued the following circular in that City as a bulletin of our paper, the Louisiana Progress:

WHY THE ZEMURRAY [54] MILLIONS   ·
SUPPORT THE RING—
THE BLOOD OF AMERICAN SOLDIERS THAT IS SPILLED
FOR ZEMURRAY—
HIS REASON FOR BACKING RANSDELL—
WHY RANSDELL FOUGHT HIS PEOPLE ON FLOOD
CONTROL—
THE BARTER OF THE JUDICIARY AND SEATS IN
CONGRESS—

It is not a matter of very common knowledge, but it is nevertheless a fact, that the United States has kept a standing army down in Central America to fight for certain interests "making in-

---

[54] Zemurray referred to in this article is now the Chief Executive Officer of the United Fruit Company, a multi-millionaire, and at the time the sole owner of an interest in Central America. He is generally known to have assisted and financed several revolutions in Central America carried on by General Lee Chrismas and Guy Malony.

vestments" in such countries as Nicaragua and
Honduras. The story runs that, when one of
these large American interests is not pleased with
what he can get at the hands of the Central
American governments, they "change the government."

Among the men who have made millions in Central America out of the work of the soldiers of this
country is one Sam Zemurray of New Orleans. He
has many concessions in the Central American
countries. Time after time, except for the blood
of the soldiers of this country, his "concessions"
would have gone up in smoke. Wherever he drove
down his stob and laid claim to a few hundred
miles of property, no matter what side of a revolution he bought from, he was able to make good
his claim by the fact that the United States would
send soldiers there to back him up.

It took influence to have the army of the United
States in a constant war to make money for
Zemurray. There was no war declared, and yet
the U. S. soldiers spent their blood for the cause
of the financial gain of Mr. Zemurray, just the
same as if war had been declared. Why? Mr. Zemurray took in as an associate, we find, a nephew
of Senator Joe Ransdell, one Joe Montgomery,
and this Zemurray and Ransdell's kinfolks' combination made millions on top of millions that anybody else could have made if they had only been
furnished with the United States army to back
them up in their concessions and grants, in the
revolutions of Central America.

Many a mother's son lies in an unmarked grave
in the tropics for the cause of Zemurray's mil-

Cartoon in Louisiana Progress.

lions and Senator Ransdell's nephew's good association with Zemurray.

And that isn't all: It suited the cause of the
Zemurray millions better, while getting protection from the American soldiers, to register their
trade ships under a foreign flag, thereby keeping
from paying their share of taxes to the United
States and to the State of Louisiana. So, the
Cuyamel ships, the Zemurray line, sailed the flag
of a foreign nation, depriving the United States
of its taxes, while at the same time being protected by the blood of the soldiers of America.

But, how did Ransdell get such a pull with the
Republican administrations who are now sending
their army men here to help him in his campaign?
Why did Ransdell stand so well with the War
Department and the President? Why are U. S.
Army engineers and office-holding doctors being
sent down to Louisiana at this time to give dinners for Senator Ransdell, when, out of a thousand doctors and engineers in Louisiana, there are
not enough that can be found in the State who
are willing to fill the seats at the Ransdell "banquets?" Why such demonstrations so that Senator
Ransdell can continue to help the cause of Zemurray and help spill the blood of the American
soldiers for the advancement of Zemurray's millions, including his nephew Joe Montgomery?

ENTER MR. JOE RANSDELL, REPRESENTING THE PEOPLE
OF LOUISIANA:

So, today, we are presented with a spectacle,
rather we are faced with two spectacles, Why has
Sam Zemurray taken charge of the Old New

Orleans Ring's financial problem in New Orleans and agreed to pour out barrels of gold in Louisiana to elect Senator Ransdell back to Congress? Why did Ransdell fight his own people, until congressmen and senators from other States took up the fight for the people in Louisiana and have begun to get us some relief (not nearly enough), in spite of Ransdell's stand against the government's paying for the work and in spite of all his record in Washington for thirty-two years?

Zemurray's gold is now poured out by the barrel to re-elect Ransdell. Queer transactions have occurred.

Pay no attention to this lying newspaper effort to play up Ransdell with banquets supposed to be by "doctors" and "engineers." Out of every 100 or 200 engineers and doctors, they manage to get about one to come to one of these Ransdell dinners.

Then the lying Times-Picayune puts out a picture showing Ransdell as having been endorsed by the "Louisiana Society of Engineers" and the "Louisiana Medical Society." It's all a lie-lie-lie. Neither of these have or will make such endorsement of political candidacies.

Ransdell's engineers and doctors to attend his "banquets" have been chiefly imported from the Republican administration departments in Washington.

Two sets of whiskers (Ransdell and Spearing) from Louisiana are coming out of Congress this time and two real men of service are going to be put there instead.

The lying newspapers and the New Orleans

Ring propose to keep the people from completing
the Good Roads' System in this State. They propose to keep the people from having a right to
say whether they do or do not want the good roads
and free bridges without any increase in taxes.

A Square Election—It's Awful!

Cartoon in Louisiana Progress.

Now, they have emerged to barter, to trade, to
swindle, to lie with anything or for any purpose,
just so the rule of the people may be broken up
and such men as Ransdell returned to the United
States Senate.

Zemurray and his millions, the blood of the American soldiers, the sacred judiciary of the State, a seat in the highest Congress of the land, —all of these are traded in as part of the Ring boodle, along with the vituperation of the lying newspapers, against the welfare of the State.
THEY SHALL NOT PASS!

When this circular had covered the City of New Orleans, such a storm was created that, while the leading candidates who had opposed the Regular Organization in the previous City election joined with them for Ransdell, none the less the rank and file of their candidates and political workers came to our banner. It also created confusion and lack of harmony in the ranks of the City Regulars.

While the campaign between Senator Ransdell and myself occupied a period of approximately seven weeks, in bitterness and intensity it exceeded any campaign this State has ever known. Copies of the Louisiana Progress to fight the unanimous press opposition were printed by the hundred thousand, then by the quarter million and finally by as many as one million copies to the issue.

Every parish in the State was combed by the opposition with a list of speakers that invaded the most isolated communities. I delayed my course of taking the rostrum until speakers of the opposition had fairly well covered the State. Then I began a tour, covering only the parish seats, taking my time, compared to other campaigns, making only from three to five speeches a day. When I had covered the State, however, I had spoken to practically every voter within its borders.

It was in that campaign that I invented our sound truck,—the first portable appliance of its kind ever used in a political campaign. With its aid, I took my time in my speeches and spoke for as long as was necessary to explain clearly and succinctly each and every matter and transaction connected with affairs of the State.

### Newsprint Versus Agricultural Products

Early in the Senatorial campaign, I drew an issue.

There was a cotton warehouse in New Orleans, which had been built by the Port of New Orleans at a cost of $6,500,000. The newspapers were allowed free storage on newsprint in that warehouse for a certain length of time and very low rates thereafter. The rates were so low that had cotton been stored at prevailing cotton rates in the same space as that used for the newsprint the charges on the cotton would have been $185,200.00 more than the amount the papers paid for their space!

I secured a material reduction in cotton rates. That order was sufficient. It caused the facilities to be over-crowded with cotton. The newsprint had to be removed.

I lambasted the newspapers with the statistical data on this transaction.

I displayed the debts that had been piled up by my predecessors in office and how I had undertaken to discharge them; how I had merely asked the right to present the issue to the people for a decision, and

then, how the Legislature had been paralyzed by a filibuster, instituted by the Constitutional League.

The frantic opposition resorted to every kind of
"faux pas." Again I was accused of attempting to

### THE FIRST TREE SITTER

Campaign Cartoon of the Louisiana Progress.

murder someone; of kidnapping others and proceedings were instituted in the courts to investigate the
affairs of State bodies. The Attorney General, who
instituted them, pursued none of these tactics after
election.

The most publicity of all was given to a supposed kidnapping charge during the three or four closing days of the election. An Assistant Attorney General of the State filed a suit in the United States Court alleging that certain persons (not including me) had illegally held two men.

The scene changed, however, into an effort of the New Orleans police to arrest the men when one of them spoke over the radio in our favor.

The day after the election the two men appeared in the United States Court, denouncing the charges.

The court rendered judgment dismissing the suit. The Attorney General blandly declared that the Assistant of his office had appeared in his own right, without warrant or authority from him.[55]

The day of election in the City of New Orleans saw two of the most determined line-ups that ever engaged in a political struggle in the history of that City. For time immemorial, on election days, Louisiana newspapers always published on their front pages the pictures of the contesting candidates. They changed the custom that day. Only Senator Ransdell's picture was printed.

An arbitration committee had been appointed, three to each side. Except for that committee, what might have occurred in the election of that day will never be known.

---

[55] Times-Picayune, page 1, Friday, September 12, 1930, says: "The Attorney General said he had nothing to do with the case, as it was strictly a private matter of Mr. Schowalter and reports connecting it with the Attorney General's office were erroneous."

### Mansion Row

When I went to Baton Rouge to enter upon my duties as Governor, the old Mansion was occupied by Governor O. H. Simpson, my predecessor. Under the law, he remained in the Mansion until the day of my inauguration. In the meantime, I took up quarters at the Heidelberg Hotel.

Mrs. Long and I had a home in the city of Shreveport which had cost us $40,000, and which we did not wish to give up entirely. When I had become Governor, we had expected to live between the old Mansion and our home in Shreveport, with the ultimate object that near the end of my term of office I would retire from public life and live again in the private practice of law in Shreveport.

But when we moved into the Mansion, the old structure was in such condition that living in it comfortably was practically impossible. It had been built about 1860. For a part of the time, it had been used as a public hospital. Various Governors had added to and patched the building from time to time. Rats and other vermin ran through the building unrestrained. Half the windows could neither be raised nor lowered. Termites had destroyed the lower sills.

We, therefore, concluded not to try to establish a home in the old Mansion. I asked the office of the city building inspector of Baton Rouge to give me a report on the Mansion. He did, declaring it unsafe for occupancy. Thereupon, my family remained in my home in Shreveport. I applied to the Board of Liquidation and members of the Legislature for authority to construct a new Mansion, and, upon receiving such authority, tore down the old building and let a contract for the new one.

Before construction could be started on the new Mansion, however, the impeachment proceedings began, at the conclusion of which I moved to New Orleans to perfect a political organization. About the time the organization was perfected, the 1930 session of the legislature convened. I was able to open the new Mansion, though in somewhat unfinished condition.

In offering my candidacy for the United States Senate following the 1930 session of the legislature, with the understanding that either I would be elected to the Senate or resign as Governor, I was still undecided as to what I would do. In the meantime, my family continued to live in our home in Shreveport until the spring of the following year, when we moved into the new Mansion.

A former governor's wife made the statement: "That old building was plenty good enough for us."

"It was too good for them," I replied.

Another ex-governor charged: "The people never expected to see a governor live in such a palace."

"That was because the people never expected to have such a wonderful governor when his kind were in office," I replied.

Another speaker made the assault:

"Some of the greatest governors this State has had lived in this mansion, but only Huey Long had to tear it down and build a big one."

"I can see where that criticism is sound," I replied. "It reminds me of the old man who kept a boarding

Wading Through the Throngs Gathered Around the Old Capitol During the Impeachment Fight, 1929.

Old Executive Mansion Before Long Administration.

Executive Mansion Built by Long Administration.

house. When one guest complained that the towel was dirty he said: 'People have been wiping on that towel for a month without complaining; I don't see what's the matter with you.' "

The new mansion, however, probably the most modern in the United States, was promised in my campaign for Governor.

### Election Results

The results of the election between Ransdell and myself were overwhelmingly in my favor.

While I lost the City of New Orleans by 4,600 votes, we carried all the adjoining parishes and, overcame the scant city lead to elect two candidates for Congress. I carried the State by over 38,000. Senator Ransdell immediately wired his congratulations.

On Wednesday, following my election, the Constitutional League of Louisiana was announced as deceased.

Early Thursday afternoon the Mayor of the City of New Orleans, accompanied by the Clerk of the Council, with a banker and a few lawyers and business men, called at my rooms in the Roosevelt Hotel.

"Well," said the Mayor, "we've accepted your proposition. We're ready to go through."

There was no time to be lost. We agreed to support the program that had been previously outlined by the Commercial Affairs Committee of New Orleans, with additional reforms which I had advocated in my campaign for Governor, including refinancing of the City of New Orleans.

A large banquet was almost immediately tendered

Drawing in Louisiana Progress.

me in New Orleans, attended by practically all the men of political and civic affairs, presided over by Judge Rufus E. Foster, Judge of the U. S. Court of Appeals. A few excerpts from remarks are here given taken from the New Orleans Item, Thursday evening, September 18, 1930:

### LONG GETS PRAISE FOR PROGRESS

"A new era of prosperity," said Judge Foster, the toastmaster, referring to the future that is wrapped in the governor's measures now before the special session of the legislature. "An era that will make Louisiana a leader among the States of the Nation!"

"The most constructive program the city and state have seen since the Civil War," said A. D. Danziger, President of the New Orleans Association of Commerce. "A program made possible by the industry, the energy, the ability and the leadership of our governor."

"The highway system that Long will leave will be a greater monument to his foresight than the Appian Way of Rome," said P. M. Milner, who knows something about good roads—an ardent toiler in this particular vineyard for a quarter of a century.

As Toastmaster, Rufus E. Foster said, "This marks a new era in the history of Louisiana. Here have met men of all creeds and nothing but good holds sway."

And when Mayor Walmsley rose and said, "I'm glad to be here," the diners somehow felt that at last the wounds of battle had been healed and all was well.

But the keynote speech of the evening was delivered by Rudolph Hecht, President of the Hibernia Bank, who described himself as a nonpartisan business man. He said:

"All of you in this room have been as much re-

CLEARING THE PATH

Campaign Cartoon of the Louisiana Progress.

sponsible as I for bringing together the warring factions for the industrial and commercial welfare of Louisiana."

Mayor Walmsley said in part: "I am glad to be here tonight, because I feel it an obligation I owe to my people and the people of this State to

join hands with Governor Long and bury our political tomahawk, so that the city and State can
forge ahead.

"After the election, a friend of the Governor,
and a friend of mine, called upon me and said we
should rise to the occasion and forget our petty
differences for the good of the State and the city.
I said I was willing. He then assured me that he
had the Governor's authority to say that he, the
Governor, wanted to join in any broad co-opera-
tive and constructive measure. That man is Mr.
Hecht, and he deserves the approbation of every
citizen of New Orleans for what he has done in
bringing about the present situation.

"The Governor worked hard to develop a program we could all unite on; he was the victor, and
he showed himself more generous.

"At no time has the Governor tried to sacrifice
a single friend who was faithful to him during his
campaign.

"Prior to the campaign, the Governor made a
proposition to the city more generous--than the
one finally adopted. The city of New Orleans will
be about $300,000.00 poorer, as things are, the
price of battle. But the manner in which the Governor has come to us is appreciated.

"The program he has laid out means more to
the peace and prosperity of this city and State
than you can realize.

"You would have thought that he was the
mayor of New Orleans, if you had seen the inde-
fatigable way he took hold of the problems of
New Orleans and worked to solve those problems.

"Even in the hour of our defeat, we feel that

he has stretched to us the hand of friendship for
the good of the State.

"When the roads and bridges he is planning are
completed, more of the city people will be going to
the country, and more people will be coming to the
city.

"Parish lines will be obliterated as a result of
the Governor's far-seeing policies. We can all
look forward to a mighty era of prosperity.

"Louisiana is going to be one of the most pros-
perous States in the Union.

"Let us, therefore, forget all the bickerings,
and let the capitalists and the laboring interests
follow the example of our two parties and join
hands as we have joined hands. Capital needs labor
and labor needs capital; both must cooperate with
full understanding for the material prosperity and
welfare of this city and State."

Mr. Hecht declared that the Governor had in-
stigated the movement resulting in the present
reconciliation.

"Weeks before the election," said Mr. Hecht,
"the Governor said to me, 'On September 10, the
day after the election, when I am chosen Senator
by a majority of about 38,000, I am going to
come to you and ask if you don't think we can
take up again the plans that went into the dis-
card some months ago, plans for the advancement
of New Orleans and of the State.'

"And I said to him, 'Governor, if you win by
such majority as that, I don't believe you will be
wanting to talk peace on such favorable terms.'
But you see for yourselves, the Governor kept his
word."

Mr. Danziger described the new Senator as a "genius," paying tribute to his "industry, energy, ability and leadership—all qualities of a man loyal to his friends and dangerous to his enemies."

"We are gathered to felicitate the Governor for the most constructive work to be done for the city and State since the Civil war," he began. "He is the cleverest and the most successful man in the rolls of Louisiana history, not only of this but also of preceding generations."

"The city and State will be drawn closer together than ever before through the great constructive work Governor Long is launching," he concluded. "We are all united in this mighty work of prosperity."

P. M. Milner, the next speaker, lauded Governor Long's "legal brilliance, unrivaled capacity for work and grasp of problems." His talk drew cheers at many points.

"He will make the best Senator Louisiana has ever had, just as he has been the best and the most constructive Governor that Louisiana ever had," Mr. Milner said. He concluded with a brief discussion of road work undertaken by Senator-elect Long as governor.

"Governor Parker had a chance to start concrete construction, but it remained for Governor Long to do it," he declared. He then described the road projects for Louisiana.

John H. Overton of Alexandria, said: "Long is the first man in Louisiana to be made governor at the age of 34; the first in the State at the age of 36 to be nominated for the Senate; and he is the first of any age to enjoy both distinctions at the same time."

"He has shown his earnest desire to serve Louisiana; he has given you ample proof of his untiring ability."

"I am glad to see by today's papers that the Legislature has removed the blot on its escutcheon —the impeachment proceedings."

W. C. Ermon, speaking as a traffic man, declared that he was first drawn to Long because of the latter's ability in handling problems so vital to the development of New Orleans, the question of rates. He discussed the governor's efforts to improve conditions, and to make it possible for the port to cure its sore spots.

T. H. Harris, State Superintendent of Education, said that "peace and good will and constructive cooperation have taken the place of ill-feeling, prejudice and hate."

He said that Senator Ransdell is "one of the most lovable and distinguished citizens of the United States.

"The people elected Long to the Senate because they believe he can be of more use to them there," he added. "The people trust Long."

"I find it mighty easy to get on with Governor Long. I have seen the school appropriations increased by $1,900,000 during the past two years. I have seen the appropriations for the State colleges increased by half a million dollars in the same time. I have seen 125,000 men and women who were illiterates learn the rudiments of education."

John Klorer said: "Anyone who withholds his

Cartoon of Louisiana Progress following Peace and Victory.

support of the governor now is not a true friend of the State. The problem of flood control will not suffer through this change in senatorial representation. Governor Long understands the situation; he has given ample proof of that."

Only a few days previously I was not mentioned in the daily public press except where someone had charged graft, corruption, embezzlement, even attempted murder. Now the happy turn of their words caused me to say to those assembled for the banquet:

"Ladies and gentlemen, up in my country once a man died, leaving a weeping widow as well as a mother-in-law who probably knew his faults and virtues better than the community at large. As the dead man lay in his casket beside the grave, the preacher delivered a funeral sermon, recounting from his memory the good deeds and kind virtues of the deceased's lifetime. He spoke of his goodness at heart; whereupon the mother-in-law rose, stepped forward to the casket, took one look at the deceased, and resumed her seat.

"The preacher continued. He told of the kindnesses which the dead man had shown in his home. Again the mother-in-law rose, gazed at the deceased, and resumed her seat. Then the preacher proceeded to enlarge upon the glowing improvement which had been wrought as a result of the sacrifices of the dead man. Immediately the mother-in-law rose, took her stand by the coffin, looked at the countenance of the deceased and never resumed her seat. The preacher turned to the good lady and said:

" 'Madam, I know you are grieved; what is there that the neighbors can do to soften your heartache on this sad occasion?'

"The mother-in-law replied: 'I just want to stand here, parson, to be sure that that man you are talking about was my son-in-law.'

"I am still hoping it's me here tonight with all these former opponents as well as my friends."

When some people start to finding out how "great" one is they know no limits.

It was about this time that rumors and reports began to circulate to the effect that the late Chief Justice Taft had paid me some high compliment. Later, even the *Vanity Fair Magazine* reported:

> The late William Howard Taft told Congressman Aswell that Huey Long was the most brilliant lawyer who ever practiced before the United States Supreme Court.

If all the good could but be true!

At least why could not enough be remembered that one, thus so highly pictured, is not found to be an exact partner of Satan because he undertakes to spread the wealth of the land among the people.

# CHAPTER XVII

## EXTRA SESSION OF 1930

AN extra session of the Louisiana Legislature was called immediately.

The banquet which I had attended afforded me little pleasure. My youngest brother, holding the position as Inheritance Tax attorney under appointment from me, had set up in Baton Rouge with whatever opposition elements he could arouse, to fight certain parts of my program, particularly the building of a new capitol.

The newspapers and my enemies had frequently charged that I had gone back on a promise to abolish the position my brother held just because of my intense desire to favor him. He was regarded as very close to me. I would have strenuous difficulty convincing my friends and supporters that in some manner I was not connected, or at least in sympathy, with the opposition he was urging.

Immediately following the banquet tendered to me, tired as I was, I took an automobile and drove for several hours that night back to the capitol at Baton Rouge, where I set about taking steps to counteract any break in my lines by some act of my brother.

Except for that, the dove of peace not only was perched on the State capitol for the extra session of the legislature of 1930, which met in September, but its wings fluttered and feathers scattered throughout both halls of the Legislature for the five days of that session. Two of the New Orleans newspapers earnestly urged that the time to fight had ceased; that the will of the people had been expressed and re-expressed and that all might as well bow and forget it.

The Times-Picayune, hurt over its switch of fronts in the impeachment for such palpably unworthy motives, followed by heavy oil trust advertising, hid its face and said nothing. But in all negotiations I would not allow a single newspaper publisher to be consulted, pro nor con. I laid the blame to them for the unnecessary agitation.

The extra session of the Legislature of 1930, comprised of the same men who had sought to bring about my impeachment, submitted to the people for adoption the following:

1. A new State capitol at a cost of $5,000,000.

2. A $75,000,000 road and free bridge program, to be directed by my administration. I should here say that the men appointed by me as an advisory committee in 1928 to safeguard the road funds voted in that year were, at this special session, created into the State Advisory Board, empowered so that none of the road funds thus voted could be spent without their approval.

3. A bill to refinance the debts of the city of New Orleans.

4. An increase in the gasoline tax of one cent, half of which was to be applied to the benefit of the public schools, and the other half to pay the interest and maturities of bonds issued by previous Governors for

the port of New Orleans, for which they had provided no means of payment, as well as to give additional support to the Port of Lake Charles.

5. Both houses of the Legislature adopted a resolution formally declaring that the impeachment charges which had been brought against me in the preceding year were at an end and dismissed. This was passed almost unanimously.

I thought that I had checkmated the efforts of my brother to prevent the building of the new capitol, but to my dismay, when the lights of the votes were flashed on the board in the House of Representatives, only sixty-five members cast their votes for the proposition. It required sixty-seven. My friend, Speaker Fournet, was in the chair. I motioned to him. He understood. He declined to announce the vote.

I took the floor, asking some members to change their votes. I noted a situation I could not understand. Members of the body declined to believe I was serious. Finally I caught the point—my enemies, using my brother, holding a high salaried position under me, had told the legislators that I wished the proposition voted down; that I would make a public display at the eleventh hour in order to appear sincere; but that friends of mine, wishing to serve my wishes, should vote to defeat it, and that my brother was simply serving my real desire.

Representative Cheston Folkes said to me:

"Whisper in my ear, so nobody can know what you are telling me; do you really want it?"

The clamor could not make Speaker Fournet, seasoned by the fire of many battles. announce the vote

A Crossing on Dixie-Overland Highway (Bayou Mason)
Before Long Days.

Same Crossing at Bayou Mason Built by Long Administration.

Type of Bridge Built in Louisiana Before Long.

Type of Bridge Built in Louisiana by Long Administration.

until I had seen enough members to roll the proposition up to seventy-three votes.

And thus the extra session of the Legislature of 1930 adjourned with Huey P. Long, Governor and United States Senator-elect, endorsed and successful in everything he had ever advocated. All enjoyed peace, harmony and good will, except the exiled who were left to their own devices.

The depression then afflicting the nation was fought by a united front in our State.

There was, in the 1930 extra session of the legislature, a little scattered opposition left to the program of erecting the new capitol. Representative Gilbert L. Dupre, who was quite deaf, came to me during the session, complaining that his seat in the hall of the House of Representatives was immediately under a leak in the roof. He demanded that I cause an immediate repair to be made. One had to write on his pad. I took it and wrote:

"Are you going to vote for the new capitol?"

"No!" he shouted.

I took his pad and wrote again:

"Die, damn you, in the faith!"

He was much amused and almost came over.

When I proposed my latest road program to the Legislature in the Special Session of 1930, I wrote into the Constitution a provision for a State Advisory Board composed of the same membership as had previously composed the citizens' committee and the State Board of Liquidation. The Board thus composed, consisting of seven State officials, of the President of the State Police Jury Association, and of eleven outstanding citizens of the State, was required to pass upon the sale of all bonds, to scrutinize all proposed contracts before they were made, to authorize the same and to approve the payment of sums in fulfillment of such contracts. I put some of my leading enemies on that board as a guarantee of our integrity.

Never was there one protestant who ever came before the Board with one single charge that a contract was irregular; that a preference was unduly shown to anyone, or that anything had been done in the expenditure of the money other than that which was right and proper for the public interest. Not one vote was ever recorded against a project, even by our enemies.

And even until this day, when silly criticisms are made as to the road construction work done in Louisiana, it is done in the teeth of the fact that the Board in charge of same was composed of men of high standing in the State, including several of my most vicious political enemies, none of whom ever registered a protest or a dissent to the authorizations and expenditures as the work progressed.

### TRYING TO QUELL THE STORMS

I did not await the popular vote in favor of the constitutional amendments before setting out on the work. Their ratification was a foregone conclusion.

When we had reinstated a highway engineer to have charge of the paved road work, I asked that he make plans for the construction of at least 1,000 miles

Bogalusa to Sun Road before Long Administration.

Same Bogalusa to Sun Road Built by Long Administration.

One of the Few Miles of Paved Roads in Louisiana before the Long Administration. (Near Lake Charles, Louisiana.)

Same Road Paved by Long Administration.

of paved highways within the succeeding twelve months.

"That is impossible," the engineer told me. "Five hundred miles per year is the most any State has ever tried to construct."

"This is one Highway Commission," I said. "Could two Highway Commissions construct 1,000 miles if one can construct 500 miles?"

"Yes, I guess two could construct twice as much as one," he replied.

"Then you run this one, and Allen and I will go and organize another one," I told him.

"Well, if you want to do it that way, I guess I could double it up here," he finally said.

He was able to double up the work, and do better than that.

# CHAPTER XVIII

BANKS were closing all over the United States by the thousands. Louisiana had an unusual class of banks and bankers, to have avoided the catastrophies which beset the balance of the United States before and after 1929.

Soon the Bank of Lafayette & Trust Company, a rather fair-sized institution of the Acadian sugar section, telephoned that a run had developed which it could not weather much longer. I was in bed with fever but I dressed and drove to New Orleans. The President of the Lafayette bank ran to me.

"Governor," he said, "I've never been for you politically, but if you'll help save this bank I'll be for you for life."

"Never mind about your being for me; do whatever you please about that. We've got to save the bank."

I acted just in time to catch some of their clearances in the Federal Reserve bank, which were being returned for lack of funds. Through the assistance of other banks and State departments I managed to clear the situation for the time being.

The situation would not hold in that bank for very long, even with the help we could give. We were compelled to force a reorganization on a larger scale. After meetings held in my rooms at the Roosevelt Hotel in New Orleans, plans were fairly well perfected.

Monroe to Bastrop Dirt Road before Long Administration.

Same Monroe to Bastrop Road Paved by Long Administration.

Old Capitol of Louisiana Built 1842.

New Capitol of Louisiana, Long Administration, 1932.

We feared the consequences in the community on the next morning, by reason of which, accompanied by the local officers of the two institutions, I took an automobile and drove the entire night until I reached Lafayette.

The following morning, there was an urgent call for me to hurry to the bank. Some of the depositors had arrived before opening time to withdraw their funds. The bank officials escorted them into the directors' room.

"I understand," I said to them, "that you have come here to draw your money out of this bank. Is that it?"

One spoke up:

"We don't like any reorganization."

"I don't like it either," I replied, "and the people going into their organization don't like to do it. But we're all trying to save the situation."

"But some of us think we'll feel better with our money out of here."

"I feel the same way," I said.

No one responded.

"Since you gentlemen are going to draw your money out, I am going to take advantage of the preference given the State and draw out our funds," I continued.

"How much does that amount to?" one of them asked.

"A great deal more than the bank has in cash," I answered.

One man rose from his seat.

"You mean you're not going to let us get anything?"

"No. I mean that I am not going to let you take your money out of the bank and leave me with mine in here. You leave your money here, I'll leave my money here; and we'll all carry on our customary business and keep a bank for everybody."

All agreed.

They made no further efforts to withdraw. The reorganization plans were perfected after considerable wrangle. The bank remained open until all the banks in America were closed.

All such bank activities were before the creation of the Reconstruction Finance Corporation.

Trouble developed with a large national institution. The failure of that bank with branches scattered in various sections, meant a spreading of trouble we would be unable to overcome. It would require large sums to save it.

We called for the national bank examiner and for the Governor of the Federal Reserve Bank of the Atlanta District, who came to New Orleans.

Up to that time I had never met Governor Black, now the head of the Federal Reserve System of the United States. The meeting had been in conference but a few moments when the bankers had stated their views and I had stated mine. Without hesitation, Governor Black turned to the bankers:

"Gentlemen, your system won't work. Governor Long is right. He has the only plan that will save this situation."

My plan was carried out, and that large national

bank, with all its branches, continued to operate until the country-wide collapse of March, 1933.

Louisiana struggled through all the disasters with practically no big bank failures and with very few small ones, until the national collapse.[56]

---

[56] Federal Reserve Board compilation of March 27, 1933, placed in Congressional Record of 1933 at pages 5403-4.

# CHAPTER XIX

GENERAL WILLIAM TECUMSEH
SHERMAN became the first president of the
Board of Supervisors of Louisiana State University,
before the Civil War. When the clouds of trouble
gathered and Louisiana seceded from the Union, he
resigned from the University and joined the Union
Army.[57]

Efforts were renewed from the time I became Governor to improve the standing of the institution. In

---

[57] Sherman's letter of resignation to Governor Moore of
Louisiana reads:
"Sir:
"As I occupy a quasi-military position under the laws of the
State, I deem it proper to acquaint you that I accepted such a
position when Louisiana was a State in the Union and when the
motto of this Seminary was inserted in marble over the main
door: 'By the liberality of the general government of the United
States. The Union—esto perpetua.'
"Recent events foreshadow a great change and it becomes all
men to choose. If Louisiana withdraws from the Federal Union,
I prefer to maintain my allegiance to the constitution as long as
a fragment of it survives and my longer stay here would be
wrong in every sense of the word.
"In that event I beg you will send or appoint some authorized
agent to take charge of the arms and munitions of war belonging to the State or advise me what disposition to make of them.
"And furthermore as president of the Board of Supervisors,
I beg you to take immediate steps to relieve me as superintendent the moment the State determines to secede, for on no
earthly acount will I do any act or think any thought hostile or
in defiance to the old government of the United States."
See Sherman—Fighting Prophet, page 142.

November, 1928, it was given "A" rating by the Association of American Universities which established it on a parity with the best in the country.[58]

There were some 1600 students enrolled in the institution at the time of my inauguration. But there was much necessity for the school's extension. Though the law had for a number of years provided for a medical school, to make the institution complete, such a school had never been established and other departments were operating under severe difficulties because of the lack of equipment and buildings.

Upon the selection of a new President, November 17, 1930, following the retirement of President Thomas Atkinson by reason of ill health, I was presented with a budget showing the needs of the University. The enrollment had increased from the time I had become Governor, despite the depression, almost 100 per cent. Students who had completed their pre-medical courses were unable to secure admission at the other medical school in the State, operated by Tulane University, because of lack of that institution's facilities.

"Go ahead with your buildings," I said to the Louisiana State University administration. "Get your architect and start out on what you need."

"But where is the money?" I was asked.

"That will be my part of the job," I said.

I had told the President of sources from which I felt available sums might be had, but I said:

"You have got to dare a bit if you build this school.

---

[58] Louisiana State University has made considerable improvements since acquiring its "A" rating.

Start ahead. Let the people see what we propose, and we will find a way to do it."

Plans were immediately prepared for a number of needed buildings and for a School of Medicine, to be established in the grounds of the State charity hospital in New Orleans, with facilities comprising every modern detail recommended for medical training and education. Architects drew plans; contracts were let and signed and buildings began to rise. But every one still wanted to know from where the money would come. Particularly the contractors. To them all I gave the same answer:

"That is my part of the job."

When the matter could be delayed no longer, I disclosed my plans. Five million dollars had been voted for a new capitol. The State University sold part of its old grounds for the Capitol site for $350,000. The Highway Commission needed permanent offices, test grounds for roads and space for garages. It purchased from the State University part of the older buildings and grounds, adjoining the Capitol site, at a price of $1,800,000.

Clamor went up from my enemies; they charged that I had diverted the funds of the State departments. Suits were brought asking for injunctions.[59]

---

[59] Unsuccessful litigation was filed by Joseph Barksdale, now the President of Louisiana Bar Association, and his law partner, former State Senator H. B. Warner, to prevent the Louisiana State University from having the funds allowed it in transactions. Both Mr. Barksdale and Mr. Warner had been unsuccessful candidates for public office, the latter having blamed Long friends for having defeated him on two separate occasions for the State Senate.

School of Medicine, Louisiana State University, Founded by Huey P. Long, 1931.

Dormitories for Women L. S. U. Constructed Under Long Administration.

Music and Dramatic Arts Bldg. The L. S. U. School of Music Constructed Under Long Administration.

But we went on with the work until that $2,150,000 had played out. More money was needed to complete the contracts. The contractors were called together. Again I said to them:

"Go ahead with your work, and within a short time after you have completed everything we will find your money."

We did.

Louisiana State University developed from 1600 students when I became Governor until now, nearly 5000 are enrolled. On February 12, 1933, the School of Medicine was approved by the American Medical Association and rated as Class A.

# CHAPTER XX

IN the meantime, I had been operating under the title of "Governor-United States Senator-elect." The time came when I could have claimed my compensation as Senator, March 4, 1931, but I had requested the Secretary of the Senate not to send me either salary check or expense allowance; that I would not claim my office there until I had practically served out my term as Governor.

The Lieutenant Governor, Paul N. Cyr, began to clamor that, with my election to the Senate, I had vacated the office of Governor. He drove to my old home in Shreveport and with some acclaim, took the oath of office as Governor, thereby occasioning some momentary confusion. I was in New Orleans at the time. Hurrying back to Baton Rouge, I placed a few guards around the State house and the Mansion. I ordered that Cyr should be arrested as an impostor if he appeared upon the premises.

Soon thereafter he filed suit in the district court at Shreveport, claiming title to the office.

When Cyr took the oath to the governor's office, I claimed he had vacated the office of Lieutenant Governor. My friend, Senator Alvin O. King, was President pro tempore of the Senate. Under the constitution of Louisiana, when the office of Lieutenant Governor becomes vacant, the President pro tempore of the Senate succeeds to it.

With Brother Cyr suspended in mid-air about the Governor's chair, Senator King took the oath of office as Lieutenant Governor and took the executive seat.

At last I was through with Mr. Cyr as Lieutenant Governor. I had only to beat him in a lawsuit over the Governor's office to put him out altogether. What a pleasant scene to contemplate!

# CHAPTER XXI

## *Broussard Announces Final Break*

THE attitude of Senator Broussard perplexed our group not a little as the campaign of 1932 approached. He had made no statement one way or the other in the impeachment trouble, although one of his close allies who represented his parish, had voted to impeach me. In the campaign between Senator Ransdell and myself in 1930, Broussard's official secretary had managed my opposition in the home parish of Senator Broussard. But Senator Broussard made no statement. The camp of our forces gave such information as to leave it beyond question that his influence was against us in the campaign.

"Edwin," I said to the Senator, when I was running against Ransdell, "you have never yet come out and said that you wanted Huey Long elected to anything. I supported you. Senator Ransdell did not. Now what are you going to do?"

"I have not decided to announce my position as yet," he replied.

"Well, I'm here to get you to announce it, if I can, either way. I want it known how you stand in this campaign."

Then we parleyed back and forth for several minutes. I became impatient.

"Well," I finally said, "I have but one rule in

politics for politicians, where I have supported a man and my opponent hasn't: 'he that is not for me is against me.' "

This made no impression on the Senator. Then I said:

"I want to do something for you. I can make a contribution of $200.00 to your next political campaign. I'll make it now if you will declare your position, and let you declare for Ransdell. I'm going to sweep this whole country; you can't prevent it. You couldn't control two hundred votes in this election to save your life. But I want you to say it."

The Senator did not become aroused over my suggestion. He retained a calm attitude, and I finally left.

With the approach of the 1932 campaign, we were uncertain as to what Broussard's position would be.

But the Senator finally gave us the necessary relief. On Sunday morning of the 26th day of July, 1931, eight column headlines streamed across the papers of the State, reading:

"BROUSSARD TO FIGHT LONG SLATE—URGES PEOPLE TO DEFEAT TICKET OF GOVERNOR"

At last the skies were clear. We could not have it said of us that we had ever, without good cause, turned our hand to oppose a friend. While Senator Broussard had never announced for me for any office in our campaigns, none the less we had supported his candidacy.

I immediately answered Senator Broussard's attack with circulars, one of which was laid on the porch of his home the same night, reading:

### GOVERNOR LONG'S REPLY

Senator Broussard's demand that Cyr be made Governor and—the Senator's example of "Gratitude."

To the People of Louisiana:

I am having to make this statement by circular because we cannot get the truth printed in some of the newspapers.

Senator Broussard's attack on me and his demand that I allow Paul Cyr to become Governor at once does not concern me very much. Although we helped Senator Broussard to the Senate in 1926, Senator Broussard has been opposing us for years, and has made a very poor showing in his home parish and in his home district thus far.

It seems, from what I read of Senator Broussard's remarks, that, if I vote for or support any one for office, that such is all the reason he needs to make such a candidate a bad man for the office. That being true, why not let Senator Broussard get out of the United States Senate? I supported him and he hasn't a friend in the State who would say that he could have been elected to the Senate in 1926 if it had not been for me. Why not let Senator Broussard set a good example, if he means what he says?

I am not going to be drawn into a political discussion for some months, because, were I to engage in politics, I would be almost compelled to arouse opposition from at least some of the officials in Baton Rouge, Lake Charles, New Orleans,

Shreveport, Monroe, Alexandria, and in the Parishes; and to arouse such opposition would mean that I would have to stop or retard some of our work until the politics was over.

We are building roads ten times as strong and for less than half the cost of the roads built by other administrations before us, notwithstanding the fact that Senator Broussard cast the deciding vote for a 30c. per barrel tariff on cement so as to cost us $1,000.00 per mile more for concrete roads than we would now be paying; we are building so many big bridges that it seems almost impossible that one administration would dare to undertake that much work; we are modernizing the ports of New Orleans and Lake Charles, having already reduced the insurance rates at New Orleans from $1.04 to 28c.; we are on our way to unify terminals at New Orleans and bridge the Mississippi at both New Orleans and Baton Rouge; the Louisiana State University is leaping into the position of one of the world's greatest and most complete institutions of learning; Louisiana, so the reports from Washington say, is leading the world in having the smallest number of bank failures during the period of depression; we are stamping out illiteracy; we have increased our capacity and reduced the death rate at our State hospitals; the State Capitol is now on the road to completion; the free school book law is a settled fact; the free bridges are up over Lake Pontchartrain and a 40-foot wide concrete road leads all the way to them; the four-year farmers' road program is again just under way—all of which simply means that we cannot mix in politics

and destroy any harmony among those with whom
we now have to work, if we are to complete the
job.

Now as to the uncalled for attack made on me
by United States Senator Broussard (just arrived from Washington), let me say to my friends
and co-workers that Senator Broussard's pronouncement does not create enough concern or
give us any cause to turn aside from our work
to engage in politics. Mr. Broussard has not spent
enough time in Louisiana to know what it is all
about down here. I fear he has been depending on
the newspapers for his advice and information. If
so, he has lots to learn. It may be that the Senator will not ride over the paved roads built by us
in his absence, because of his apparent, terrible
dislike for the work of this administration and because he may feel that, having by his vote added
$1,000 per mile to the cost of such roads, he would
rather go afoot than to travel on Huey Long concrete.

Senator Broussard is not such a powerful boss
in the politics of his Parish, or of the Third District, or of the State, as the newspapers would
have him appear to be, by the eight columns
spreading headlines he is given. His great power
has been more or less demonstrated in some recent campaigns. I have never seen any friend of
Mr. Broussard who thought he would be in the
United States Senate today if it had not been for
me. Are his attacks on me a return of such favors?
Is that the way some people have of repaying
others for help that they get from them? He now
praises J. Y. Sanders and his wonderful example

when he was elected to the Senate in 1910. It was in 1926 when I helped to save Senator Broussard from Sanders when Sanders was all powerful in Louisiana. Now Senator Broussard attacks me, without cause, and praises Sanders.

Mr. Broussard took some hand in the State campaign last Fall, when I was running for the Senate. He openly fought my running mate, Mr. Montet, for Congress in the Third District, and was generally reported to be against me for the United States Senate, though he would not publicly declare himself on my race. His official secretary came down from Washington and was on the streets leading the fight against me in the City of New Iberia. Broussard was on the scene himself. I carried the Third District in that campaign by a majority of 7,909 votes and Mr. Montet carried the Third District by a majority of 4,904 votes. We both carried Senator Broussard's home Parish of Iberia.

Senator Broussard says that he wants me to get out of the Governor's office, which would let Paul N. Cyr step in and become Governor of this State. Mr. Broussard cannot make Mr. Cyr Governor now, nor in one year from now, nor in ten years from now.

No one knows better than Senator Broussard that, in my race last fall, I told every one that I would serve out my term as Governor before going to the United States Senate. I spoke those very words in New Iberia, Senator Broussard's home town, on the day when Senator Broussard's political ally, Sheriff P. A. Landry, would not allow me to speak on the courthouse square, where everyone had spoken for years. That fact, that I would not go to Washington until May, 1932, was seized upon by my opponents and by the newspapers as a leading argument against my election. The people have decided the matter. Is Mr. Broussard to dictate to the contrary?

Senator Broussard knows that I have not taken the oath of office or drawn a dollar's salary as a United States Senator. He ought to know that no term of office begins, whether it be constable, justice of the peace, Governor or Senator, until such officer is sworn in. He ought to know that several other Governors before me, who were elected to the United States Senate, did the same thing that I am doing now. David B. Hill, of New York; Robert M. LaFollette, of Wisconsin; and Hiram Johnson, of California, are among the Governors who delayed taking their seats as Senators until they could serve out their terms as governors.

It is six months before the political campaign. I am not going to be drawn into politics now or at any time soon for the reasons stated. But, when the time rolls around, I am willing to tender the issue to the people again on whether they do or do not want Paul N. Cyr to be the Governor of Louisiana. I would be recreant to my duty and foul on my promise to the people if, in order to get a better salary, I would turn loose the reins of this State government and allow Paul N. Cyr to step in at this momentous period, when we are at the threshold of completing more improvements than have been made by all the State administrations during the past seventy-five years.

Sincerely,

HUEY P. LONG.

# CHAPTER XXII

## BROTHER AND A FAMILY AGAINST BROTHER

MY youngest brother became an attorney about two years before I became Governor. He had wished to start out in the practice of law in New Orleans. He desired that I appoint him to the position of attorney for the Inheritance Tax Collector, concerning which position, during the course of the campaign, I had spoken very disparagingly. I indicated in one of my speeches that I might see fit to advocate its abolition. It had. been held by a campaign manager of one of my opponents for Governor.

Under the circumstances I hesitated to appoint my brother to that particular position. I was almost certain to be condemned for such an act. The urgings of those closest to my administration, the forces in my office, the Speaker, John B. Fournet, and my Senate floor leader, O. K. Allen, were very persistent and convincing in his behalf.

This brother had been at all times a political supporter, a good and faithful worker. It was almost impossible, with the forces which prevailed in his favor, for me to decline any reasonable request made by him or in his behalf.

Senator Allen insisted that, if I would send his name to the Senate, there would not be a vote in that body against his confirmation. Finally I yielded and handed in the nomination. It was, as Allen predicted, unanimously confirmed.

The job was probably the best to be had in the State. In some good years it paid as much as $15,-000.00. Criticism and condemnation followed, to which I paid no attention, and it soon became of no great moment.

I had agreed on the candidates whom I would support in the election of January, 1932. They were O. K. Allen for Governor, John B. Fournet for Lieutenant Governor, and others.

My young brother began to announce his ambition to run either for Governor or Lieutenant Governor. I sought to discourage him, stating that it would be disastrous for a brother to undertake to have a brother succeed him in the office or to have him elected as Lieutenant Governor.

It was already being charged that I was a dictator and that I had allowed many relatives to be placed on the State payrolls. To have added a family name to the head of the ticket either for Governor or Lieutenant Governor would have been disastrous to the whole ticket.

My brothers and sisters, however, could not see the matter in that light.

I gave everyone to understand that I was irrevocably committed to Allen for Governor and Fournet for Lieutenant Governor. This youngest brother again announced that he would either run for Governor or Lieutenant Governor, and most likely for the latter.

I finally declared openly and publicly that I would not be his supporter for either office; that I was under lasting obligations to others; that I had done the best I could for my brother, but that I could not and would not undertake to persuade any of the candidates to whom I had given my promise to step aside.

Eventually, however, my brother came forward with his early and open pronouncement that he was a candidate for Lieutenant Governor. Certain of my political opposition, particularly that part of the public press always ready to strike, gave front page publicity to all members of my family which might be required to encourage the candidacy of my brother for Lieutenant Governor. Thereupon, the discouraged, distracted and almost annihilated opposition took heart and began again to fight against the election of officers friendly to my administration.

My brother's entry into the campaign and the general family barrage against me was the rift in the sky for which they had looked.

But, while giving my brother and other members of the family such front page space as they might desire to attack me, the opposition had likewise proceeded to list from time to time a number of my relatives to whom positions had been given by State departments. I was caught coming and going in a very clever ruse set by my alert opponents. There was a fair list of relatives on the pay roll, not due to the relatives having been preferred, as much as to the large number of relatives which I had in the State, and the fact that only naturally they were among my political supporters of longest and most arduous service—therefore, under the fair rules of politics as practiced everywhere, entitled to consideration.

Brothers and sisters, first aggravated at my failure to support my brother, later became angry until finally well-defined and displayed articles of the press fanned their anger into flame and then to a madness.

In addition to our candidate, there were four other candidates for Governor on the ticket in January. Our candidate, and my brother and several others were candidates for Lieutenant Governor. In the first and only primary of January, 1932, Senator O. K. Allen's majority over all his opponents, combined, was stupendous. The entire administration ticket of nine candidates were elected, all campaigning under a ticket labelled "Ticket to complete the work of Huey P. Long."

# CHAPTER XXIII

## COTTON REDUCTION PLAN—POTLIKKER EPISODE

IN the late summer of 1931 it became apparent that there would be a tremendous cotton surplus in the United States. I proposed that no cotton should be planted in the United States in 1932, and that thereby the farmer, in possession of his 1931 crop, might reap for this one crop a price much in excess of what he would get for two crops, should one be raised in 1932.

The plan and suggestion met with such immediate favorable response that the Louisiana Legislature, meeting in special session, unanimously passed favorably upon the plan in both houses. The plan was later adopted by the Legislature of South Carolina. It was desired by the farmers of Texas, Alabama, Georgia and Arkansas, and might have been passed in all of those states, had it not been that the Governor of Texas threatened to veto the law should it be passed by the Texas Legislature.

We are now watching the farm relief plans. None will succeed permanently except one which balances production with consumption, and no plan is capable of accomplishing that, save and except that which has been prescribed in the Scripture, which is "to let the land lie barren in the days of surplus," the plan which I proposed.

When I saw hard times ahead in this country, I undertook to encourage the people of the South, and, for that matter, of the United States, to raise gardens and to feed themselves and their children food products which they might not have the money to buy in days of stress. I began the propaganda with regard to potlikker and corn pone, which can be fed to a family for a few cents per week and the whole family kept strong and healthy.

Potlikker is the juice that remains in a pot after greens or other vegetables are boiled with proper seasoning. The best seasoning is a piece of salt fat pork, commonly referred to as "dry salt meat" or "side meat." If a pot be partly filled with well-cleaned turnip greens and turnips (the turnips should be cut up), with a half-pound piece of the salt pork, and then with water, and boiled until the greens and turnips are cooked reasonably tender, then the juice remaining in the pot is the delicious, invigorating, soul-and-body-sustaining potlikker. The turnips and greens, or whatever other vegetable is used, should be separated from the juice; that is, the potlikker should be taken as any other soup and the greens eaten as any other food.

Corn pone is made simply of meal, mixed with a little salt and water, made into a pattie and baked until it is hard.

It has always been the custom to eat corn pone with potlikker. Most people crumble the corn pone into the potlikker. The blend is an even tasting food.

But, with the progress of education, the coming of "style," and the change of the times, I concluded that refinement necessitated that corn pone be "dunked" in the potlikker, rather than crumbled in the old-fashioned way. So I suggested that those sipping of potlikker should hold the corn pone in the left hand and

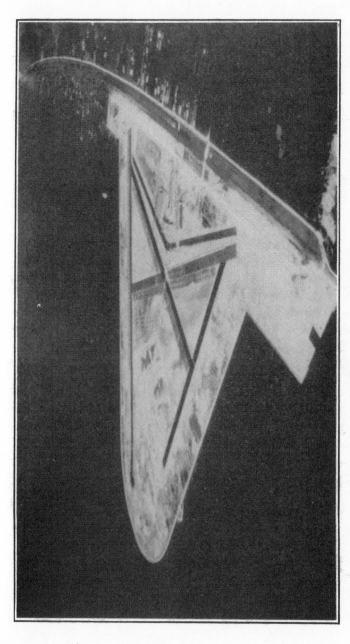

Shushan Airport, New Orleans. World's Largest Base for Land and Sea Planes. Constructed Under Long Administration Without Tax Increase.

Seven Mile Concrete Sea Wall and Driveway, New Orleans. Built by Long Administration.

the spoon in the right, sip of the soup one time, then dip the corn pone in the potlikker and bite the end of the bread. My experience showed this to be an improvement over the crumbling.

But upon my undertaking not only to advertise and to bring about a wider use and distribution of potlikker and corn pone, but also to introduce a more elegant method of eating this delectable concoction, I met with opposition, first State-wide, then nation-wide, later international.

When Franklin D. Roosevelt, the present President of the United States, sent his telegram to the Atlanta Constitution, lining up his forces with the crumblers, I compromised—I compromised with all foes on the basis that it would be a commendable pursuit to eat potlikker with corn pone, whether it be done by crumbling or by dunking.

But the serious strain here is that the health of the entire nation would be marvelously improved if people would boil their vegetables and eat the juice left after such vegetables are removed from the kettle, as there are in these foods properties such as iron, manganese, and others which are needed for health and complexion, sound bodies and minds, and "the perfect 36."

# CHAPTER XXIV

### THE NEWSPAPERS' REVERSE

WHILE it had been so that newspapers had done whatever they could to present me in an unfavorable light to the State of Louisiana and to the outside world, for a time at least some of them exerted just as strenuous efforts to record some favorable news. On an occasion when I had done a courtesy to a woman and her children, in such a manner as to make it practically certain that it would not be known, some newspaper was so eager in my interest that on the following day I found myself confronted with the following headlines and story:

### BIG HEARTED HUEY

Hitch-Hiking Mother, Two Tots,
Helped by Governor Long.

Executive Finds Penniless Family
Trudging to Missouri—Buys
Tickets and Gives Money
for Long Trip.

(By the Associated Press)
ALEXANDRIA, LA., Feb. 14—Governor Huey P. Long played the role of Good Samaritan to a poor mother and her two children here today.

En route to Shreveport in his automobile, Governor Long's attention was attracted at Willow

Glen, a suburb of Alexandria, by a woman and two small children trudging along the road. He commanded his chauffeur to stop the car.

The Governor alighted from his automobile.

"Going my way?" he inquired.

"Yes, we are headed for Missouri," the mother replied.

Without revealing his identity the Governor invited them to get in his car, and while driving the six miles to Alexandria, learned that they were penniless, cold and hungry, and were trying to get to Charleston, Missouri, by the hitch-hike method, where, the mother explained, relatives lived.

Arriving in Alexandria the Governor drove the mother and her two children to the depot where he escorted them to the ticket office, purchased tickets amounting to $18.30, and placed a ten dollar bill in the hands of the mother. Seeing that they would be cared for until time for the departure of the train, the Governor departed.

"Who was that man?" the mother asked the ticket salesman.

"Why, didn't you know?" the ticket agent replied. "That was the Governor of Louisiana, Huey P. Long."

A gratifying result of some of the favorable publicity was the return of my former friend, Col. Robert Ewing, to praiseworthy comment on my course of conduct.

Editorials in Colonel Ewing's "New Orleans States" frequently abounded with such expressions as the following:

Governor Long gives best Christmas present—
Father of eleven given back his job on Dock
Board—
Governor establishes right to dismiss then or-
ders Longhauser restored. (December 18, 1930)

We commend His Excellency on an act that
does credit to both his head and heart. (December 20, 1930)

Such a situation is utterly intolerable, and we
have no doubt, if Governor Long were not ill, he
would either put his foot heavily down on Mr.
Barnes, or forthwith dismiss him for his con-
tumacious defiance. (January 24, 1931)

It is a matter for congratulation that within a
comparatively short time—for the money is available—that the program will be pushed with all
possible celerity. (January 20, 1931)

In sum, therefore, we are to have a capitol perhaps surpassed by no other in the country as respects architectural impressiveness, and ample
room to meet the needs of the State for a century
to come. (December 12, 1930)

### GOVERNOR HELPS IN CRISIS

Even the Governor's critics must admit that
he is keeping his promise, carrying on at a high
pressure the modernization of the road system of
Louisiana and doing his share toward the solution
of the problem of economic depression. He is not
only doing this, but he is giving Louisiana a tremendous amount of favorable advertising, not only
in the United States but abroad, for we have on
our desk a recent copy of the Shanghai (China)
Daily News, presenting a large spread with maps

and pictures of the Governor and Chairman Allen of the Highway Commission in connection with the State's last road program. (February 12, 1931)

### SAVING ON SCHOOL BOOKS

Before Governor Long carried his plan by the votes of the people, Louisianians spent hundreds of thousands of dollars annually for school books. On the other hand, thousands of poor children were kept out of school because their parents and guardians could not afford the expense. Now, no child need miss an education for the want of books, and as a result, there is a steady increase in enrollment throughout the State. Among the achievements of the present administration none will be longer remembered than that which furnished free school books without discrimination between the rich and poor and as between public and private schools. (February 27, 1931)

The Governor is in sympathy with the proposed solution. He is counted on, as others who have congressional leanings, to stand aside at this time and contribute to the avoidance of a fight. Mr. Overton is making a sacrifice in agreeing to go to the House, when he is to be a candidate next year for the Senate. He is doing it in a spirit of harmony and setting an example to others we hope will be followed. . . . Mr. Overton is a lawyer of commanding ability; he is a finished speaker. He keeps constantly in touch with public affairs. He will fit particularly well into the seat made vacant by Dr. Aswell's death. (March 28, 1931)

"Colonel Ewing was a generous friend, but as an enemy his energies knew no bounds; that is, he asked

and gave no quarter," was a comment I made when
Colonel Ewing died. Before our break I had caused
him to be named National Committeeman to the
Houston Convention, in 1928. He died April 27,
1931.

When I was suggested for Democratic National
Committeeman to succeed Colonel Ewing I announced my willingness to accept provided my selection could be made without any opposition whatever.
Upon the Democratic State Central Committee's being called into session, the state was in such condition
I was nominated and by acclamation declared the
unanimous Committee selection for National Democratic Committeeman for the State of Louisiana.

# CHAPTER XXV

I N the course of my administration as Governor, I undertook the work of combining in substantive order the several Constitutions of the State of Louisiana. There had been eight of them, beginning with the one of 1812 and ending with the one of 1921. With the help of members of my administration, we prepared a volume by which each article, as it appeared in each of the Constitutions, was chronologically arranged. We presented such work with the extracts of the court decisions on each of them as they appeared at the time of their existence.

While the credit for the compilation was due as much or more to those working under my direction, I none the less received considerable acclaim for the value of the volume from the bench and bar of the State, and particularly from instructors in several of the universities of the United States.

Soon thereafter the Loyola University of New Orleans, the only university of high standing in the State of whose supervising board I was not a member, accepted this work as a thesis for the presentation of the degree of doctor of laws. Thereupon, with quite a demonstration, attended by the justices of the Supreme Court and many of the administrative officers and professors of some of the other colleges and universities of Louisiana and of other States, in recognition of my public service and my work in compiling the constitutional history of the State, the university presented the following:

TO ALL WHO VIEW THESE PRESENT LETTERS
FROM THE PRESIDENT AND FACULTY OF
LOYOLA UNIVERSITY
NEW ORLEANS, LA.

One peculiar characteristic of our Nation is that we place our hopes, not so much in laws, as in men; not so much in force, as in individual responsibility. We make our act of faith, as our forefathers did, in democracy as the safest means of social organization, believing that the best in man is developed where there is the largest play for individual initiative and choice. The framers of our Constitution, after mature consideration, concluded that our form of government would find its bulwark in the brave and generous hearts of its individual citizens. Such citizens must pay the price for the boon of liberty, and that price is the development of their own characters and will power. This latter is not the result of a mere wish or whim but the product of constant watchfulness and effort. Self-sacrifice, self-discipline, the glad acceptance of tasks that are hard, these are the factors which strengthen the fibres of the will. In Old World countries man's greatness usually consists in his ability to make men serve him, but in our Republic an American's greatness is measured by his ability and willingness to serve others. If he stays at his post and is loyal to his convictions he is dubbed one of America's noblemen. The honorable gentleman, around whom are gathered tonight such representative citizens of our State and Nation, has been judged by the Board of Directors of Loyola University as a true Son of Columbia, a man of action, with ideas born of outstanding vision, who dares to fight for the realization of his ideals, watchfully waiting, working continually. In the words of Lucan, describing the great Cæsar, "Nil actum credens, qum quid superesset agendum," he believes nothing accomplished as long as anything remains to be done. He has dedicated the best of his energies to public service. What a service that has been! He lives for his State and labors unceasingly for the common good. As a member of the Louisiana Public Service Commission he has helped to stabilize and to render more effective the relations between the people and the common carriers. He has brought to the masses a fuller use and benefit of the moneys derived from the Severance Tax. He has opened wide the gates of Education by his stand on free text-books. His resourcefulness and determination have begun a network of roads far surpassing Italy's renowned Via Appia, known as the "Queen of Long Ways," "Longarum Regina Viarum." He has played a conspicuous part in the profession of Law, but, not content with being an advocate, he has issued a vade mecum, a manual of sure guidance for the legal profession, in his masterful "Compilation of the Constitutions of the State of Louisiana."

Because Loyola University is entitled to honor worth and wisdom, by her sanction, whether they glisten within or without her walls,

Because she deems her guest on this occasion a

true representative of Americanism and a real leader of his people,

We, the Senate of Loyola University, have the honor to present to you, the Reverend President, for the degree of Doctor of Law, "honoris causa,"

HIS EXCELLENCY HUEY PIERCE LONG,

Governor of Louisiana

United States Senator Elect for the Aforesaid State. February second nineteen hundred and thirty-one.

# CHAPTER XXVI

MY friend, Mike Conner, the former Speaker of the House of Representatives, had run for Governor of Mississippi in 1923 when I had run for Governor of Louisiana. We had both been defeated and had exchanged condolences. In 1927, we both were again candidates for the office of chief executive in our respective States. He was defeated and I was elected. I sent him condolences and he wired me congratulations. We continued good friends.

Many of the Louisiana roads, having outlet into Mississippi, needed the adoption of a "good roads" project in Mississippi before their full use could be available. In connection with my good roads program, I had undertaken to persuade some of the members of the Mississippi Legislature to help out on a road program during Governor Bilbo's administration. Nothing came of the effort, however.

I encouraged Mr. Conner to try again for the governorship of Mississippi. When the time rolled around for a campaign, my friends in Louisiana and I, and some friends I had in Mississippi, whom I knew when I was in that State, were doing all that we could to help Mr. Conner.

In the first primary election, Mr. Conner was one of the two highest candidates and therefore entitled to enter the run-off. In his other races, he had never been able to get in the run-off. If he had, he might have been elected.

When the second primary opened between Mr. Conner and his opponent, Mr. White, who had led him in the first primary, our friends redoubled their efforts to try to be of better service to Mr. Conner. Our activity was nothing out of the way. Quite frequently, Mississippi politicians had commended various officers in Louisiana, and vice versa. But Mr. Conner's opponent was a very wealthy candidate and set upon making me the issue of the campaign, even going to the extent of saying that the sole issue of the race was my effort to be of help to Mr. Conner.

I answered in kind to attacks made and at times made statements about them without waiting for them to attack me further. Whether because of or in spite of my having been injected in the campaign, Mr. Conner was an easy winner in the second primary.

# CHAPTER XXVII

IN the course of our several political battles we from time to time termed various of our political enemies the "Kingfish," most prominent of which was in our designation of a certain corporation lawyer as the generalissimo of the political policies of a newspaper.

It so happened that in our writing the bond laws of the State I so worded the last road statute as to have the highway bonds sold by the Highway Commission instead of by the Governor, a change which I did not notice for some time, because the Governor was still required to sign the bonds.

On one occasion when we were considering bids submitted for bonds, one of the prospective bond purchasers made the point that under the statute the sale of the bonds had to be awarded by the Highway Commission and not by the Governor, although members of the Commission had always sat with me when such bids were opened. Upon glancing at the law I readily recognized that the official award must be made by the Commission instead of by the Governor.

"I am participating here anyway, gentlemen. For the present you can just call me the Kingfish," I said.

Having dubbed so many of my political opponents by such a title, the newspapers instantly took advantage of the incident and heralded my name far and wide as the self-styled Kingfish. It has persisted ever since. It has served to substitute gaiety for some of the tragedy of politics. I have made no effort to discourage it. The sound of the name and the word "Long" over the telephone for some reason is a bit difficult to understand. It has saved time and effort on many occasions to say, "This is the Kingfish."

# CHAPTER XXVIII

## ARRANGING TO LEAVE PRISON

FROM the day of May 21, 1928, when I took the office of Governor, I had not dared to leave the State of Louisiana. I did leave the State a few times, but only for such intervals that I could return before Lieutenant Governor Cyr was aware of my absence. On one occasion when he had learned that I had made an overnight trip to Jackson, Mississippi, he started from his home to the capitol at Baton Rouge, but I crossed the ferry over the Mississippi River, returning to the State just as he drove in front of the State House.

At that time we were still friends. He had been trying to persuade me to appoint Nicholas Carbajal a member of the Dock Board of New Orleans, which Colonel Ewing and Sullivan insisted should not be done. When Cyr glanced up and saw me in the capitol he laughed.

"Well, you beat me to it," he said.

"What's the matter, Paul?" I asked.

"I want Nicholas Carbajal made a member of the Dock Board, and you ought to do it."

"Paul, I would like the best in the world to do that, if you can just get Ewing or Sullivan to consent."

Strange things develop. Carbajal became disappointed over such refusal and later joined the opposition. Ewing and Sullivan went the same route. So did Cyr. The four men gathered in the camp of my opposition, all with grievances against me, although two of them had kept me from doing what the other two wanted.

So I remained, as certain publications termed me, "a prisoner within the boundaries of Louisiana."

The Supreme Court had handed down an opinion holding that Cyr had no claim to the office of Governor. He was then neither Governor nor Lieutenant Governor. Lieutenant Governor King would step into my shoes when I left the State, until Governor Allen's term began in May.

I called in the department heads of the State government and surveyed the situation:

The capacity of the charity hospitals had been doubled. In the larger one at New Orleans, the capacity of 1600 patients per day had risen to 3800 per day, the death rate had been reduced from 4.1% to 2.8%, such improvement having been made despite a reduced daily per capita cost from $1.74 to $1.31. Similar improvement was being effected at the Shreveport Charity Hospital.

I had become the founder of the great School of Medicine of the Louisiana State University. There had been completed the magnificent structure for that school in the midst of the buildings of the Charity Hospital at New Orleans. That new school, upon examination, was found to have been supplied with every modern device or contrivance suggested and recommended by the national medical organizations. It was given "A" rating by the American Medical Association before it had been in operation more than eighteen months.

Main Highway, Leesville to Alexandria Before Days of Long.

Same Leesville to Alexandria Highway as Built by Long
Administration.

The two hospitals of the State that were treating mental diseases had abolished the barbarous plan of chaining insane patients' hands to plow stocks, locked chairs, straight jackets, etc., instituting in lieu thereof modern therapy and other progressive scientific forms of treatment. The capacity of these two State institutions was increased more than 35% to take care of many for whom admission had been sought; there had been a material increase in the percentage of cures. Dental service newly supplied for those institutions resulted, in the space of a few days' time in one institution of more than seventeen hundred rotted and abscessed teeth being taken from the mouths of long suffering patients.

A new institution and home had been established for the treatment of persons suffering from epilepsy and for mentally deficient or backward children.

The Louisiana State University had more than doubled its enrollment despite the depression; its standing had risen to Grade "A"; dormitories and buildings for departments of music, dramatic arts and physical education had been completed; other buildings were soon to start, and costs of attendance had been lowered within the reach of many.

The free school books had instantly brought a 20% increased enrollment and the public school system of Louisiana was declared by national authorities to be the best anywhere in America; night schools had given the adult illiterates an opportunity by which out of 238,000 shown from the United States census to be in Louisiana, a reduction was made of more than 100,000, credited with being the greatest percentage of reduction of illiteracy achieved by any State in the same length of time.

An overdraft of $5,000,000 in the accounts and finances of the City of New Orleans had been paid through a bill which I had sponsored. Funds had been provided to enable the ports of New Orleans and Lake Charles to discharge obligations and proceed with improvements.

Natural gas had not only been provided for the homes and industries of New Orleans, but for practically every population center of the State, and no one even charged that the promise made and never filled by other governors had failed of fulfillment at my hands.

The charges of the Port of New Orleans on such agricultural commodities as cotton, had been reduced from 25 to 50%. The port had adopted a modern sprinkler system, reducing insurance charges from $1.04 to 28¢ per thousand.

The banks of Louisiana had been operating without any very serious breakdown or collapse, while they had closed by the thousands in many other States. Except for the national collapse when all banks closed throughout America, Louisiana might have continued to escape such trouble.

The Orleans Levee Board had completed a sea wall along the shores of Lake Pontchartrain, long the dream of the city, and was in the course of constructing the great Shushan Airport, the largest and most modern of its kind for the arrival and departure of planes by both land and sea.

The road system of the State which we had taken

$5,000,000 in debt without money for maintenance or improvements, had been so restored that all indebtedness had been paid, farmers' gravelled roads had been rehabilitated and thousands of additional miles built; nearly 2,000 miles of concrete highways had been laid and 1,000 miles surfaced with asphalt had been completed at a cost (including bridges) lower than those prevailing for similar construction anywhere in America, notwithstanding soil difficulties in Louisiana and the unusual necessity for bridges in the State by reason of numerous and extra wide streams.

The system of free bridges was coming into full bloom. The free bridges over Lake Pontchartrain had been in operation for some months; over the Red River a bridge had been completed at Coushatta; over the Ouachita River one had been completed at Sterlington; over the Black River the bridge was in service at Jonesville; a free bridge was open over the Atchafalaya at Krotz Springs. In addition, free bridges were in course of construction over the Red River at Shreveport, Alexandria and Moncla; over the Ouachita at Monroe and Harrisonburg; over the Atchafalaya at Morgan City, with contracts signed for an eleven million dollar free bridge over the Mississippi River at New Orleans.

The new state capitol was nearing completion, the modern wonder of architecture and sculpture of all public buildings of America, at a cost surprisingly low when compared with those more simply built in other States.

A set of modern books and records had been placed in all departments open to the inspection of the public, so that by the merest glance one might determine any particular regarding any project or affair of the State.

I felt I could turn the State into worthy hands. There was a necessity for additional revenue being raised to care for additional requirements of the State's institutions, but plans had been made to that end at the first convening of the Legislature in May to follow, at which time the same were perfected.

Therefore, I notified Lieutenant Governor King that I was ready to leave the State, and upon his reaching Baton Rouge, I departed for Washington on the night of January 23, 1932.

### PERSONAL GAINS AND LOSSES

But while I could recount the gains my administration brought to the State of Louisiana and to its people, my personal account showed an entirely different score.

I had gone into the Governor's office with a lucrative law practice; I had considerable money in cash, some bonds and some good stocks, a home that had cost me $40,000.00, and other property, some money owing to me, and a large amount of life insurance. I owed nothing.

As I left for the Senate there were plain evidences of what had been wrought to my personal fortune as the result of the difficulties and political fights through which I had passed. My law practice was gone, my home in Shreveport was to go for debts; I was undertaking to buy a home in New Orleans and to mort-

Home of Huey P. Long, Shreveport, La., Before His Election as Governor, 1928.

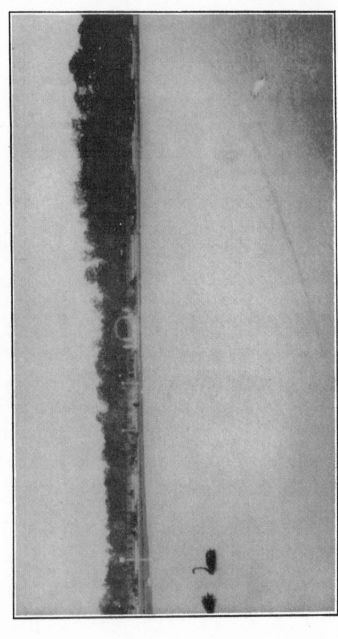

TYPE OF FISH HATCHERIES BUILT THROUGHOUT STATE

The "Huey P. Long" Fish Hatchery, St. Tammany Parish.

gage it for the purchase price, which I succeeded in doing. I was compelled to borrow all that I could on my life insurance and depend upon the indulgences of my friends in the future for the funds which I would need if I cared for my family and myself near so well as I had done before taking the office of Governor, realizing that to repay such loans would some day necessitate my returning to private life. When?

# CHAPTER XXIX

I ARRIVED in Washington January 25, 1932. Soon thereafter I met our Democratic leader, Senator Robinson of Arkansas. He escorted me to the lounging room immediately adjacent to the Senate, where I sat awaiting the time when I would enter the Senate and be administered the oath of office.

My old friend, Senator Broussard, whom I had not seen for eighteen months, walked up to me while I sat there.

"Huey," he said, "there is a rule here that a Senator from one State should escort a new Senator from that State when he takes the oath."

"Edwin, I will be glad to have you do that," I said, "but I don't want you to misunderstand me. When I reached here this morning I read in the newspapers remarks attributed to you, saying that you had not decided whether you would or would not introduce me. I was asked concerning your remarks, and I made the statement that that was a matter you were not going to decide. Now, I just want you to know that."

The Senator was angry.

"I won't introduce you unless you ask me to," he said.

"Don't hold your breath until I do, Edwin," I replied.

Senator Robinson returned, and I told him of the conversation.

"Well, would you have any objection to his introducing you, just dropping matters?" he asked.

"No, not particularly," I said.

He left to talk to Senator Broussard; but on returning he said:

"All right; I'll introduce you."

I had been in the Senate but a few days until I discovered it to be composed of 96 men of varied and sundry political complexions, informed on all subjects and questions, separately and collectively, far better than I had ever expected any ninety odd men to be.

Within a few days I found in that body the uncurbed kind of versatile intelligence which will be the bulwark of support to democratic government in the United States for trying centuries to come.

### CYR SETS UP ANOTHER GOVERNOR'S OFFICE

I had settled to such a situation but a few days when news came that Mr. Cyr, who had abandoned the office of Lieutenant Governor, and lost his suit for the office of Governor, was undertaking to create a furor in Louisiana by purporting to act as a sort of rebel leader. I was telephoned to come home. I started for Louisiana.

Upon arriving I was presented with the press accounts showing that the former Lieutenant Governor Cyr had announced to the world that he had set up Governor's offices in the Heidelberg Hotel in Baton Rouge, and was there ready to transact the business of the State. Certain officers of the militia were guarding the executive mansion and Capitol under the direction of Governor King.

I advised in the matter for a few moments and telephoned to the owner and manager of the Heidelberg Hotel.

"Roy," I said, "what are you doing with the Governor's headquarters there in your hotel?"

"I'm not having anything to do with the Governor's office, Senator," he answered.

"You're not? You've got the Heidelberg Hotel advertised as the capitol. You're not saying or doing anything about it?"

"Well, what do you think I should do?"

"I'd put the Governor's office out of there, and do it quick, if I were in your place."

"It will be done right now," he answered.

The next thing that happened the doctor had been invited to depart with his Governor's office, and with great haste he landed his office at Jeanerette, one hundred miles away from the capital. He sued Governor King and lost.

### PRESIDENTIAL SITUATION DEVELOPING

When I reached Washington on January 25, 1932, newspapermen generally inquired what I thought of the approaching presidential election. My reply was that I thought most any Democrat could win; that I thought some one like my friend Senator Joseph T. Robinson or my friend Senator Pat Harrison would be the best choice. I spoke kindly of Garner as a prospective candidate, as well as of Al Smith, but I expressed contrary predictions on the then Governor of New York, Franklin D. Roosevelt.

I had been in the Senate but a few days, when the famous sales tax fight developed; much of our Democratic leadership in Congress was either favorable to this policy which was being advocated for Mr. Hoover, or, at least, was not unsympathetic to it.

I regarded the sales tax as a disaster. It was diametrically opposed to what I considered the only course which the nation must take to relieve itself from the distress which then and now afflicts it. I was soon looking away from my early inclinations, and eventually toward Governor Roosevelt, who all the time, day by day, made commitments exactly consistent with my belief and understanding of correct government.

Progressive members of the United States Senate, particularly Senators Norris and Wheeler, played a material part in my inclination for the then Governor of New York and present President of the United States. They were the boldest, most courageous men I had ever met.

# CHAPTER XXX

## THE EFFORT TO SPREAD THE WEALTH AMONG THE MASSES

I HAD come to the United States Senate with only one project in mind, which was that by every means of action and persuasion I might do something to spread the wealth of the land among all of the people.

I foresaw the depression in 1929. In letters reproduced in this volume, I had predicted all of the consequences many years before they occurred.

The wealth of the land was being tied up in the hands of a very few men. The people were not buying because they had nothing with which to buy. The big business interests were not selling, because there was nobody they could sell to.

One per cent of the people could not eat any more than any other one per cent; they could not wear much more than any other one per cent; they could not live in any more houses than any other one per cent. So, in 1929, when the fortune-holders of America grew powerful enough that one per cent of the people owned nearly everything, ninety-nine per cent of the people owned practically nothing, not even enough to pay their debts, a collapse was at hand.

God Almighty had warned against this condition. Thomas Jefferson, Andrew Jackson, Daniel Webster, Theodore Roosevelt, William Jennings Bryan and every religious teacher known to this earth had declaimed against it. So it was no new matter, as it was

290

termed, when I propounded the line of thought with the first crash of 1929, that the eventful day had arrived when accumulation at the top by the few had produced a stagnation by which the vast multitude of the people were impoverished at the bottom.

There is no rule so sure as that one that the same mill that grinds out fortunes above a certain size at the top, grinds out paupers at the bottom. The same machine makes them both; and how are they made? There is so much in the world, just so much land, so many houses, so much to eat and so much to wear. There is enough—yea, there is more—than the entire human race can consume, if all are reasonable.

All the people in America cannot eat up the food that is produced in America; all the people in America cannot wear out the clothes that can be made in America; nor can all of the people in America occupy the houses that stand in this country, if all are allowed to share in homes afforded by the nation. But when one man must have more houses to live in than ninety-nine other people; when one man decides he must own more foodstuff than any other ninety-nine people own; when one man decides he must have more goods to wear for himself and family than any other ninety-nine people, then the condition results that instead of one hundred people sharing the things that are on earth for one hundred people, that one man, through his gluttonous greed, takes over ninety-nine parts for himself and leaves one part for the ninety-nine.

Now what can this one man do with what is intended for ninety-nine? He cannot eat the food that is intended for ninety-nine people; he cannot wear the clothes that are intended for ninety-nine people; he cannot live in ninety-nine houses at the same time; but like the dog in the manger, he can put himself on the load of hay and he can say:

"This food and these clothes and these houses are mine, and while I cannot use them, my greed can only be satisfied by keeping anybody else from having them."

Wherefore and whence developed the strife in the land of too much, beginning in the year 1929.

I was standing in the lobby of the Roosevelt Hotel in New Orleans on the 23rd day of October, 1929, at lunch time. Mr. R. S. Hecht, President of the powerful Hibernia Bank & Trust Company, walked to the middle of the lobby, approached me and said:

"Governor, hell's broke loose; the biggest crash of everything that you have ever seen. It is going to be sixty days before this country will get back to normal."

"I have expected this crash for three years," I replied. "It is here for many, many years. It cannot end until there is a redistribution of wealth. Make your plans on that basis."

We argued and wrangled for some moments. A few days later I was informed by a member present that at a meeting of the board of directors of his bank he had repeated, without approval, what I had prophesied. I made known my opinion of the then prevailing cause of the national collapse to the people generally. Time is bearing out all I then said.

# CHAPTER XXXI

M Y philosophy for sharing the work and sharing the wealth by shortening hours and limiting fortunes was first delivered in the United State Senate on April 4, 1932:

> Machines are created making it possible to manufacture more in an hour than used to be manufactured in a month; more is produced by the labor of one man than was formerly produced by the labor of a thousand men; fertilizers are available whereby an acre of land can be made to produce from two to three or even four times what it formerly produced; various other inventions and scientific achievements which God has seen fit to disclose to man from time to time make their appearance; but instead of bringing prosperity, ease and comfort, they have meant unemployment; they have meant idleness; they have meant starvation; they have meant pestilence; whereas they should have meant that hours of labor were shortened, that toil was decreased, that more people would be able to consume, that they would have time for pleasure, time for recreation—in fact, everything that could have been done by science and invention and wealth and progress in this country should have been shared among the people. . . .

> But, oh, Mr. President, if we could simply let

the people enjoy the wealth and the accumulations and the contrivances that we have. If, with
the invention of every machine, we could secure the
education of every man; if with increased production of every kind there could be less toil, more
hours of pleasure and recreation; if there could
be a happy and contented people enjoying what
the Almighty has made it possible to provide; if
there could be people clothed with the materials
that we have to clothe them with today, and no
place to put them; if the people could be fed with
the food that we have to feed them with, and no
place to put it; if the people could be sheltered
in the homes we have today, that the Federal
Land Bank has taken away from them because
they cannot pay the interest on the mortgages—
if that could be done, if we could distribute this
surplus wealth, while leaving these rich people all
the luxuries they can possibly use, what a different world this would be.

We can do this. If we do not, we will leave these
masters of finance and fame and fortune like the
man in the book of old, who said to himself, so
the Bible tells us:

"I will pull down my barns, and build greater;
and there will I bestow all my fruits and my goods.

"And I will say to my soul: Soul, thou hast
much goods laid up for many years; take thine
ease, eat, drink and be merry.

"But God said unto him: Thou fool, this night
thy soul shalt be required of thee."

While the tax bills were pending before the United
States Senate in 1932, I proposed a resolution which

provided that the tax bills should be so revamped that no one man should be allowed to have an income of more than one million dollars a year; that no one person should inherit in a lifetime more than five million dollars without working for it.

The effect of that resolution was that when a man made one million dollars in a year, the government of the United States would receive the balance; and when a rich man died, he could not leave one child more than five million dollars, and the balance would go to the government of the United States.

This would have meant that much of the taxes would have been paid by the so-called upper classes, and that instead of the funds of the government being sucked from the bottom and exploited by the classes at the top, the classes at the top would have paid the taxes to be filtered out to the masses at the bottom, through the various general works and compensations supported by the government.

My resolution, however, received only a few votes.

### A Comparison

Consider the horrible way of the gangster, and then compare his practices with the greed of our mighty fortune-holders in America:

The gangsters have killed hundreds, maybe thousands, to carry out their nefarious rackets to extort money.

The hoarders of wealth have destroyed humanity by millions in their quest for greater accumulation.

From the newborn babe to the man bowed with age, some have been denied the sustenance for life:

they have been thrown from the shelter above their
heads; to keep children warm they have been placed in
the ground, to start a life not in the cradle, but in the
grave; half naked bodies have been thrown against
the winter's wind; some have become beggars, some
thieves, and some have been murderers; others have
been driven insane and still others to suicide—all in
the wake of the drive that the masters of fortunes may
own and control so much that, even in the land of too
much to eat and too much to wear, people perish in
their shadow.

Jefferson, Jackson, Webster, Lincoln, Theodore
Roosevelt and Bryan have clamored to spread our
work and our wealth among all the people.[60]

---

[60] Abraham Lincoln said: "Inasmuch as most good things are
produced by labor, it follows that all such things of right
belong to those whose labor has produced them. But it has so
happened in all ages of the world that some have labored and
others have without labor enjoyed a large proportion of the
fruits. This is wrong and should not continue. To secure to each
laborer the whole product of his labor, or as nearly as possible,
is a worthy subject of any good Government."

On December 29, 1820, Daniel Webster said: "The freest government, if it could exist, would not be long acceptable if the
tendencies of the law were to create a rapid accumulation of
property in few hands and to render the great mass of the population dependent and penniless. In such a case the popular
power would be likely to break in upon the right of property,
or else the influence of property to limit and control the exercise
of popular power. Universal suffrage, for example, could not
long exist in a community where there was a great inequality
of property.

"The holders of estates would be obliged in such case, either
in some way to restrain the right of suffrage, or else such right
of suffrage would soon divide the property. In the nature of
things, those who have not property, and see their neighbors

It is the law of God that a nation must free and re-free its people of debt, and spread and re-spread the wealth of the land among all the people.[61]

"Wherefore ye shall do my statutes, and keep my judgments, and do them; and the land shall yield her fruit and ye shall eat your fill, and dwell therein in safety." Leviticus, Chapter 25, verses 18 and 19.

What cycle of events brings the crime wave of robbery and extortion, murder and destruction?

"Who gave Jacob for a spoil and Israel to the robbers? Did not the Lord, for they would not walk in his ways, neither were they obedient unto his law." Isaiah, Chapter 42, verse 24.

In my never changing course for relief and compensation for the Veterans of our wars, livable wages

---

possess much more than they think them to need, cannot be favorable to laws made for the protection of property. When this class becomes numerous it grows clamorous. It looks on property as its prey and plunder, and is naturally ready, at all times, for violence and revolution."

President Theodore Roosevelt said: "I feel that we shall ultimately have to consider the adoption of some such scheme as that of a progressive tax on all fortunes beyond a certain amount, either given in life or devised or bequeathed upon death to any individual—a tax so framed as to put it out of the power of the owner of one of these enormous fortunes to hand down more than a certain amount to any one individual."

The Declaration of Independence contains: "Whereas, all men are created equal."

William Jennings Bryan said: "Behold a Republic! where every man is a King, but no one wears a crown."

[61] Law of Moses, Leviticus, Chapters 25, 26, 27, provides for freeing and refreeing all persons of debt every seven years and for distribution and redistribution of wealth every fifty years. See also Nehemiah, Chapter 5; St. James, Chapter 5.

for public employees, a recognition of all hirelings to unite and bargain for the sinews they have to offer,— all to be supported from top heavy accumulations,— I have merely carried through a philosophy to insure diffusing our wealth into the hands of all who must consume our products.

But I saw to it that my views were known to Mr. Roosevelt, then Governor of New York and now President of the United States. Early in his candidacy in a speech delivered in Atlanta, Mr. Roosevelt said:

> The millions who are in want will not stand by silently forever while the things to satisfy their needs are within easy reach.
>
> Many of those whose primary solicitude is confined to the welfare of what they call capital have failed to read the lessons of the last few years and have been moved less by calm analysis of the needs of the Nation as a whole than by a blind determination to preserve their own special stakes in the economic disorder.
>
> We may build more factories, but the fact remains that we have enough now to supply all our domestic needs and more, if they are used. No; our basic trouble was not an insufficiency of capital; it was an insufficient distribution of buying power coupled with an oversufficient speculation in production.

Soon thereafter on the basis of such declarations, I became convinced that the best chance for a solution of America's difficulties was through the election of Franklin D. Roosevelt as President.

# CHAPTER XXXII

## F. R. B. C.
### (For Roosevelt Before Chicago)

THERE was an unsettled matter in Louisiana requiring my attention before I could go to the national convention in Chicago. It was to require certain interests to more fairly pay what was necessary to support the schools and colleges of the state. It rankled many of us that our effort to place a tax of 5c per barrel on the business of refining oil had resulted in my near impeachment in 1929. The impeachment assault was at least successful in preventing such taxes on their business. The time for suspension of hostilities had expired. The feelings we had smothered in the meantime had been somewhat lightened by winning the suits for a severance tax on oil before going to Chicago. On Governor Allen's call I returned to the 1932 regular session of the Louisiana legislature. I drafted three laws: one imposing a tax on insurance premiums collected in the state, another imposing a tax on the electric power interests not to be passed on to the people, and a third bill to place a franchise tax on all corporations. We gave notice to the oil trust that if they lent any support to oppose these bills we would add to them the 1929 bill to place a tax on their business of refining oil. The oil companies privately agreed that our proposals were just. The power companies announced they would not oppose us. Chambers of commerce,

299

newspapers, so-called tax leagues, etc., appeared to make a fight but the stimulus and sinews for their fights against us were not present when the big interests folded up. Our bills passed almost unanimously. We calculated we have secured revenues from them far more than the tax on refining oil would have yielded.

During the time that I was practically ready to declare as a Roosevelt supporter, a group of the generally recognized leaders of the Democratic Party met in Washington. They agreed on behalf of the prospective candidates, Roosevelt, Smith and the rest, that Senator Alben W. Barkley of Kentucky, a Roosevelt supporter, should be the temporary chairman, but that Jouett Shouse, aligned with the anti-Roosevelt forces, should be the permanent chairman of the Chicago Convention. It was alleged and stated in the newspapers that Mr. Roosevelt's leaders and Mr. Roosevelt himself had sanctioned that agreement.

I no sooner read this statement than I knew that it was tantamount to the Roosevelt forces trading the presidential nomination to anybody except Roosevelt.

It was patently necessary that someone remain outside the breastworks for a sufficient length of time to be able to say that they were not parties to such an understanding, and not bound by an agreement, whether the Roosevelt leaders had concurred in it or not.

Before saying a word, I had occasion to talk to Senator John S. Cohen of Georgia. He sat beside me in the Senate.

"Huey," Senator Cohen said to me, "why, this

thing trades our man out of the nomination. You
know the fight that we are going to have there if we
ever get across. The most trivial of rulings from the
chair against us will blow us out of the water. The
chair will control the situation if it wants to. Politics
is politics."

"I have already taken that in view," I said. "Now,
your crowd from Georgia is instructed for Roosevelt.
You had better get to the Roosevelt forces as soon as
you can to start a counter-action."

I learned later that Senator Cohen saw Governor
Roosevelt early in the game, and that several others
prominent in Roosevelt's support began to advise
both Governor Roosevelt and his leaders of the illegal-
ity of, and against allowing, the Shouse deal to stand.

Those standing with me at that time, enrolled under
no banner whatever, could in the very best of faith
decline to be bound by any such agreement, or to
allow others to be bound by it. It later fell to my lot
to write a letter rejecting the matter.[62]

On my way from New Orleans to Washington one
night I met Clark Howell of the Atlanta Constitution on the train. I gave him to understand that I was
inclined to Roosevelt. Soon thereafter I received a
letter from Governor Roosevelt telling me that Mr.
Howell had informed him of what I had said. He
paid me a few compliments and closed by saying:

"You and I are alike for the rights in behalf of the
common man of this country."

I was more than ready to join him.

[62] Proceedings of Democratic National Convention, 1932,
pages 516-517.

Soon, however, the election occurred in Massachusetts. It was overwhelmingly against the Roosevelt cause. It marked the possible beginning of a slackening of the Roosevelt movement. My friend Al Smith had issued his statement saying that a chunk had been put under the old Roosevelt band wagon, and that things from then on would take a different course.

Senator Norris had argued with me in favor of Roosevelt for some months. I immediately went to his office. We discussed the situation.

"Senator," I said, "I have been ready to declare publicly for Roosevelt. I have wanted to do it when I thought it would do the most good. He has had a setback in Massachusetts that his opposition is going to play up to the utmost."

"I think that your coming out for him now might be the best time," Senator Norris answered.

"I have a further suggestion to make to you, Senator," I said. "While you are a Republican, if I can say that if Roosevelt is nominated you are going to support him against Hoover, it will carry much more weight than my announcement. We should lead out everything we can for him right now."

The Senator questioned me a little further as to what the best method would be to make such an announcement. I told him that Clark Howell in Atlanta had spoken to me about the Roosevelt matter on the train; that he would be very glad to give any publicity he could to help Roosevelt.

"What I want to do, Senator," I said, "is to get off the train at Atlanta and hand Howell a statement declaring that Louisiana will vote for Roosevelt and that you are going to support Roosevelt as against Hoover, and that I am making such a statement after conferring with you. Senator Cohen has the other paper in Atlanta and he is also for Roosevelt," I continued, "and we will get the best publicity from that source."

The Senator was in agreement that such would be the best thing to do.

I telephoned to Mr. Howell in Atlanta, asking him to meet me on the train passing through that city on its way to New Orleans. He did. I gave him a statement I had prepared.

Senator Norris, when questioned in Washington, confirmed my statement that he would support Roosevelt as against Hoover.

My friend Jim Farley rang me from New York, asking for some help in lining up delegations. I immediately set to work in other States. Farley had telephoned me particularly about the State of Mississippi, and I had asked that he trust me to look into that matter. I did what I could in other southern States, particularly Arkansas.

When I was invited to Oklahoma to deliver a speech before the Young Men's Democratic Club of that State, I accepted. It was my hope that while there I could so arrange matters that when Alfalfa Bill Murray withdrew, the delegation of that State could be put in line for Roosevelt.

# CHAPTER XXXIII

## BEFORE AND BEHIND THE SCENES AT THE CHICAGO CONVENTION

AT the request of Mr. Farley, Mr. Roosevelt's manager, I reached Chicago some few days ahead of the scheduled opening date of the convention, which we considered necessary; first, because a contest was to be filed against several delegations, including my own, and second, to continue efforts to secure support from delegates of other States.

News soon developed that the opposition to Roosevent would undertake to sponsor as many "favorite son" candidates as possible until Roosevelt's strength had worn away. To my surprise, I immediately heard that efforts would be made to sponsor favorite son candidates both from Arkansas and from Mississippi. I devoted my first work to countering that effort.

Early one morning I undertook to talk to Bill Murray, of Oklahoma. I went to his bedroom just at daylight, and knocked on the door. He opened it.

"You're the farmers' candidate, aren't you?" I said. "Most farmers are up before this time of day."

Alfalfa Bill was very gracious. He naturally assumed that I had eaten breakfast before coming to visit him. Presently he telephoned for some breakfast for himself.

While we talked at length, he dwelt upon the virtue in the possible candidacies of everybody except

Roosevelt and himself, even to suggesting me as a candidate. He understood the favorite son game.

I soon saw that I was fencing with a past master in politics. Had I listened to him very long he would have been at work to make a favorite son candidate out of me. I was then moving Heaven and earth to keep down other favorite son candidates. My deflection or that of anyone else along that line might have meant a spread to others at once. Favorite son moves were the most dangerous things we had to fight.

Soon the breakfast came; but while my friend Bill Murray was undertaking to shave, absent-minded as I sometimes am, I ate some of the breakfast and left.

Afterward when I realized what I had done, I concluded, on further reflection, that Alfalfa Bill was properly punished and had justified my action when he undertook to exuberate me.

Fencing against Bill Murray was time lost.

I mingled with several other delegations and delegates until and after the convention was under way.

In the early hours of the Democratic Convention at Chicago a tall, middle-aged gentleman approached me.

"Do you know who I am?" he asked.

"No, but I won't be surprised if you don't know whom I am," I replied.

"Well, I am William Jennings Bryan, Jr."

"Well, if you knew me, I believe you'd say that I ought to know you."

He gave me a gold fountain pen which had been presented to his father by the school children of Mexico.

A deadlock had developed at Madison Square Garden in 1924, preventing the nomination of William Gibbs McAdoo. The rules which have governed in every Democratic convention are that for one to be nominated he must hold two-thirds of the votes of the delegates to that convention.

Several of us had canvassed the situation. We saw considerable danger in the effort to secure two-thirds of the votes.

A contest was filed by the factions from Louisiana which had been defeated in the preceding eight or ten elections. These were viciously opposed to Roosevelt and included former Governors Sanders, Parker and Pleasant, with John P. Sullivan, E. R. Rightor and other New Orleans ex-politicians. They claimed that a rump convention in Shreveport had selected other delegates to oppose our regular delegation at Chicago. I had been given to understand, in advance, that a declaration in favor of Roosevelt would result in a contest against our delegation. As an attorney, aside from his general gambling businesses, Sullivan had represented concerns connected with the power combine. They were a prolific source for Roosevelt opposition.

The Louisiana delegation, of which I was a member, had been selected in a convention of the Democratic State Central Committee, composed of the members of that body, 104 in number, who had been elected directly by the people. The delegation of our opponents claimed an election through a self-asserted group, or rump convention, elected by nobody in particular.

The preliminary organization of the convention was in the hands of the Chairman of the Democratic National Committee, Hon. John J. Raskob, who, together with Mr. Jouett Shouse, were known leaders of the opposition to Roosevelt's nomination. The convention was to be a strictly Roosevelt and anti-Roosevelt affair.

Mr. Raskob appointed a sub-committee to pass on the contest of delegations from the various States. When those of us in the Roosevelt camp took one glance at it, we immediately saw there were about three members of that committee against Roosevelt's nomination to one in favor of it.

A meeting was therefore held in my room in the Congress Hotel, attended by the leaders of the regular delegations from Minnesota, Porto Rico and Louisiana. We concluded that a preliminary disadvantage might result from presenting our claims to the sub-committee as selected by Mr. Raskob. Thereupon, acting for all of the delegations, with the Roosevelt management co-operating, I directed the following letter:

Chicago, Ill., June 22, 1932.

Honorable John J. Raskob, Chairman,
National Democratic Committee;
Honorable Jouett Shouse, Working Chairman,
National Democratic Committee.
Gentlemen:

I find it proper that I should address this communication to inform you that as National Committeeman for the State of Louisiana and as delegate duly elected to the National Democratic Convention I cannot recognize or be governed by two unprecedented and unauthorized arrangements which I understand you to have made or participated in the making. They are as follows:

1. There never has been a Permanent Chairman selected for the National Democratic Convention except by the convention. The so-called arrangements for the appointment of temporary officers have never applied to the selection of the Permanent Chairman.

From the public press I understand that some few members of the Democratic National Committee, after having agreed to recommend a Temporary Chairman, went so far as also to attempt to recommend a Permanent Chairman to the convention. It does not make any difference what candidate or candidates approved of the so-called process of electing a Permanent Chairman; it is unprecedented, and I must assume that all persons giving such understanding their hasty approval did so without due consideration, and upon proper reflection they are bound to recognize these facts.

2. I understand that you have assumed, even without agreement, to appoint a sub-committee of the Democratic National Committee to review and pass upon contests of delegations and delegates. There has been no resolution passed by the National Democratic Committee, so far as I know, that allows anyone to select any sub-committee for this purpose. There was a Committee on Arrangements appointed, naturally, to hire halls, install fans, print platforms and hire bands, and I un-

derstand that even in those acts there has to be ratification by the entire committee; but certainly the matter of arrangements does not include your having the right to include a committee to pass upon credentials, which is, in effect, what you have undertaken to do, and you have purported to appoint this sub-committee to conduct hearings before such appointments and selections can be confirmed by the Democratic National Committee.

We have been advised by several members of the National Democratic Committee that they consider this action is, on your part, wholly unwarranted, and we feel we would give cause for offense should we recognize any such unprecedented procedure.

So far as the State of Louisiana is concerned (and I believe the duly elected delegates of Minnesota and Porto Rico will agree), we will present whatever case we may find necessary in our behalf before the Democratic National Committee as a whole, or to such other agency as may be authoritatively designated by or through that committee, and to none other.

Please acknowledge receipt of this communication to me in Rooms J-10 and 12, Congress Hotel.

Very truly yours,

(Signed) HUEY P. LONG.

In this letter we concur.

(Signed) JOSEPH WOLF,
Democratic Committeeman of Minnesota.
(Signed) JEAN SPRINGSTEAD WHITTEMORE,
Democratic Committeewoman for Porto Rico.

On the same day Mr. Raskob and Mr. Shouse replied to my letter as follows:

Chicago, June 22, 1932.

Dear Senator Long:

In reply to your letter of even date, perhaps you are laboring under one or two misapprehensions. To clear your mind, let me state the following facts:

1. It is within the power of the National Committee to make any recommendations it chooses to the National Convention. These, of course, are mere recommendations and are in no way binding, because the convention always handles its own business in such matters as it deems best.

2. The National Committee, at a meeting held in New York July 11, 1928, passed the following resolution:

"Be it

"RESOLVED, that the Chairman of the National Committee be and is hereby empowered to create an Executive Committee and such other committees as he may deem necessary to expedite the work of this committee, the members of which may or may not be members of the National Committee; and to create such other positions and appoint such persons as he may deem necessary or desirable to the conduct of the affairs of the committee."

Under the terms of that resolution I appointed a sub-committee of the National Committee to hear all contests. You will understand that the work of this sub-committee is intended merely to expedite the work of the National Committee itself. Its report is made to the National Committee, is in no way binding, and can be rejected or adopted by that committee when read.

You are hereby advised that a meeting of the

sub-committee, which has been properly appointed in line with the above-mentioned resolution and also in line with precedent established by previous Chairmen, will meet on the Mezzanine Floor of the Congress Hotel tomorrow, June 23, at ten o'clock, and all parties interested in contests should be present at that time.

Notice of this meeting was sent last week to interested parties. I am sending a copy of this letter to Joseph Wolf, National Committeeman from Minnesota, and to Mrs. Jean Springstead Whittemore, National Committeewoman for Porto Rico, as they affixed their signatures concurring with the views as outlined in your letter of this date above-mentioned.

Very truly yours,
JOHN J. RASKOB, Chairman,
Democratic National Committee.
JOUETT SHOUSE, Chairman,
Democratic National Executive Committee.

The Roosevelt forces stuck by our letter and declined to make any appearance before the sub-committee appointed by Messrs. Raskob and Shouse. As a result, that body took but very little action. What it did take was rejected at the first session of the Democratic National Committee, which thereupon proceeded to hear arguments on the contest from Minnesota, Louisiana and Porto Rico in the order named, after which all the regularly chosen delegations, including our own, were temporarily seated.

An appeal was taken to the Credentials Committee. Before that body, all of the regularly chosen delegates were again ordered seated.

Appeals were taken to the floor of the convention.

The Democratic National Convention assembled in its first formal session in the Chicago Coliseum on the 27th day of June, 1932. The first controversy was the dispute between contesting delegations. Contests were heard alphabetically, beginning with Louisiana. This was the original test of strength of the Roosevelt forces in that convention.

We knew an effort would be made on the first contest, regardless of what it might be, to break through our lineup; furthermore, in the seating of delegates, the Roosevelt forces did not dare to sacrifice a vote, for the selection of a permanent chairman bade fair to be a nip and tuck contest due to the early commitments certain of our forces had made.

The opposition to the seating of our delegation was most ably presented by two distinguished anti-Roosevelt Democrats from Illinois and Iowa. Our floor leader, Arthur Mullen, and myself replied for the Roosevelt forces.

The final vote stood 638-¾ to 514-¼ and our delegation was seated.

It was the initial victory for the Roosevelt forces at the National Convention in Chicago.

It was a queer turn when, after Mr. Roosevelt's election, my failure to support certain legislation including that to reduce the compensation allowed to disabled veterans of our wars, brought the newspaper comment that the same persons who had appeared at Chicago to fight us, including the gambler and power trust lawyer Sullivan, were to be recognized for patronage in Louisiana.

**Surrounded by Newspaper Men upon Arriving at Chicago for National Convention—1932.**

Initial Fight for Roosevelt Delegations, Chicago Convention, 1932.

# CHAPTER XXXIV

## EVERY MAN A KING!

I T would serve no cause to the reader were I to
undertake to relate such activities as I have pursued in the United States Senate, my further par-
ticipation in the convention at Chicago, or the campaign speaking tour I made for the Democratic
National Ticket headed by Mr. Roosevelt. All are
of no consequence.

### THE CARAWAY AND OVERTON CAMPAIGNS

When the United States Senate had recessed, fol-
lowing the Chicago convention, I campaigned in the
State of Arkansas for the election of Mrs. Hattie W.
Caraway to the United States Senate.

Mrs. Caraway and I campaigned together for
exactly seven days. She could never forget nor cease
to laugh over the plans we made for caring for
obstreperous infants in the audience so that their
mothers might listen to the speeches without the
crowds being disturbed.

I remember when I saw her notice one of our cam-
paigners take charge of the first baby. The child began fretting and then began to cry. One of the young
men accompanying us immediately gave it a drink
of water. The child quieted for a bit, and resumed a
whimper, whereupon the same campaign worker
handed the baby an all-day sucker, which it immediately grasped and soon fell asleep.

313

Mrs. Caraway did not understand that it was a matter of design until it had been repeated several times.

I left Mrs. Caraway at Jonesboro, Arkansas, on Monday evening, taking a train at Memphis at midnight for my home in New Orleans. The election occurred the next day. Over the radio early in the next night I learned that she had received more votes than the combined vote of all of her opponents.

Returning to Louisiana I had but a few days in which to engage in the campaign of my friend, John H. Overton, who was a candidate for the United States Senate against Senator Broussard. We made a hasty tour of the State. He was elected, carrying nearly every parish in the State, by the largest vote that was ever given to any candidate for that office in Louisiana.

"John," I said to him in the course of the campaign, "you have always been very kind to me. You have let me speak in your meetings every time you have run for the Senate, this time and last time."

He had run in 1918 and was defeated, when I was elected to the Railroad Commission.

### ROOSEVELT'S PRONOUNCEMENT AGAINST SWOLLEN FORTUNES—HOOVER'S "CONVERSION"

My hopes for the cause of a distressed humanity rose to great heights through the utterances of our Democratic candidate, Mr. Roosevelt, who said:

> Just as freedom to farm has ceased, so also the opportunity in business has narrowed. It still is true that men can start small enterprises, trust-

ing to native shrewdness and ability to keep
abreast of competitors; but area after area has
been preempted altogether by the great corporations, and even in the fields which still have no
great concerns the small man starts under a handi-
cap.

The unfeeling statistics of the past three dec-
ades show that the independent business man is
running a losing race. Perhaps he is forced to the
wall; perhaps he cannot command credit; perhaps
he is "squeezed out," in Mr. Wilson's words, by
highly organized corporate competitors, as your
corner grocery man can tell you.

Recently a careful study was made of the concentration of business in the United States.

It showed that our economic life was dominated
by some six hundred and odd corporations, who
controlled two-thirds of American industry. Ten
million small business men divided the other third.

More striking still, it appeared that, if the
process of concentration goes on at the same rate,
at the end of another century we shall have all
American industry controlled by a dozen corporations and run by perhaps a hundred men.

Put plainly, we are steering a steady course
toward economic oligarchy, if we are not there
already.

I, too, believe in individualism; but I mean it
in everything that the word implies. I believe that
our industrial and economic system is made for individual men and women; and not individual men
and women for the benefit of the system. I believe that the individual should have full liberty
of action to make the most of himself; but I do

not believe that in the name of that sacred word
a few powerful interests should be permitted to
make industrial cannon fodder of the lives of half
of the population of the United States.

President Hoover, in his Madison Square Garden
address, in which he referred to me and others in no
complimentary manner, felt obliged to show a "conversion" or "repentance" with the following utter-
ance:

> . . . My conception of America is for a land
> where wealth is not concentrated in the hands of
> a few, but diffused among the lives of all.

The election of Roosevelt under such commitments,
reinforced by Mr. Hoover's Madison Square Garden
"deathbed repentance," seemed to mean that where
there was an abundance of food, all the people of the
land would be fed; that where there was an excess of
clothes, all of the people of the land would be clad;
that in the land of too many houses, none would be
without shelter above their heads; that all would be
possessed with comforts for the day time and the
night time, so long as this was a land of plenty.

Such were my hopes—my dreams—some say my
imaginations, and others claim, my hallucinations;
but none the less, before and after the nomination of
our candidate, before and after his election, I drank
of the fountain of a new life as I saw, heard and read
of his expounding the principles which had guided
my activities throughout my public career.

To my heart, such pronouncements were relighting
the lamp of "America's dream."

When Franklin Roosevelt became President, I reintroduced in the first session of Congress which he convoked my proposition to limit the size of fortunes and to spread the wealth among all the people.

A vote on my proposal was: Yeas 14, Nays 50.

The pairs announced would have given my proposition the votes of almost twenty senators. Although defeated, it had grown to recognizable proportions at last. It now awaits the consideration to be given it in the future by the minds of others.

When I began to suggest to the United States Senate that there should be a limitation to the swollen fortunes of the country so that the wealth of the land might be more equitably distributed among all the people, I anticipated personal hostility. I did not, however, think that any of the swollen fortune-holding element would undertake to harm or hamper the State of Louisiana by reason of anything I might advocate in the United States Senate.

Publicity began to spread, however, indicating a motive not only to cripple my political activities, but to afflict the State of Louisiana as much as possible. Finally a news report came from New York which said:

NO MORE LOANS TO LOUISIANA IS WALL STREET
ATTITUDE

Wall Street today showed signs of growing weary of furnishing ammunition for Huey Long's war chest.

Unwittingly, perhaps, New York banks have furnished the State of Louisiana with about fifty

million dollars since the "Kingfish" took hold down
there. . . .

This contribution was in the form of bond issues
floated here and with the proceeds Long managed
to construct one of the best highway systems in the
country. . . .

In denouncing Wall Street, Huey is merely kill-
ing the goose that laid the golden egg, for each
tirade against the moneyed interests serves only to
dull the rich investor's interest in Louisiana's
bonds. . . .

Wall Street banking houses previously identi-
fied with Louisiana financing were definitely "not
interested" in the five million dollar issue scheduled
for today.—New York dispatch in Kansas City
Star, January 17, 1933.

At a later date I began to read further dispatches;
one read in part:

INQUIRY IS UNDER WAY TO "GET" HUEY LONG

Determined Effort Being Made Against "Kingfish."

A determined effort is being made to "get"
Senator Huey Long.

Whether the movement, which bears many ear-
marks of political persecution, is inspired by some
of the powerful interests he has offended since he
came to the Senate, or by his old enemies in Louisiana, or by an administration at Washington which
regards him as an outstanding Democrat, and
therefore fair game, is unimportant at this junc-
ture. . . . Secret service agents are investigating
Senator Long's personal income tax over a period
of several years; they are trying to find irregu-

larities in a loan which he obtained from the Reconstruction Finance Corporation. . . . No stone
is being left unturned. . . . Long's bank accounts
everywhere are being scrutinized. When he made
a trip to New Orleans during the Christmas holidays he was shadowed by government agents, his
telephone tapped and every movement watched.—
Commercial Appeal (Memphis, Tenn.) January
23, 1933.

I pursued diligently such things as were consistent
with my ideas of popular government.

Several national magazines directly or indirectly
affiliated with the house of J. P. Morgan & Company,
particularly Collier's Weekly, had seen fit to publish articles at least to some extent favorable to me;
but when calumny had reached its final height
through the columns of a number of publications, the
same Collier's Weekly, through the same writer, Mr.
Walter Davenport, rewrote my career and "makeup"
in a form to attribute to me all of the vices and crime
in the catalog of human sins.

A comparison of these two articles was prepared
and sent to me by some anonymous authors. It is as
follows:

PUTTING THE HOOK IN THE KINGFISH—WHAT COL-
LIER'S HAD TO SAY BEFORE AND AFTER HUEY PUT THE
HOOK IN THE HOUSE OF MORGAN—LET THERE BE
LIGHT

(From Colliers, December 1930)
(By Walter Davenport)

. . . filled with the same unconquerable confidence, cleaving to the same directness of purpose and speech, overflowing with an energy which flattens weaker beholders, ruthless as a machine gun, a political bob, has overcome enough obstacles and achieved successes enough to make up two or three robust careers.

I have met many men, many politicians, but I have never met one so quick to turn an enemy's thrust against the attacker or to convert a mean situation into a personal triumph.

(Anent the problem of free textbooks for the children of Louisiana:)

Huey met the situation with characteristic simplicity. Huey is one of the earth's perpetual children, anyway. All he did was to draw up a bill which provided that every child in Louisiana should be given free schoolbooks. That's all —schoolbooks. It mattered

(Collier's, June 1933)
(By Walter Davenport)

To see him for the first time is something of a shock. You would expect a picture of power, the intensity of a zealot, the burning eye of fanaticism, the uncompromising jaw of the crushing autocrat, the lean asceticism of a prophet, the austerity of a despot. But nothing like this. He's pudgy. His cheeks are blotched, flabby. His uncertain nose is red, betokening either bad circulation or entirely too much. His face is weak, willful, and there is no discipline in it. But his eyes— soft, protruding robin's eggs—are nevertheless bold. Hit-and-run eyes that roll upward as he talks.

And then out of the car steps Huey—the Honorable HUEY P. LONG, general manager and business agent of the State of Louisiana, United States Senator, protector of the poor, Hotcha Huey (Tell 'em nothing and make 'em

not where that child went
to school, just so long as it
was enrolled in a school.
Free schoolbooks—and God
love 'em.

His opponents, chagrined
that so old a problem should
be solved by this irrelevant
upstart, appealed to the
courts. . . . And Huey
himself, admittedly one of
the best lawyers in the
South, went along arguing
to victory after victory until it appeared in the Supreme Court of the United
States. There Huey de-
fended his naive legislation
with such conviction and
enthusiasm that it was not
only declared wholly constitutional but Huey was
commended by Mr. Justice
Brandeis.

Even if he weren't a
good lawyer, he'd be a
prominent one because of
his love for a fight. . . .
The truth is that the Long
mind is usually five or six
laps ahead of any political
rival's.

(Anent the attempted
impeachment of Huey:)
Presently they dropped
the whole impeachment, ad-
mitting thereby that Huey
was boss. Not only that,
they adopted his magnifi-
cent road program. . . .
His plan is to lay 3,000

like it), Get-'em-while-
they're hot Huey, Let's go-
LONG, the hardest-work-
ing demagogue in America.

Among the first things
they tell you about Huey
in Louisiana is that he
lacks physical courage,
that he sleeps behind a machine gun, and that his
slumbers are guarded by
such staunch lads as Joe
Messina, Wheaton Stillson,
Two-Gun Thompson, and
Squinch, or Squinch-Eye
McGee. There's a boy for
you—Squinch. Listen, mis-
ter, don't lay no hand on
the Senator; just don't lay
no hand on no Senator,
pal, and you and me will
be okay.

There's no handshaking.
Not that Huey's above
handshaking, but some-
times, particularly these
days when hatreds have
boiled to the surface and
one's enemies are putting
everything they have into
one roundhouse wallop,
Huey is taking no chances.

In his suite at last, Huey
makes ready for the affairs
of State. It's quite warm,
so he sheds his coat and
vest, hurling them from
him. They are picked up
by retainers who either
stand there holding them
or hang them in the closet.

miles of concrete roads and 6,000 miles of gravel highways. Somebody discovered that this will cost $99,000,-000. . . . Not that Huey pauses. He simply refers you to his new tax on gasoline (he raised it from 2 cents a gallon to 4) and says the solution lies there, because with better roads there will be additional motorists and with more cars to consume gasoline the aggregate taxes will . . .

There was nothing in Huey's campaign to indicate he was interested in national affairs. Hardly once did he mention a national issue. He won on his good-roads issue and his tremendous appeal for the rural vote. To compensate for the enmity of all the daily papers in the State he started a newspaper of his own—a weekly—the Louisiana Progress. In no time it achieved a circulation of 50,000 and the right to its claim to being the livest and frankest journal in the State.

──────────

ure of speech, although where virtually everything worth having belongs to Mr. Long, why quibble about the ownership of a hat?

And while Huey is making himself comfortable on the bed, pillows at his back and his hands hooked behind his head, let's look over the assemblage. We'll have time because Huey is delivering himself of a few snappy commands and a brisk summary of the situation in general. Too bad we can't quote him; but, except when delivering himself for the papers, Huey isn't very quotable. To try it on paper is to lose all the salty flavor of the man's tongue.

Presently, when he needs him, Huey will telephone Baton Rouge, and Gov. Oscar K. (Okay) Allen will come galloping in with his hat in hand. "Hi-yah, Allen, where the hell have you been?"

In Louisiana, primary elections are actually pulled out of a hat. And statesmen, too. Anybody's hat will do; the make, shape, style, and quality have nothing whatever to do with the result. Your hat will serve, or mine would, were we on the scene at the time and in line for such honors. Of course, the growing but still disorganized minority in New Orleans will have it that it is Huey's hat, but that is only a fig-

One thing before Huey paid his respects to the House of Morgan; something else when Huey took up for the interests of the common people.

It's enough to make a polecat detour!

## THE COMMITTEE OF THE COMMON PEOPLE

On the 9th day of June, 1933, when the committee of the United States Senate was inquiring into the affairs of J. P. Morgan & Company, I appeared before that committee and asked that I might be permitted to propound a few questions to a leading partner of that concern, the Hon. Thomas W. Lamont.

The committee accorded me that privilege.

I asked Mr. Lamont whether or not he was a director of the concern publishing Collier's Weekly. He said that he was not.

Thereupon I asked him if he was affiliated with the concern that owned the corporation that did publish Collier's Weekly.

He answered that he was.

Further questions elicited from Mr. Lamont the information that the "dummy" concern publishing Collier's Weekly is owned by the Crowell Publishing Company, affiliated to the House of Morgan. It also owns the American Magazine, The Woman's Home Companion and the Country Home.

I then asked Mr. Lamont to explain if he could why this Morgan Publication printed one article praising and commending certain of my activities in public life, and later published another article condemning the same activities which they had previously praised and all by the same writer.

Mr. Lamont professed an ignorance and lack of understanding of the entire proposition. He admitted, however, that at the same time of this attack on me, the same magazine was publishing articles from his pen, undertaking to commend and to extol various transactions and personages of the House of Morgan.

When the program I proposed for a fair sharing of the wealth of the country among all the people had but three or four United States Senators to sponsor it, the criticisms directed against me were confused and sprinkled with a few compliments here and there for the constructive service I had rendered in Louisiana, and even with some laudatory references for what I was doing in Washington.[63]

But when it appeared that my proposals would attract such definite notice that some twenty United States Senators would declare for it in toto (backed by the utterances of both Roosevelt and Hoover in the last campaign), the publicity directed at me and everything I had ever done or tried to do took on organized form with definite purpose.

The interests have always had my Louisiana enemies to start with. The kind of veracity one might expect from such enemies as I had and now have, is demonstrated by a colloquy between the head of their organization, the Constitutional League, and myself, as reported in an organ for the League:

---

[63] Other notes contain proof of this statement.

(Taken from the Baton Rouge State Times, Nov. 15, 1929.)

At the end of the discussion, Governor Long invited Governor Parker to visit him at his office in the Whitney-Central Bank or at his bedroom in the Roosevelt with any alleged irregularities on which he had information.

"I promise you, governor," Governor Long said, "that I will either remove the person responsible or convince you that you are wrong."

"Do I understand you now, governor," Mr. Parker said, "to say that you will take immediate action on any charges I may file?"

"Yes, if I don't convince you that you are wrong."

"Very well," Governor Parker said, and waved a salute as he retired from the room.

But neither Mr. Parker nor the League, nor any of its members charged an irregularity, either to me or to the State Advisory Board (some of the members of which were members of the League of my enemies).

It was the same Parker, however, who years later headed petitions declaring fraud in the course of work.

I have tried hard to find a spark of honor in characters practicing such conduct.

Time and again have I called the attention of the people of Louisiana to the millions of dollars, funds of the State and funds contributed by the special privilege interests of Louisiana,—to pursue various investigations relative to all affairs connected with

my administration, and to the further fact that never
has one material iota of proof been submitted by evidence that would be competent in any court. I have
said to the people of Louisiana:

"Once on the farm we had to go a long ways from
the house we lived in to the field where we worked.
We had a little fice dog that always dragged along
with us. Just about the time that we got the mule
hitched up to the plow, sharpened the hoes and got
well under way, that little dog would begin to bark
out in the woods like he had treed something.

"So we would lay down the hoes and tie the mule
up to the rail fence and run over in the woods to find
the dog.

"When we would get there we would find him with
his shaggy nostrils buried in the hole of a tree yelping
for dear life. So we would send one of the boys up to
the house to get a saw and ax and when he came back
we would cut down the tree and saw off a cut and
split it open, then to find that there was not a single
thing in that tree.

"So we would go back to work, but about the time
we would get started the dog would begin yelping
three times as hard as he had before. Then we would
figure the dog had evidently missed the game the
first time but that it had slipped over to another tree.

"Out in the woods we would go again and cut down
some more trees and split them open, but never to find
any game.

"We kept up that practice until we had cut down
and split open about all of the trees there were in
those woods.

"We lost the crop, but we convinced the dog."

An article appearing in LABOR on June 27th, 1933, noted:

> The campaign to discredit, and if possible destroy, Senator Huey Long of Louisiana, is pressed with ferocity seldom equalled in our political history.
>
> Just who is doing the planning and paying has not come to the surface, but anyone familiar with the mysteries of propaganda knows there is a plethoric pocketbook and a directing brain some place in the background. . . .
>
> Senator Long fought vigorously and intelligently to set up the six hour day. . . . At a time when the railroad boys needed friends, he was 100% back of them. . . . He possesses one of the most remarkable minds in the Senate. He has detailed and accurate information on an immense number of subjects. . . . He never "picks" on the little fellow. . . . He fights as well when he is alone as when he has company. . . . He is entitled to a sympathetic hearing from everyone who believes that this government should be run in the interests of the many and not for the enrichment of the few.

To support the propaganda, irregularities in uncontested elections were colored and painted.

The State of Louisiana was pictured as heavily loaded with debt and groaning under a heavy increase in taxes, as a result of my administration.

The debts of cities, towns, villages and districts,

some created before I was born, were added, and then re-added to the State debts, many of which also were made before I was either born or in politics in Louisiana, to get a figure big enough to advertise as "What Huey Long has cost Louisiana."

All such notwithstanding that the State of Louisiana can be rated America's most modern State in improvements, that regardless of the national collapse it has discharged its obligations, including principal and interest, without default, holds down its tax rate and shows an administrative cost of government below that of any State in the Union.[64]

In the election over any office, even where there is a contest, an irregularity of a thousand or so votes in any state is nothing startling.

In Louisiana, a presidential election is a formality. There is no contest. Usually there are amendments to the State constitution and other proposals attached to the presidential ballot, most of the times a formality also.

On November 8, 1932, on the Roosevelt-Hoover ballot in Louisiana there were seventeen other propositions on which to be voted. To count and tabulate as many as six hundred of these long ballots in one precinct requires many hours and, where the election commissioners are inexperienced, they sometimes count through all the next day.

Some hatched up thing was needed as a basis to stir up some more publicity over Louisiana, and if it

---

[64] Report of Association of State Auditors, Comptrollers and Treasurers, 1932 Richmond Convention; page 21 reports Louisiana's percentage for administration at 1.2%, the nation's lowest.

Senator Huey P. Long.

could be over Louisiana, it was then simple to make it all over Huey P. Long.

Ha, a great thought! The long and complicated ballots of the uncontested election in November, 1932, would supply the sinews for muckraking.

Why not count the ballots of some election over an office where there was a contest? The Overton-Broussard primary election ballots were still sealed and untouched. Our enemies had urged fraud in that election. There was a contest in that race. Why not count them? Because such ballots were short, simple and easy to count; there was not a chance for much irregularity in them; election commissioners in a precinct of six hundred ballots could correctly count and tabulate them all within two hours.

And further, with the kind of publicity that is sent out when Huey P. Long is to be concerned, soon the newspapers are so confused that their stories read that the whole matter is over the senatorial election anyway.

So the drive went on to call the Grand Jury to ransack the ballots of the *uncontested* November election for fraud. Our enemies were supposed to have had grounds for belief that these ballots would not all show correct tabulations. Much of the commissioners' work had been entrusted to the unemployed, people needing that day's work, but who never expected they were going to have to work all night, too, to count the ballots. By the time the polls had closed at 7:00 P.M., Central Standard Time, returns of the presidential election were coming in over the radio. By 9:00 P.M., before the commissioners could have tabulated one-third the way on the uncontested ballot, the whole City of New Orleans was a fanfare. The first Democratic President in twelve years, the third since the Civil War, had been elected. No place forgets everything to turn out to celebrate and parade like New Orleans, the home of the Mardi Gras, where they quit all business for weeks during the Carnival; for years it was advertised, "The City that Care Forgot," until I changed the slogan to: "All Roads Lead to New Orleans."

"Don't you know," our enemies reasoned, "that all those commissioners didn't stick around to go through those ballots when nearly all ran the same anyway?"

Others were known to have said:

"They made as quick a job as they could in a couple of hours. They may have just averaged them like they ran the first hour."

In some precincts it developed that some of our enemies had actually said to commissioners engaged in tabulating ballots near midnight:

"What difference does it make? There's no contest. Do the best you can and call it a day."

The Court, however, impanelled a Grand Jury to go into the matter. Early in 1933 that body, after going into boxes and hearing witnesses, reported no charges against anyone.

In March of 1933, a new Grand Jury was selected. Again was the effort made to have that body go into the ballots of that uncontested election. It did. It reported "No True Bill," a Louisiana term meaning a Grand Jury exoneration, on every election commissioner.

Put the picture of a small bore politician, two columns wide, on page one of a newspaper, with a few complimentary headlines, and it takes most of them many days to come to earth. They have them all running for Governor, President or something. The members of the two grand juries, their faces, their sterling lives and careers, with photographs of their wives and children, were played up on page one of the newspapers, amidst the prophecies of how they would "save the country," but somehow did not respond. They declared the flare ridiculous.

How would these pent up publicity mills get going? They were ravenous.

A marriage had occurred! Judge Alex O'Donnell was an old time, good Irish and hardened ringster politician. He had lived a bachelor for many years. He had practically ceased to try cases in his court; he was in failing health and not given long to live.

Suddenly Alex married a society matron of wealth and standing, a big stockholder in the Times-Picayune. Alex's name and picture began to adorn the front page and society columns. The distinction was deserved and noticeable.

The last remaining streak of authority left to John P. Sullivan was the office force of the Criminal Sheriff. Sullivan's odium by reason of his varied career and gambling businesses, was such that he had been dismissed from all political caucuses. The asset of such job holders in the Sheriff's force could not compensate the loss inflicted upon any crowd having Sullivan with them.

Judge Alex O'Donnell's picture continued to

cover several columns on page one. Society notes fluttered over him. The publicity was dazzling.

He was asked by the newspaper interests to decline to honor the last grand jury's report. He responded. He even went to the grand jury to beg them not to file their report.[65] When this second grand jury reported anyway, he announced he would not accept it (something he couldn't help having done).

But Judge Alex, in charge of his court, allowed the Sullivan sheriff force to physically throw the grand jurors out of their own court quarters; [66] he allowed that crew to actually take into their physical possession the opened ballot boxes in the grand jury room, and to keep them five days and nights.

When some of those boxes finally came back from this force's control, out of 600 ballots in one of them, 215 were reported not voting, and 186 of the remainder were declared "spoiled ballots," a showing never equalled by any ballot box fixer since the days of Pharaoh.

On that basis, in the "recount," irregularities are reported and a difference of a few thousand or so, votes are reported changed, never enough to show anything approaching significance in results, but for the fanfare of renewed attack because I live in Louisiana and hold office there.

A Senatorial election investigation over the Overton-Broussard primary campaign was held in

----

[65] Petition of Grand Jury dated July 31, 1933, (Office of Secretary of State) signed by eleven jurors certifies this fact.

[66] Page 1 of Morning Tribune and Times-Picayune, July 6, 1933, headline: "Deputies eject Grand Jurors."

New Orleans for weeks. It was guided by the cele-
brated "General" Ansell, whose word that Grover
Cleveland Bergdoll wanted to go into the woods to
look for a pot of gold, resulted in Bergdoll's escape
to Germany. He caused my private and public career
to be explored from the cradle down, but never once
called for the ballots of the election or submitted one
line of competent proof, under any rule of evidence,
of any irregularity in the election. The ballots remain
sealed and not counted to this day.

If election commissioners were ever to be trained
to miscount ballots in New Orleans, I would not have
been one to have shown them anything. They came
ahead of my time.

In 1924 I led Governor Fuqua by nearly 14,000
votes until I reached New Orleans, where he overcame my lead and had over 7,000 to spare.[67]

In 1929 I had several thousand more than the combined votes of Governor Simpson and Congressman
Wilson until New Orleans came up with Wilson leading me there by 20,425 and Simpson leading me there
by 4,505.

For the United States Senate in 1930 New Orleans
showed a majority against me for Senator Ransdell
of 4,600 votes, which the country overcame, with
38,000 to spare.

Can liars never be persuaded to desist from ascrib-

---

[67] The vote in the Governor's race for 1924 outside of New
Orleans was Long 61,798; Fuqua 48,188; Bouanchaud 60,862.
The vote in New Orleans was Long 12,187; Fuqua 33,194;
Bouanchaud 23,300 (Reports of Secretary of State).

ing my success in politics to a machine in New Orleans?

Louisiana can stand the attack; except for being a part of the United States, it would never have known a depression.

# CHAPTER XXXV

AMONG the clap trap is certain propaganda spread through a use of names of the wives or other women relatives of my enemies. This seemed to find its culmination in a petition filed with the Vice-President. This feature of the enemy is advertised as an attack "by the women of Louisiana."

Who are these women?

Among them and most to the forefront are: Mrs. John M. Parker, her daughter and daughters-in-law; the womenfolk of others defeated by me in politics and of those dismissed from State service. For a fair cross-section of this so-called "women's uprising," these names, most often paraded and published are noticeable:—(1) Hilda Phelps Hammond, the sister of the railroad and power trust lawyer and Times-Picayune dictator, Esmond Phelps, the wife of Arthur Hammond, who was found on two State payrolls and "fired" from both; (2) Gladys Brezeale, of the Rump delegation which were denied seats at the Chicago Convention; (3) Mrs. Charles Dunbar, wife of the law partner of Esmond Phelps; (4) Mrs. Joseph Montgomery, wife of the young man taken into the Zemurray organization (so mentioned in the circular in the Senatorial Campaign) and Mrs. Roger T. Stone, daughter of Sam Zemurray.[68]

---

[68] Zemurray is the head of the United Fruit Company and was formerly connected with the revolutions of Central America. He

But the drive to stop the wealth of this land from being concentrated into the hands of a few men has begun to attract enough notice and support to make certain that the calumny directed at us cannot obscure the issue.[69] All recent pronouncements from the

was the financial backer of the campaign against Huey P. Long and mentioned in circular issued.

[69] Washington News, August 17, 1933, contains United Press article,

"DARROW SAYS CRIME CAN BE TRACED TO CAPITALISTIC CONTROL.

"Famous Lawyer Says More Equitable Division of Wealth is Solution; Poor Man Suffers.

"CHICAGO—Capitalists indirectly plant the seed for crime and to crush the criminal society must check the big money interests, Clarence Darrow, internationally famous lawyer and humanitarian, declared today.

"A more equitable division of wealth is the real remedy for crime, Darrow said.

"Poor Man Suffers.

" 'Every time a crime campaign is made,' Darrow said, 'the little fellow, the poor man, suffers the most. He is put away for life or given the maximum of the law, while sight is lost of the big money interests which are responsible, after all, for the existence of crime.

" 'Look into our prisons and you will see them there. Do you think if there were an even division of wealth that crime would exist?'

" 'Kidnapping is the newest way for making money,' Darrow said. 'But those criminals are pikers compared with the big fellow who manipulates against the masses.

"Publicity Forgotten

" 'The capitalistic practice of collecting wealth for the few while the poor man has not a chance to make a living is responsible. The depression of the past three years has been hard on the little fellow.

" 'We had a brief investigation of capitalistic practices recently but the publicity given it by the newspapers has been forgotten. Other crime gets daily attention.' "

authorities at Washington admit necessity to spread the wealth among the masses.

---

The Baltimore Sun, June 4, 1933, contains Associated Press article,

"WEALTH-CONTROL MEASURES STUDIED.

"Senate Group Ponders Restrictive Steps as Outgrowth of Morgan Probe.

"NO PROPOSAL ADVANCED.

"Question of How Far It Is Wise to Let One Concern Rule Industry Is Raised.

"WASHINGTON, June 3—Legislation to prevent the concentration into a few hands of control of industry and finance is being studied seriously by members of the Senate Banking Committee as a result of the disclosures in the investigation of J. P. Morgan & Co."

# CHAPTER XXXVI

## THE MADDENED FORTUNE HOLDERS AND THEIR INFURIATED PUBLIC PRESS!

THE increasing fury with which I have been, and am to be, assailed by reason of the fight and growth of support for limiting the size of fortunes can only be explained by the madness which human nature attaches to the holders of accumulated wealth.[70]

What I have proposed is:—

### THE LONG PLAN

1. A capital levy tax on the property owned by any one person of 1% of all over $1,000,000; 2% of all over $2,000,000 etc., until, when it reaches fortunes of over $100,000,000, the government takes all above that figure; which means a limit on the size

---

[70] "By these examples any one may learn how many and how great instances of wickedness men will venture upon for the sake of getting money and authority, and that they may not fail of either of them; for as when they are desirous of obtaining the same, they acquire them by ten thousand evil practices; so when they are afraid of losing them, they get them confirmed to them by practices much worse than the former, as if (no) other calamity so terrible could befall them as the failure of acquiring so exalted an authority; and when they have acquired it, and by long custom found the sweetness of it, the losing it again; and since this last would be the heaviest of all afflictions, they all of them contrive and venture upon the most difficult actions, out of the fear of losing the same."—Josephus, Book VII, Chapter I, Verse 5.

of any one man's fortune to something like $50,-000,000—the balance to go to the government to spread out in its work among all the people.

2. An inheritance tax which does not allow any one person to receive more than $5,000,000 in a lifetime without working for it, all over that amount to go to the government to be spread among the people for its work.

3. An income tax which does not allow any one man to make more than $1,000,000 in one year, exclusive of taxes, the balance to go to the United States for general work among the people.

The foregoing program means all taxes paid by the fortune holders at the top and none by the people at the bottom; the spreading of wealth among all the people and the breaking up of a system of Lords and Slaves in our economic life. It allows the millionaires to have, however, more than they can use for any luxury they can enjoy on earth. But, with such limits, all else can survive.

That the public press should regard my plan and effort as a calamity and me as a menace is no more than should be expected, gauged in the light of past events. According to Ridpath, the eminent historian:

> "The ruling classes always possess the means of information and the processes by which it is distributed. The newspaper of modern times belongs to the upper man. The under man has no voice; or if, having a voice, he cries out, his cry is lost like a shout in the desert. Capital, in the places of power, seizes upon the organs of public utterance, and howls the humble down the wind.

Lying and misrepresentation are the natural weapons of those who maintain an existing vice and gather the usufruct of crime."
—Ridpath's History of the World,
Page 410.

In 1932, the vote for my resolution showed possibly a half dozen other Senators back of it. It grew in the last Congress to nearly twenty Senators. Such growth through one other year will mean the success of a venture, the completion of everything I have undertaken,—the time when I can and will retire from the stress and fury of my public life, maybe as my forties begin,—a contemplation so serene as to appear impossible.

That day will reflect credit on the States whose Senators took the early lead to spread the wealth of the land among all the people.

Then no tear dimmed eyes of a small child will be lifted into the saddened face of a father or mother unable to give it the necessities required by its soul and body for life; then the powerful will be rebuked in the sight of man for holding that which they cannot consume, but which is craved to sustain humanity; the food of the land will feed, the raiment clothe, and the houses shelter all the people; the powerful will be elated by the well being of all, rather than through their greed.

Then, those of us who have pursued that phantom of Jefferson, Jackson, Webster, Theodore Roosevelt and Bryan may hear wafted from their lips in Valhalla:

EVERY MAN A KING

# INCIDENTAL PUBLICITY

*American Progress Bulletin No. 1*

## J. P. MORGAN & COMPANY POINTS WAY FOR CAPONE'S RELEASE

*Can receive original gold medal and fund collected for "unknown hero" at Collier's office owned by Morgan & Company.*

### AN OPEN LETTER

Alphonse Capone,
    United States Penitentiary,
    Atlanta, Georgia.
Dear Sir:—

The newspapers report efforts to secure your release from the penitentiary. A way is open for you to do it. Somebody (it makes no difference how many) made an assault on United States Senator Huey P. Long and then made a clear get away, while he was attending the Charity Benefit at Long Island on Saturday, August 26th.

Glorious worship has been printed for several days for whoever was guilty of this crime. No one has yet found the criminals to get any version from them, but, just the same, certain newspapers and magazines have given various "what might have been" reasons for the assault, and while each "reason or excuse" contradicts all the other "reasons and excuses," none the less these papers declare that the assault should be highly extolled and commended.

Now the House of Morgan editors, particularly one Owen P. White, of Collier's Weekly, owned by Morgan & Co., are receiving contributions to give to the unknown criminals, or to put it their way, "only one criminal, but a very strong man capable of doing the job alone."

The fact that Collier's magazine is owned by Morgan & Co. was admitted by Mr. Thomas W. Lamont, a Morgan partner in answer to questions propounded by Senator Huey P. Long before a U. S. Senate Committee.

The New York Evening Post, owned by the House of Morgan but later turned into the name of one on its preferred list, says: "Money and messages rolled in to Mr. White at his office at Collier's Magazine."

This Morgan editor, Owen P. White, has announced that large sums are coming in cash currency so that the Morgan firm can swell it to immense proportions, thus concealing that they are really just putting up the money. (You know, Al, while they've got you in the penitentiary for not reporting all your income tax, J. P. Morgan and all his partners paid none at all and the government ordered them "not investigated because anything they returned was O. K.")

So now, here is your chance: You haven't yet been charged with having anything to do with trying to beat up or kill any U. S. Senators, particularly one of those who advocates a limitation on big fortunes. Furthermore, you have been in a small fry business. Morgan and our other international bankers swindled the people out of more money on Kreuger & Toll and Insull stocks, on Argentine, German and Brazilian floatations and caused more starvations, suicides and murders than a million such men as you could do in a hundred years.

But, now comes your chance if you can rise to it: Wire at once to Collier's Weekly, the Evening Post, or any other magazine or newspaper in with the House of Morgan and other big fortune holders (and that gets most of them), wire them at once that you had Senator Huey P. Long beat up at the Charity Benefit on Long Island and that the only reason he wasn't killed was because he managed to get away too soon for the men to finish the job. Immediately they will send you the contribution and this Morgan gold medal. That puts you in their class. Then you are not expected to pay any income tax and the government will owe you back whatever money you did pay.

Wire them that you will complete the job on Senator Long if he goes too far again. And, to make it sure, wire them also that you have your eyes on the other U. S. Senators who voted for the "Long Plan" to put some limit on the big fortunes and to spread some of the wealth among all the people in America. Let it be known that from the sign left on the forehead of a U. S. Senator, (who escaped before he could be worse handled) is a mere warning of "events that are casting their shadows before." Those Senators who have persisted in voting to place taxes on the big man at the top, so as to relieve and help the little man at the bottom, should be announced as your special luminaries for future notice and attention, with Senator Long as the fair sample.

If you send this wire and qualify for the credit of this attack then, overnight, you become the hero to America that Morgan's magazines are now looking for; you get the big "contribution" being taken up by Morgan's editors, or at least the swag Morgan's outfit has to give for "the work." Becoming thus honored and aligned with Morgan & Co. the government has to release you from jail and pay you back whatever you paid on income taxes. Instead of being classed with small fry criminals, you will stand with the crew that has starved and killed by the millions, not just a few now and then; you will rank with the extortioners who filched the last penny of the laborers, widows, and orphans for the worthless paper floated by the swollen fortune element.

We advise that you make connections early. Otherwise someone else may claim this honor if you delay.

# INDEX

Allen, Oscar K.: 186, 259, 299; early friendship with Long, 19-22; aids Long in first campaign, 40; as floor leader, 118-119; in impeachment, 148; elected governor, 260-262
Anders, Ben L., 32
Anders, Joe, 32
Ansell, Samuel, 333
Atkinson, Thomas, 247

Barkley, Alben W., 300
Bernstein Case, 78-79
Bilbo, Theodore, 275
Black, Eugene, 244
Bouanchaud, Hewitt, 78
Bozeman, Battling, 143
Brezeale, Gladys, 335
Broussard, Edwin S.: 139, 286-287; in campaign of 1926, 82-83; opposes Long in 1932, 252-258
Brunot, H. F., 62-63
Bryan, William Jennings, Jr., 305

Caddo parish, 114-115
Caraway, Hattie W., 313-314
Carbajal, Nicholas, 279
Cellini, Benvenuto, 1
Chipley, Hunt, 53
Coco, A. V., 67-68
Cohen, John S., 300-301
*Collier's Weekly*, 319-323
Conner, Mike, 275-276
Constitutional Convention of 1921, 56-57
Constitutional League, 183-184, 191

Cumberland Telephone and Telegraph Company, 52-55, 66-69
Cyr, Paul N.: 142, 146, 211; elected lieutenant governor, 103; breaks with Long, 126-132; claims governorship, 250-251, 257, 279-280, 287-288

Danziger, Alfred D., 196-197, 231
Davenport, Walter, 319-323
Dawkins, Tom, 95
Dawson, K. W., 10
DeLoach, Martha E., lawsuit, 23-25
Dore, Hugo, 172
Dreher-LeBoeuf Case, 126-130
Drew, H. C., 187
Dunbar, Mrs. Charles, 335
Dupre, Gilbert L., 239

Ellis, Harvey E., 94, 96
*Emden*, 192-199
Ermon, W. C., 232
Ewing, John D., 94-96
Ewing, Robert E.: 269-270; in campaign of 1928, 94-96; breaks with Long, 119-121; in impeachment, 155-156, 159

Farley, James A., 303, 304
Folkes, Cheston, 238
Foster, Rufus E., 69, 105, 227
Fournet, John B.: 238, 259; elected speaker, 107; attempt to remove, 136-137, 203; elected lieutenant governor, 260-262
Fuqua, Henry L., 78, 87, 91, 92